COORDINATING COMMUNITY RESPONSES TO DOMESTIC VIOLENCE

Sage Series on Violence Against Women

Series Editors

Claire M. Renzetti
St. Joseph's University

Jeffrey L. Edleson
University of Minnesota

In this series . . .

COORDINATING COMMUNITY RESPONSES TO DOMESTIC VIOLENCE
Lessons from Duluth and Beyond

Melanie F. Shepard
Ellen L. Pence
Editors

Sage Series on Violence Against Women

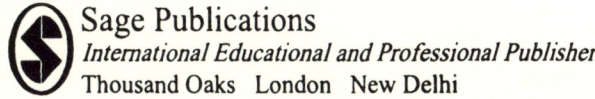

Sage Publications
International Educational and Professional Publisher
Thousand Oaks   London   New Delhi

For information:

Sage Publications, Inc.
2455 Teller Road
Thousand Oaks, California 91320
E-mail: order@sagepub.com

Sage Publications Ltd.
1 Olivers Yard, 55 City Road
London EC1Y 1SP

SAGE Publications India Pvt Ltd
B-42 Panchsheel Enclave
PO Box 4109
New Dehli 110 017

Printed in the United States of America

Library of Congress Cataloging-in-Publication Data

Main entry under title:
    Coordinating community responses to domestic violence: Lessons from
Duluth and beyond / edited by Melanie F. Shepard and Ellen L. Pence.
        p.   cm.—(Sage series on violence against women)
    Includes bibliographical references and index.
    ISBN 0-7619-1123-5 (cloth: alk. paper)
    ISBN 0-7619-1124-3 (pbk.: alk. paper)
    1. Domestic Abuse Intervention Project (Duluth, Minn.).   2. Wife
abuse—United States—Prevention.   3. Family violence—Law and
legislation—United States.   4. Victims of family violence—Services
for—United States.   5. Abused women—Services for—United States.
    6. Abusive men—Rehabilitation—United States.   I. Shepard, Melanie.
II. Pence, Ellen.   III. Series.
    HV6626.2 .C66   1999
    362.82'92'0973—dc21   99-6048

            01   02   03   04   05   7   6   5   4   3

Acquiring Editor:	C. Terry Hendrix
Production Editor:	Denise Santoyo
Editorial Assistant:	Patricia Zeman
Typesetter:	Lynn Miyata
Indexer:	Julie Grayson

Contents

PART I

EIGHT KEY COMPONENTS OF COMMUNITY INTERVENTION PROJECTS

1

An Introduction

Developing a Coordinated Community Response

Ellen L. Pence
Melanie F. Shepard

In 1975, every advocate for battered women in Minnesota met in the upstairs office of Women's Advocates, the only battered women's shelter in the state. We could very likely have fit every advocate in the country in a slightly larger room. For many of the feminists in the emerging movement, this time was filled with excitement and the sense of radical possibilities. Much has happened in the years that have followed: substantial reforms in the criminal justice system, greatly expanded shelter and advocacy services, an industry of domestic violence treatment programs for offenders, and steady growth in research and evaluation activities. An important development was the initiation of community intervention projects to modify, coordinate, and monitor the response of community agencies.

The Domestic Abuse Intervention Project (DAIP), located in Duluth, Minnesota, was initiated in 1980 after legal advocates in other cities had effected changes in every aspect of criminal court intervention, from dispatching to sentencing. The DAIP gained national recognition as the first community-based reform project to successfully negotiate an agreement with the key intervening legal agencies to coordinate their interventions through a series of written policies and protocols that limited individual discretion on the handling of cases and subjected practitioners to minimum standards of response (Pence, 1983). The Duluth project's most well-known accomplishments have been its work with the Duluth Police Department to develop a mandatory arrest policy in the early 1980s and the creation of an educational curriculum for batterers that focuses on power and control as the purpose and function of battering (Pence & Paymar, 1993).

Many domestic violence agencies have adopted what has been termed the *Duluth model*. The DAIP has conducted more than 600 training sessions and seminars in the United States and at least five other countries. Communities in the United States, Scotland, New Zealand, and Germany have adopted aspects of Duluth's community intervention model. However, when the "Duluth model" phrase is used in these different communities, it can take on different meanings. For example, it may be understood as the men's curriculum, the use of a mandatory arrest policy, the use of a tracking system to monitor the criminal justice system, or interagency coordination. This book is designed to give a comprehensive description of the Duluth model. It is hoped that it will be used by domestic violence practitioners in developing a coordinated community response in their own communities.

The first part of this introductory chapter will lay the groundwork for understanding the social and historical context that led to the development of the DAIP and other institutional advocacy projects. The second part of this chapter will provide an overview of the book, including the eight components of a community intervention project, adaptations of the DAIP model in different settings, and areas of controversy. Throughout this chapter, quotations drawn from interviews conducted by one of the coauthors (Ellen Pence) will be used to illustrate key points. For her doctoral dissertation, Dr. Pence conducted an investigation of the Duluth civil and criminal court system using an approach called institutional ethnography. Dr. Pence used data from a variety of sources, including interviews with practitioners in the criminal and civil court system, advocates, and battered women (Pence, 1996).

Understanding the Social and Historical Context

To understand the purpose and function of community intervention projects, it is necessary to reflect on the historical developments
that led to their creation. In the past 20 years, activists in the U.S.
battered women's movement have argued successfully that the state
has an obligation to intervene in personal relationships to protect
women from their abusive partners, that it can and should remove
violent husbands from their private homes to protect women in their
private homes, that the police should arrest husbands for assault, and
that the state should prosecute them (Dobash & Dobash, 1979;
Schechter, 1982). These shifts in the legal status of women marked a
monumental achievement for the women's movement, not unlike the
gains in the abortion and divorce rights efforts.

None of the new measures was implemented as a matter of
course. In every state, in every courthouse, and in every squad car,
there has been resistance to the full measure of what this social
movement seeks to gain for women. Still, for the first time in the
history of the struggle against "wife beating" that began as early as
1640, the contemporary battered women's movement has won public
acknowledgment that the state has the obligation to render full
protection to abused women (Dobash & Dobash, 1979; Pleck, 1989).

Every state has expanded the obligation and authority of police
to arrest abusive partners. Every state has passed some version of a
protection order that allows the court to exclude abusive partners
from their homes. The National Council of Family and Juvenile Court
Judges (1994) has published an extensive model state code recom-
mending that state lawmakers adopt a comprehensive legislative approach to the reform of the antiquated legal system. The American
Medical Association and the American Bar Association, two of the
most powerful professional lobbies in Washington, D.C., have both
adopted far-reaching positions on domestic violence (Flitcraft, 1992).
Public opinion, though far from fully enlightened, has dramatically
changed as court watch groups, community-based legal advocacy
projects, and battered women's shelters have put the spotlight on
practitioners, their failures to respond to domestic violence, and the
ways abusers escape social sanction. Men who beat their partners can
no longer expect to use violence and remain immune from social
sanction, nor can practitioners who fail to respond to the violence be
assured of anonymity.

The suffrage and progressive social reform movements of the late 19th century produced legislative changes, ending more than 200 years of regulating wife beating, and criminalized the practice regardless of the woman's behavior. By 1911, laws forbidding wife beating had been passed in every state. Because no infrastructure of local efforts existed to advocate for the implementation of the new laws, they were noted in law books and shelved until 70 years later, when the next wave of feminism gained momentum and activists insisted on their enforcement (Dobash & Dobash, 1979; Pleck, 1989).

In the United States, the battered women's movement emerged in the mid-1970s on the heels of the social activism of the 1960s. It attracted people of diverse political commitments to advocate for women's right to freedom from violence in marriages. It has been a pragmatic movement that, in its early years, drew much of its strategy from the progressive social struggles of the 1960s and much of its theory from the feminist movement. In the early 1970s, when the first shelters opened, the feminist movement was organizing largely through locally based consciousness-raising groups. From these groups rose a voice of and for women that had been absent in the public discourse for half a century. As the women's movement developed its political analysis, it called into question the European notion of the "natural family unit" held together by love. Feminists argued that the nuclear family, which evolved over centuries of European patriarchal feudalism and capitalism, was held together not so much by love as by the concrete conditions of women's subordinate economic and social status in the public and private spheres (Schechter, 1982).

The battered women's movement did not develop a radical critique of the family or of the capitalist state or of heterosexism. Rather, *safety* became to the battered women's movement what *liberation* was to radical feminism. This means that the battered women's movement is not a feminist project the way the antipornography, the antiprostitution, or abortion rights movements have been. It cannot be adequately understood or critiqued unless we account for its political diversity and its corresponding absence of a radical critique. This was an undertaking in which feminists and progressives played a primary role but were not the sole or even perhaps the majority of workers. Of course, political positions can change. As one shelter-resident-turned-activist remarked, "I never considered myself a political person or a feminist, but then there is nothing more politicizing than a fist in the face followed by a little chat with 10 other women with black eyes" (interview, May 19, 1995).

Although much of the analysis of the feminist movement regarding relations of dominance and subservience has been taken up by the battered women's movement, its two-decade history nevertheless has been marked by a reproduction of the race, class, and heterosexist oppression that dominates social relations in this country. White women, often from middle-class backgrounds, have held many of the structural leadership positions (e.g., coordinator, program director, fundraiser) and have written the majority of the literature.

Movement strategies, including legal reform strategies, were developed with women of color often in reactive rather than proactive leadership roles. In these roles, women of color have been far more cautious in mapping out strategies for reform that would involve an expanded role for police and the courts in women's lives. Much of the early work of legal reform efforts was marked by a certain naïveté on the part of the White middle-class leadership about the role of the legal system in maintaining existing relations of ruling.

> I think White women talked more as if the courts belonged to us [all women] and therefore should work for us where we [women of color] always saw it as belonging to someone else and talked more about how to keep it from hurting us. (Legal advocate, interview, September 19, 1995)

In every state, advocates formed coalitions of locally based programs to work for legislative changes as well as for changes in the state's regulation of local welfare, police, and funding agencies. The new legislation merely authorized change. Many of the laws and regulations passed were either ignored or cynically turned against battered women or against men in marginal positions in society. Thousands of women in the United States have been charged with assault when they have fought back against an abuser; many others have been punished for failing to cooperate with the prosecutor's efforts to enforce criminal statutes against batterers. As a direct result of the reform efforts that envisioned a more active role for the courts in intervention, battered women have been charged with filing false police reports, failing to obey subpoenas, and neglecting their children (Pence & Ritmeester, 1992).

However, the grassroots nature of the battered women's movement created an infrastructure through which the misuse of legislative reforms could be challenged over a long period. Policy changes secured at the state or legislative levels would be taken up by advocates by means of local training programs for professional groups. Through constant pressure, advocates kept raising issues about how particular cases were being mishandled by the system.

Few of the women who organized the battered women's movement were economically self-sufficient. Most were part of the working poor. Some were dependent on their husbands or dependent on the state, either as welfare recipients or as civil service workers. As women seeking refuge in the shelters turned to the state for financial resources or legal protection, the state's role in reproducing relations of dominance and subordination was repeatedly demonstrated. Lawmakers, police officers, judges, prosecutors, probation officers, and social workers consistently failed to use their institutional powers to protect women from further abuse or to sanction men for their violence.

Even when the movement had secured legislation that expanded the institutional power to intervene, practitioners frequently refused to use their new powers. It was this reality that politicized movement workers. Feminist theory offered them an analysis of what they were experiencing each day they walked through the shelter door to begin a work shift or to escape a batterer. As women crowded into shelters, their stories revealed a disturbing pattern of specific actions on the part of legal and human service practitioners that seemed to collude with men's violence and intensify women's vulnerability to domination by violent men.

> It got so I could finish a woman's story halfway through it. There was this absolutely eerie feeling that these guys were getting together and deciding what to say and do. The people in the system were saying a lot of the same things that the men were saying: "It's her fault, too. She has to take some responsibility for what's happening, it takes two to tango." Back then there were no arrests, no prosecution, no special visitation orders. It's as if everyone just had blinders on to how violent some of these men were. Some women weren't shocked by this—they had been on welfare or in this system for a long time and had that jaded attitude toward the system. I was a novice, I was shocked at it. I remember thinking, "But the squad car says 'to protect and serve' on the door—how could the police just walk away?" (Shelter advocate, interview, June 15, 1995)

Advocates began to understand that the failure of the courts and police to protect women was not simply a matter of an attitude on the part of individual practitioners. It was a lack of legal tools to intervene in a legal system that did not take into account the inequality of the possibilities of parties seeking court intervention in family matters or the complexities of women's experiences in a society in which citizens' access to resources and social privilege is determined by their sexuality, race, gender, and class position. These realizations led advocates to form legislative coalitions and criminal justice reform projects at the state level. Successful legal reform efforts in one state were quickly taken up by advocates in other states. Reform initiatives—such as laws that authorized civil courts to remove abusive parties from their homes, expanded police authority to make arrests, required jailers to notify victims when releasing offenders from custody, and allocated funds for shelters—would be passed in one state and within 3 to 5 years passed in more than half of the country's state legislatures (National Council of Juvenile and Family Court Judges, 1996).

Activists also organized criminal justice reform efforts on the local level, either as separate projects within shelter programs or, in cases such as the DAIP in Duluth, as independent sister organizations of the shelters. The first community-based advocacy projects focused on specific aspects of legal intervention. For example, Evergreen Legal Services in Seattle set up the first legal advocacy project for women who wanted to prosecute their abusers. The San Francisco Family Violence Prevention Project was the first major project to locate a feminist advocacy program within a prosecutor's office (Schechter, 1982).

Within the battered women's movement, there was little disagreement that it was the role of advocacy programs to challenge institutional practices that prevented women from getting the full protection of the legal system. There was, however, sharp disagreement over the extent to which battered women's activists could or should initiate reforms that would increase the presence of the police and courts in the lives of battered women. Activists debated efforts to require police to arrest batterers and require prosecutors to pursue convictions as the multiple realities of women's lives came into sharp relief. Even when police uniformly apply their arrest powers to men of different or ethnic backgrounds, arrest does not mean the same thing to a Latino man and an Anglo man, to a poor man and a middle-class man, or to a gay man and a straight man; nor does it have the same impact on their partners. Movement activists were demanding the protection of women from an institution that has been instrumental in maintaining social inequalities. The movement was caught in the tensions of responding to immediate needs of women and working toward long-term institutional change. Like tensions within all social movements, they took on complex meanings (Costain, 1982; hooks, 1984).

> It was one of those you're damned if you do and you're damned if you don't things. When we started talking about arrest, I knew it was going to be used against Black men for reasons other than hitting a Black woman. It was things like the Birmingham police arresting 10 Black men to every White man that made me argue against it, but then I didn't want police walking away when a Black woman was beaten either. So in the end I supported a policy which meant in most cases the man would be arrested and Black women would be down there to get him out. That's the way it is. (Legal advocate, interview, June 23, 1995)

Politically, the battered women's movement has been oriented toward the very practical legal, financial, emotional, and medical needs of battered women. The sheer numbers of women coming into shelters necessitated a pragmatic approach (Costain, 1982). Women called the police when they were being beaten, sought legal relief in divorce court, and were dragged into juvenile court as allegedly bad mothers. The question of whether we should use the courts to protect women was in a sense rhetorical, as women were already inextricably hooked into the legal system. The more meaningful debate centered on strategy (Currie, 1990).

As activists developed advocacy strategies at the state level and community-based programs pushed for their implementation on the local level, two distinct forms of advocacy emerged: individual advocacy and institutional advocacy. Individual advocacy involves an advocate helping a woman consider her options and then pursue a course of action in the legal system. The advocate explains various court procedures and helps negotiate around obstacles. In short, it is the job of the advocate to help a woman achieve her personal goals in the legal system. The advocate may not agree with the choice the woman has made, but she is trained to support the woman's decision unless she cannot ethically do so (Davies, 1995).

For the battered women's movement, institutional advocacy is the sum total of those activities designed to change an institutional practice (i.e., policy, procedure, or protocol) that works against the interests and needs of battered women as a group. It is rooted in individual advocacy in that institutional advocacy programs are informed by the everyday experiences of battered women as their cases are processed in the legal system. Institutional advocacy is committed to claiming the legal process for women who have very different goals in using the system than those in the system who process her case. Wittner's (in press) institutional study of women's agency in domestic violence court found that battered women used the courts for many purposes; rarely was it to secure a conviction.

In many cities, shelter or community-based advocacy program staff practice both forms of advocacy.

> I always think of my role in doing individual advocacy as helping to clear a path for women who have chosen a course of action but are coming up against obstacles. My knowledge of the system and relationships with people in the system put me in a position to help overcome those obstacles. When I am doing institutional advocacy, I think of it more as clearing a new path. When an advocate finds herself coming up against the same problem over and over again with different women, it's clear something needs to permanently change. (Legal advocate, interview, June 15, 1995)

Institutional advocacy, however, also focuses on how the state should intervene with men who beat women, regardless of the desires of an individual woman who is the victim of an individual man. Thus, the demands of the battered women's movement to criminalize violent men often conflict with the interests and desires of women who are living with those men (Edwards, 1989).

Institutional Advocacy Projects

Community-based individual advocacy projects brought women without law degrees or any official legal standing in a case into the courtroom to advocate for individual women. Institutional advocacy programs extended their presence into the administrative workings of the system, inserting advocates into discussions on the managerial practices of the court system and demanding a voice on behalf of women as a class. Their presence was met generally with resistance and occasionally with cooperation. In some cities, they were charged with practicing law without a license or accused of "man hating," gender bias, and obstructing justice (Davies, 1995).

Although many advocacy groups and shelters have had tense relationships with police departments and the courts, there was often a recognition that a cooperative relationship would be in the interest of both groups. Shelters gave police as well as the courts much-needed resources to deal with a crime they had previously been ill-equipped to handle. Besides offering emergency housing for women, shelter programs coordinated the legislative initiatives to expand police arrest powers, judicial authority to quickly remove violent offenders from the home and to hold them following arrest, and prosecutorial ability to bring certain evidence into the courtroom. With these expanded powers came rising expectations that the court should act to protect women and children in far-reaching ways.

Institutional advocacy projects attempt to achieve changes both at the macrolevel (e.g., passage of new laws or adoption of new prosecution, probation, or police policies) and at the microlevel (e.g., making changes in procedures and in daily court and police practices such as setting court calendars, arranging a safe waiting space for women and advocates, determining what information belongs in a police report, and presenting sentencing recommendations to the judge). Both levels of advocacy require careful attention to the way one change will affect another part of the case processing. In general, advocates consider any change they or others propose from the standpoint of how it will affect battered women, both as a class and as individuals.

In some cities, institutional advocacy projects have organized as independent organizations, but in others they are program components of shelters. Some projects operate almost exclusively on volunteer labor, and others have substantial budgets and staff. Some are operated by people with no previous political or organizational experience, and others are staffed by people with academic degrees in professional fields. Despite the educational, class, and social differences that separate many of these programs, they are loosely connected. What has led them to enter into coalition with each other is the experience of working with women who face horrendous institutional obstacles in securing safety for themselves and for their children.

Community intervention projects are a type of institutional advocacy project that focus on creating institutional practices and policies within a community that allow for a coordinated community response to domestic violence. Community intervention projects emphasize that it is the community's responsibility to address domestic violence, not the victims of this violence. The Duluth DAIP was the first institutional advocacy project that took this approach.

Domestic Violence Programs in Duluth

Duluth is a small city that is part of seven-county region in northeastern Minnesota called the "Arrowhead region." It is a regional center for surrounding communities that extend along the north shore of Lake Superior and north to Minnesota's Iron Range and the Canadian border. Superior, Wisconsin, which is across the bay, is the center for much of rural northwestern Wisconsin. Most of northeastern Minnesota and northwestern Wisconsin is sparsely populated. There are 12 Anishinaabeg (Chippewa) reservations in this part of Minnesota and Wisconsin.

Duluth, Minnesota, is a mostly working-class city of 85,500 people and is located in the state's sixth judicial district. The city has a history of economic difficulties and declining population. According to U.S. Census Bureau statistics, the annual income of 52% of its households is less than $25,000; only 16% have an annual income of $50,000 or greater. The population is 2% Native American, 1% Asian American, 1% African American, and 96% European American.

There are two battered women's advocacy programs in Duluth: the Women's Coalition and the DAIP. The Women's Coalition provides battered women shelter, educational groups, and advocacy in the civil and criminal court. Shelter advocates conduct almost all of the individual advocacy for battered women and, in so doing, become the central informants in the process of determining institutional advocacy goals. The DAIP, like the shelter, is a small nonprofit agency, but its orientation is not direct advocacy in individual cases for battered women. It acts instead as a monitoring and coordinating organization for all the agencies and practitioners who intervene in these cases.

The Women's Coalition was organized through the grassroots efforts of local women during the late 1970s. By 1979, the Women's Coalition staff, like that of other shelters in the state, was becoming increasingly frustrated with how new laws were being implemented and with the lack of progress in securing more substantive changes in both the police and court systems' response to battered women and their intervention with batterers. Therapy groups for men were starting to form, and there was a growing concern that these groups would give an already unresponsive system a way to further decriminalize these cases. Nationally, shelter activists were advocating for increased involvement and intervention by the courts and the police and an end to the nearly laissez-faire approach that dominated police and court response.

In Minnesota, several activists met to discuss a proposal to attempt to organize a battered women's institutional advocacy project. The notion of locating a city in which to test many of the assumptions that advocates were making about how to better protect women emerged from a series of statewide meetings of shelter workers. The similarities in the problems that women using shelters were experiencing with police, prosecutors, and judges were striking, but the resources to work simultaneously on more than 600 Minnesota law enforcement agencies and 11 judicial districts were not available. We thought if we could make headway in one jurisdiction, it would clear a path for advocacy in all of them. Because of the size of Duluth, the shelter staff's enthusiasm for working on such an effort, and the willingness of a few key people (e.g., the police chief and the city attorney) to experiment with new policies, Duluth was selected as the site of the demonstration project (Pence, 1983).

The Duluth DAIP

Before selecting Duluth as the project site, organizers met with the administrators of the police department, the heads of the city and county prosecutors' offices, the directors of three mental health agencies, the deputy in charge of the county jail, and the chief judge. A vague proposal was put forward, asking that each agency attempt to reduce repeat cases of domestic assaults by developing written policies and protocols and engaging in an interagency networking process. Each administrator agreed, contingent on the agreement of the others. This nonspecific commitment to developing policies was enough for project organizers to decide to locate the project in Duluth. A Duluth foundation made the first grant to the project of $30,000, and in September 1980, 4 years after the opening of the shelter, the DAIP opened its office (Pence, 1996).

The first DAIP staff consisted of a legal advocate from the shelter, a secretary who had been volunteering at the shelter, and an activist from Minneapolis who had been administering state shelter funds. All of the planning and strategizing was conducted with the DAIP and shelter staff. The DAIP staff contacted one person from each law enforcement and court agency whom shelter advocates had identified as friendly to the cause of making changes in the system. These practitioners provided staff with an insider's knowledge of how the system worked as well as political advice on how to accomplish the goals of the project. At the same time, project organizers were holding evening meetings with women who had used the shelter to find out how the system worked in practice and how it worked for different women. Proposed policies and procedures originated at these meetings. By the time project organizers met with agency administrators, they had a fairly good picture of how the system was designed to work, how it was actually working, what changes in institutional procedures advocates wanted to propose, and who would be sympathetic to these proposals, as well as who might be hostile or resistant.

Nine agencies were drawn into the negotiating process, although project organizers avoided suggesting any interagency meetings until after the basics of a policy or procedural agreement had been worked out with each agency. Once the decision was made to try the plan out in Duluth, it took 9 months to enact the policies. On March 1, 1981, at 2:00 p.m., the agency directors participated in a press conference to announce their new policies, which then immediately went into effect. The role of the DAIP in orchestrating this interagency experiment and then working with individual agencies to coordinate its ongoing implementation has positioned this community intervention project in an unusual insider-outsider role.

Since 1981, the DAIP has continued to promote institutional change and to monitor the response of the criminal justice system in Duluth. The DAIP also provides direct services to victims and offenders. It offers a men's nonviolence program that uses an educational group format, which serves primarily court-mandated offenders. Advocacy and support services are provided to women whose partners or former partners are involved with the men's nonviolence program. Several programs have developed in association with the DAIP: a national training project, a child visitation center, specialized domestic violence services for the American Indian community, and programming for women who use violence.

Overview of the Book

This book is organized into two parts. Part I describes the necessary components of a community intervention project. Part II examines areas for future development and the adaptation of the Duluth model in other settings. Each chapter in Part I focuses on one of eight key components of a community intervention project, as described below.

Part I: Eight Key Components of Community Intervention Projects

Community intervention projects engage in a fairly complex set of activities that occur simultaneously. The staff of the Duluth DAIP have identified eight key components that comprise a community intervention project:

1. Creating a coherent philosophical approach centralizing victim safety
2. Developing "best practice" policies and protocols for intervention agencies that are part of an integrated response
3. Enhancing networking among service providers
4. Building monitoring and tracking into the system
5. Ensuring a supportive community infrastructure for battered women
6. Providing sanctions and rehabilitation opportunities for abusers
7. Undoing the harm violence to women does to children
8. Evaluating the coordinated community response from the standpoint of victim safety

Creating a Coherent Philosophical Approach Centralizing Victim Safety

I think we spend a great deal of our time fighting against the notion that these assaults are logical extensions of relationship problems or dysfunctions. We have picked up some allies in the mental health profession, but the mainstream is still a powerful force in the legal system, and their way of seeing violence as an individual pathology has been hard to overcome. We also battle endlessly against the blatant and subtle ways that people in the system blame women for getting battered. But our biggest effort still comes down to getting systems people to develop a sense of urgency in these cases. In towns like ours, 80% to 90% of homicides are domestics, but the sheer volume of these cases lulls people into a passive intervention role. (Legal advocate, interview, May 26, 1995)

In Chapter 2, Ellen Pence discusses the philosophy that has provided the foundation for the DAIP's work in developing a coordinated community response. Successful intervention projects require a common philosophical framework that will provide the basis around which the goals of victim protection, offender accountability, and changing the social climate of tolerance for domestic violence can be achieved.

A central goal of institutional advocacy projects has been to eliminate the pervasive victim-blaming practices of the current system and to shift the onus of holding offenders accountable from the victim back to community institutions. In practice, this means changing the way practitioners think about the cases before them. It means changing how they understand domestic violence, how they understand the relationship of the offender to the victim, and how they understand the potential for further violence. It also means changing who they see as responsible for undoing the harm caused by the violence and what they understand to be the respective roles of the offender, the victim, and the community in ending the violence. In Chapter 2, Ellen Pence will examine how the DAIP looks at the causes of domestic violence and how institutions change.

Developing "Best Practice" Policies and Protocols for
Intervention Agencies That Are Part of an Integrated Response

> Training wasn't going to do it. We've had to push for written policies and protocols that provide some kind of standard of response. She calls 911 and from then 'till she's done with the whole mess there could easily be 30 or 40 people who have something to do with her case. In a city like ours, several hundred different people get involved in some part of the case. Without some fairly clear guidelines as to what are acceptable responses and what are not, we are going to be all over the map in what we do as a community. (Legal advocate, interview, June 15, 1995)

Drawing from more than 15 years of experience with the DAIP, Ellen Pence and Coral McDonnell discuss in Chapter 3 how to develop policies and protocols that enhance victim safety. Victim safety will not be achieved simply by having actors in a coordinated response system think differently. They must act differently. The actions of those located in different parts of a coordinated system need to be oriented toward victim safety and organized in ways that complement rather than undermine or subvert each other. With this goal in mind, practitioners' decisions and actions need to be guided by sets of protocol standards and, in some cases, direct policies. Chapter 3 will explicate the underlying assumptions that guide Duluth's reform efforts and provide suggestions for advancing the policy-making process.

Enhancing Networking Among Service Providers

> I can't tell you how many times I've seen a total breakdown in communication cause a case to be lost or dismissed. Every time somebody gets seriously hurt or killed, everybody scrambles to the files to make sure they didn't mess up. If they didn't, there's a big sigh of relief, but there's always this awareness that on so many cases there's a screw-up. (Court clerk, interview, January 15, 1996)

Strategies for achieving interagency agreements to enhance coordination among criminal justice and domestic violence agencies will be addressed by Denise Gamache and Mary Asmus in Chapter 4. The DAIP's approach to facilitating interagency dialogue and cooperation will be contrasted with the strategy of using coordinating councils that has been adopted in many communities. The chapter will discuss the key elements of successful networking, keeping in mind the priorities of victim safety and offender accountability.

Building Monitoring and Tracking Into the System

> We needed to keep pushing for accountability. We wanted the court to see itself as accountable to a community, to women who were being beaten, and to in turn hold the abuser to some standard of accountability. (Legal advocate, interview, June 22, 1995)

In Chapter 5, Dennis Falk and Nancy Helgeson will describe monitoring and tracking systems, drawing from the DAIP's experiences. One of the crucial functions of a community intervention project is ensuring accountability. Community intervention projects must develop monitoring systems so that they can track how cases are handled and responded to on both a macro (policy) and micro (individual) level. At the macrolevel, interagency tracking systems can be set up to monitor the movement of cases through the criminal justice system and to provide information on how well the community is responding to domestic violence cases. Agencies must be held accountable for responding according to the policies and protocols that have been set up and for giving victim safety priority. When aggregate data are examined, patterns may be identified that indicate a need for changes in how the system is responding. At the microlevel, tracking information can be used immediately by practitioners working on individual cases to enhance their response. Practitioners reviewing individual cases can respond more effectively when they have access to more complete information about a case.

Ensuring a Supportive Community Infrastructure for Battered Women

> Legal remedies are not enough. A community needs to provide some basic resources for women, like shelter, long-term housing, a decent income, and a place to talk with other women in the same situation. (Shelter advocate, interview, September 11, 1995)

In the United States, the most effective legal reform programs tend to be located in communities with strong infrastructures of services for battered women. Coordinated community responses need to ensure that essential services are available to women trying to negotiate a violence-free life for themselves and their children. These include emergency housing, legal advocacy, support and education groups, and financial assistance. In Chapter 6, Melanie Shepard shares the thoughts of a group of battered women's advocates as they examine advocacy within the context of a coordinated community response and some of the unintended consequences of reform efforts.

Providing Sanctions and Rehabilitation Opportunities for Abusers

> For me, the biggest shift was thinking about how to directly intervene with the man doing the violence. Do we try to fix him? When do we want to push for jailing batterers? Jails are not exactly places where men learn to respect women. I don't think we can claim to be standing with women if that means we say we're with you, except we won't ever deal directly with the person beating you up. On the other hand, trying to individually fix every man who beats his wife is futile. This is a tough one because as soon as you start to say, "OK, let's do something with these men," all sorts of screwballs show up to get in on it. (Legal advocate, interview, May 20, 1995)

Fernando Mederos in Chapter 7 describes the development of batterer intervention programs, compares the DAIP's approach to other programs, and raises controversial issues to be considered in future developments. A coordinated community response to domestic violence means that batterer intervention programs are one component of the response to abusers, which includes criminal justice sanctions. As the violence is understood to reinforce unequal gender arrangements in society rather than the manifestation of individual pathology, the responsibility for sanctions and rehabilitation must be assumed by the relevant social and legal institutions and community organizations rather than left to individual women. Many advocates argue that rehabilitation programs typically depoliticize and decriminalize the problem by psychologizing male violence in ways that make neither individual men nor unequal gender arrangements in society responsible for the violence. The DAIP has adopted an educational approach, drawing from Paulo Freire's (1970) literacy and popular education process, that emphasizes the cultural aspects of abuse and its influences on the individual's beliefs and actions (Pence & Paymar, 1993).

Undoing the Harm Violence to Women Does to Children

> Somehow the children are always labeled as the innocent victims of battering. I suppose that means their mothers aren't so innocent. The system needs to see that when a man beats a woman in front of her kids, there are two innocent victims. It's so artificial to separate out— this is a child protection issue and this is a criminal court issue. No matter what, mothers come with kids and kids come with mothers. (Visitation center worker, interview, September 20, 1995)

The success of advocacy projects in improving community and court interventions in domestic assault cases has not yet been matched by a similarly coherent approach to the child visitation and custody issues that usually accompany the end of a relationship in which there has been violence. Chapter 8 of this book describes the creation of a visitation center in Duluth, which is designed to provide a safe place for the exchange of or visitation with children. In this chapter, Martha McMahon discusses the challenges faced by the staff of the visitation center in addressing the harm done to children by the violence against their mothers. Children who witness violence in their homes are also its victims.

Community intervention projects can play an important role in protecting children from violence, distress, and harm as their primary relationships are reordered. One cannot think about children or the "best interests of the child" as if children stand alone and are not integral to the power relations of which violence against women is part. To protect children and undo the harm done to them by domestic violence, community intervention projects and legal advocates argue that the mother's and child's interests must not be pitted against each other. In Chapter 8, Martha McMahon argues that the response of the system must be informed by an understanding of the role violence and power play in shaping the social relationships of families.

Evaluating the Coordinated Community Response
From the Standpoint of the Victim Safety

> It's important to agree on the standard that we will use to judge our work. If it's more arrests or more prosecutions or a speedier process, we may find a successful project that's failed to improve women's lives. We need to use what's happened to the women who are being beaten as the basis for judging ourselves. (Prosecutor, interview, September 20, 1995)

In Chapter 9, Melanie Shepard emphasizes that evaluation should be considered an essential part of a coordinated community response. Evaluation findings in regard to project implementation and outcomes can be used to inform decision making and shape new programs and policies. A variety of evaluation methods should be used while taking steps to ensure the safety and confidentiality of battered women. Collaborative relationships between project staff and evaluators can strengthen the project and improve the quality of the evaluation.

Part II: Future Developments and Adaptations
of the Duluth Model

These eight components are not meant to be a definitive list of project activities but reflect essential aspects of what is termed the Duluth model. The model is expected to grow and develop over time, as continued examination and reflection lead to adaptation, innovation, and change. Part II of the book addresses some of the leading-edge issues that remain to be addressed in developing a comprehensive coordinated community response and adapting it in different settings.

A strength, as well as a limitation, of the Duluth model is its efforts to promote uniformity within the criminal justice system. In Chapter 10, Shamita Das Dasgupta describes the negative implications of this for women who have used violence against their partners. She argues that women's use of violence in heterosexual relationships is different from that of men and should be closely examined. She shares her analysis of interviews with 32 women who were attending groups for abusers. Shamita Das Dasgupta suggests that arrest policies be modified to allow for the contextualization of the violence.

In Chapter 11, Kersti Yllö raises an issue that has been made largely invisible in our criminal justice system: marital rape. Activists in Duluth, as well as in other communities, have not been successful in developing an adequate community response within the criminal justice system. Yllö describes the nature, scope, and impact of marital rape. She urges communities to create a coordinated community response to marital rape by first recognizing the problem and then developing appropriate interventions.

Each new community that seeks to use the Duluth model must adapt it to meet the needs of the unique characteristics of that community. In Chapters 12 and 13, we hear how the Duluth model has been adapted in countries and cultures other than in the United States. Roma Balzer describes the creation of the Hamilton Abuse Intervention Project (HAIP) in the North Island of Aotearoa (New Zealand). The Duluth model has widespread appeal to both Maori and non-Maori women within the refuge movement in New Zealand as it provides a framework that explains the current status of women and Maori within this country, a status that evolved through the culturally supported subjugation of both groups. Robyn Holder discusses using the Duluth model in Britain and Australia and the challenges of operating in cultural, social, economic, structural, and political contexts that are vastly different. We hope that Part II of the book will challenge the reader to think beyond the Duluth model to the next stage of action to end domestic violence.

References

Costain, A. N. (1982). Representing women: The transition from social movement to interest group. In E. Boneparth (Ed.), *Women, power and policy* (pp. 19-37). New York: Pergamon.

Currie, D. H. (1990). Battered women and the state: From the failure of theory to a theory of failure. *Journal of Human Justice, 1*(2), 77-96.

Davies, J. (1995). *An approach to legal advocacy for individual battered women.* Unpublished manuscript.

Dobash, R. E., & Dobash, R. (1979). *Violence against wives.* New York: Free Press.

Edwards, S. S. M. (1989). *Policing "domestic" violence: Women, the law and the state.* London: Sage.

Flitcraft, A. H. (1992). American Medical Association diagnostic and treatment guidelines on domestic violence. *Archives of Family Medicine, 1,* 39-47.

Freire, P. (1970). *Pedagogy of the oppressed.* New York: Herder and Herder.

hooks, b. (1984). *Feminist theory: From margin to center.* Boston: South End.

National Council of Juvenile and Family Court Judges (Ed.). (1994). *Family violence: A model state code.* Reno, NV: Conrad N. Hilton Foundation.

National Council of Juvenile and Family Court Judges (Ed.). (1996). *Family violence legislative update.* Reno, NV: Conrad N. Hilton Foundation.

Pence, E. (1983). The Duluth domestic abuse intervention project: Toward a coordinated community response to domestic abuse. *Hamline Law Review, 6,* 247-280.

Pence, E. (1996). *Safety of battered women in a textually mediated legal system.* Unpublished doctoral dissertation, University of Toronto, Canada.

Pence, E., & Paymar, M. (1993). *Education groups for men who batter: The Duluth model.* New York: Springer.

Pence, E., & Ritmeester, T. (1992). A cynical twist of fate: How process of ruling in the criminal justice system and the social sciences impede justice for battered women. *University of Southern California Review of Law and Women's Studies, 2,* 255-292.

Pleck, E. (1989). *Criminal approaches to family violence 1640-1980.* Chicago: University of Chicago Press.

Schechter, S. (1982). *Women and male violence.* Boston: South End.

Wittner, J. (in press). Reconceptualizing agency in domestic violence courts. In N. Naples (Ed.), *Rethinking feminism and activism.* New York: Routledge Kegan Paul.

2

Some Thoughts
on Philosophy

Ellen L. Pence

W hen Melanie and I first discussed editing this book, we realized
that because we had a wide variety of authors with so many different
connections to the Duluth Domestic Abuse Intervention Project
(DAIP), we ran the risk of never clearly articulating the philosophy of
the Duluth model. I naively agreed that when all the chapters were in,
I would write a short philosophy piece to help readers understand how
each chapter or program component is conceptually linked to a set of
underlying principals. Now the time has come to write this little jewel,
and I realize it is an impossible task. I am at a loss in several respects.

The DAIP is one project of a nonprofit community-based advocacy group called the Minnesota Program Development, Inc.
(MPDI).[1] The MPDI has five domestic violence–related projects: the
DAIP, the subject of this book; the Duluth Family Visitation Center;
the National Training Project; Mending the Sacred Hoop, a technical
assistance project to Native American tribes; and the Battered
Women's Justice Project, a national library and resource center on
criminal justice reform efforts. The first three projects are located in
Duluth. They emerged from the DAIP, which was the first project of
the organization. The other projects were the creation of activists in
the state who used our organization as a home base to do national
organizing.

So now I am asking myself, whose philosophy am I writing about? The board of the MPDI? The staff of the DAIP and the Duluth Family Visitation Center? The collection of agencies that participate in the interagency effort? I wonder if I should write about the articulated philosophy or the operative philosophy. Perhaps I could just make arguments for my own thinking and ascribe it to the project. Even if I can identify a standpoint from which to speak about the philosophy of the project, what aspect of the philosophy shall I address? Then, of course, I get all confused about what Melanie and I had in mind when we said we need a piece on philosophy. Is a discussion on our philosophy equal to talking about how we think about things? What things? What we think causes the violence? What we think the role of the legal institution is in stopping or perpetuating the violence? How we think institutions work or how they change? How we think about our work with the individual offenders and victims? I realize that the prospect of clarifying things for the reader is quickly diminishing.

Perhaps the way out of this quagmire is to describe some of our debates in all of these areas and try to highlight the challenges the DAIP staff posed to the system. It is, after all, the role of the DAIP staff to facilitate interagency debate and articulate a position that holds us collectively to the goals of victim protection, offender accountability, and changing the social climate of tolerance for this kind of violence.

What Causes the Violence?

This question is rarely asked at an interagency meeting, but our conflicts are almost always rooted in our different perspectives on what causes the violence. We argue over how to interpret observations and statements, what to do about a case, the role of the victim in stopping or provoking the violence, and the content of policies or educational programs. The conflict centers on the split among those who see the violence as rooted in (a) some kind of psychological problem of the offender, (b) the way the man and the woman act as a couple, or (c) how the offender understands the notion of being coupled. There are countless variations of these themes, and no one fits neatly into any one camp, but these camps are broadly representative of our individual points of diversion.

In many ways, how an individual practitioner conceptualizes the causes of domestic violence is not so important. As I discuss later in this chapter, a critical feature of institutions is that they put into place procedures, policies, categories, and language that subsume the idiosyncratic thinking and acting of individuals into institutionally acceptable responses to a case. Although the thinking of individuals in the system is not always a critical determinant of case outcome, the conceptual basis for writing institutional instructions that guide their actions is a crucial determinant.

I cannot do justice to describing the conflicting and often competing theoretical notions operative in the Duluth legal system. I can, however, try to articulate some of the thinking that was already firmly entrenched in the legal discourse of the Duluth system and then describe how the DAIP staff attempted to introduce another way of thinking about the violence and the cases before the court.

Our Thinking About the People

When the project began, most practitioners in the system linked the use of violence in marriages (intimate relationships) to the abuse of alcohol, people with poor relationship skills, or an inability of the men involved to handle stress, anger, or frustration in nonaggressive ways. These frameworks led practitioners to focus their attention on the offender's (and, in some cases, the victim's) lack of communication skills, their frustrations from unmet expectations, their inability to negotiate in a relationship, their self-destructive use of alcohol or drugs, their inability to deal with a partner who is destructive or mean, their lack of support for their partner, their poor parenting skills, and their lack of empathy needed to live in loving families. They believed that these deficiencies led some men and women to erupt in violence because they were either unwilling or unable to use healthier methods to resolve these conflicts. An offender's inability or unwillingness to act differently was seen as rooted in his own family or personal history. In addition, there was a recognition that a certain percentage of offenders were just generally antisocial and violent in many settings.

The DAIP staff raised the question, "Why, in this relationship, does the offender suddenly lose skills he seems to have in other social relationships?" If it was the alcohol, the stress, or the lack of communication skills, then why isn't he hitting his boss, a store clerk, or an incompetent barber who makes him angry? A common answer was that this relationship is different. It is more personal, more constant, and more private, and both parties must know how to negotiate in the context of a deeply personal relationship. You can walk away from the store clerk; there is no building up of tensions and resentments. You simply change stores or barbers, but the home is different.

The DAIP staff agreed that it was about the nature of the relationship but wanted to shift the focus of intervention from fixing or ending the relationship to confronting what seems to be a sense of entitlement to use coercion, intimidation, or violence in this relationship that is not permissible in other social relationships. By making this shift, it was assumed that the whole center of attention would shift from resolving conflict to challenging the use of violence. As time went on, this line of thinking led to focusing more attention on how to contextualize the use of coercion, intimidation, and violence.

We worked on developing ways to distinguish between "slappers," those who use low levels of presumably nonlethal violence, and "stalkers," those who escalate in the types and severity of violence. It led us to eventually distinguish between those who assaulted their partners and those who were engaging in a pattern of coercive and violent behaviors that resulted in the offender establishing a relationship of dominance over the victim (the latter we refer to as battering). We saw that not all domestic assaults were battering, and not all batterers escalated to the point of seriously injuring or even killing their partners.

Although the DAIP staff has argued against using causal explanations that require practitioners to assume a fairly universal psychological makeup among batterers (i.e., stress or anger control problems), we have developed some of our own truisms that also reduce complex social relationships to slogans. One was the notion that batterers use violence, coercion, and intimidation to control their partners. *He does it for power, he does it for control, he does it because he can*—these were advocacy jingles that, in our opinion, said just about all there was to say.

The Power and Control Wheel, which was developed by battered women attending women's groups, was originally a description of typical behaviors accompanying the violence. In effect it said, "When he is violent, he gets power and he gets control." Somewhere early in our organizing efforts, however, we changed the message to "he is violent *in order* to get control or power." The difference is not semantic, it is ideological. Somewhere we shifted from understanding the violence as rooted in a sense of entitlements to rooted in a desire for power. By determining that the need or desire for power was the motivating force behind battering, we created a conceptual framework that, in fact, did not fit the lived experience of many of the men and women we were working with. Like those we were criticizing, we reduced our analysis to a psychological universal truism. The DAIP staff—like the therapist insisting it was an anger control problem, or the judge wanting to see it as an alcohol problem, or the defense attorney arguing that it was a defective wife problem—remained undaunted by the difference in our theory and the actual experiences of those we were working with. We all engaged in ideological practices and claimed them to be neutral observations.

Eventually, we began to give into the process that is the heart of the Duluth model: interagency communication based on discussions of real cases. It was the cases themselves that created the chink in each of our theoretical suits of armor. Speaking for myself, I found that many of the men I interviewed did not seem to articulate a desire for power over their partner. Although I relentlessly took every opportunity to point out to men in the groups that they were so motivated and merely in denial, the fact that few men ever articulated such a desire went unnoticed by me and many of my coworkers. Eventually, we realized that we were finding what we had already predetermined to find. The DAIP staff were interpreting what men seemed to expect or feel entitled to as a desire. When we had to start explaining women's violence toward their partners, lesbian violence, and the violence of men who did not like what they were doing, we were brought back to our original undeveloped thinking that the violence is rooted in how social relationships (e.g., marriage) and the rights people feel entitled to within them are socially, not privately, constructed.

Due to the efforts that you will read about in the following chapters, we have become increasingly more able to account for the many ways that violence is used in an intimate relationship. Much of our thinking now about safety and accountability is linked to our ability to contextualize the violence—to ask who is doing what to whom. And with what impact? The DAIP still conceptualizes the violence as a logical outcome of relationships of dominance and inequality—relationships shaped not simply by the personal choices or desires of some men to dominant their wives but by how we, as a society, construct social and economic relationships between men and women and within marriage (or intimate domestic relationships) and families. Our task is to understand how our response to violence creates a climate of intolerance or acceptance to the force used in intimate relationships.

Finally, activists have for years faced the accusation that women who "claim" to be battered are often lying about the abuse. Even though the research overwhelmingly shows that women in fact minimize abuse, defense attorneys, prosecutors seeking to dismiss cases, and judges explaining nonpunitive sentences spin tales claiming that women are likely making up the abuse, its effects on their children, and the need for protection. While it is clear that every community can find the case of "the woman who lied," all women are suspect. For more than a decade, the DAIP and shelter advocates reacted to this constant undercurrent of "women are liars" by arguing that "women are saints." In many ways, we turned a blind eye to some women's use of violence, their drug use and alcoholism, and their often harsh and violent treatment of their children. There did not seem to be a way to acknowledge these problems and still argue that this was a deeply gendered issue and that women were being subjected to repeated acts of intimidation and coercion very different from what men were experiencing as a group within marriages.

Today I am sitting in a motel room with CNN on in the background. The lead story is about the acquittal of the highest-ranking enlisted man in the army faced with 18 charges of sexual misconduct. Apparently, the jury has accepted the defense that all six women, who do not know each other, lied. The next story reveals new accusations about the president's sexual activities and the corresponding White House denials insisting that these women are lying. The speculation is that the sergeant major is the victim of a racist attack and the president is the victim of a right-wing conspiracy. I have no doubt that the racists and the right-wing propaganda machine are using the claims of these women for their own purposes. Neither do I doubt that most of what actually happened will never be accounted for. Even though most of us know that this kind of sexual misconduct is rampant in the D.C. political establishment and in the armed services, we will ultimately settle for a murky conclusion because it's so easy to just say women lie.

Unlike children, few battered women are seen as innocent victims of abuse. The victim-blaming accusations in the system, coupled with advocates' false representation of women as having no agency (everything she did wrong, he made her do), plague us to this day. But we have moved beyond many of the impasses of our first decade. The work with women who assault their abusive partners described in Chapter 10 attests to our collective growth in this area.

Our Thinking About the System's Response

A second and equally contentious set of debates centers on addressing why the criminal justice system's response to these cases is so ineffective at stopping the violence. The standard response in 1980 was that the victim was ambivalent about what she wanted to do. Some practitioners were extremely sympathetic to the horrendous dilemma victims faced when trying to end this kind of violence; others were impatient, frustrated, and generally hostile to victims of domestic violence. Many moved from various forms of sympathy to victim blaming.

Again, the DAIP staff introduced a new spin to the same old facts. The system is not ineffective because "women do not react to being beaten properly"—it is ineffective because it handles cases in a generic way that does not account for this unique crime and the distinct response it requires. Although other advocacy groups were arguing that we should treat this crime like stranger assaults or barroom fights and criminalize the offense, Duluth advocates used a different argument. We maintained that assaulting your wife is not like assaulting someone in a bar or at a party or in a social setting where the victim and offender have no familial or economic or emotional ties to each other. In a barroom fight, if a victim pursues a conviction by cooperating with the prosecutor, the case will likely go forward; if the victim does not want to cooperate and expresses a strong desire to have the whole case just disappear, it will likely be dropped. But applying that same standard to domestic assault cases is problematic for many reasons; most important, it gives the offender who has control over the victim control over the state's intervention.

In our first 5 years of working toward new policies, we were conviction driven, which made us face a philosophical dilemma. We knew that most battered women had legitimate reasons for not wanting to have the state engage in a hostile criminal proceeding against their partners, yet we pushed prosecution as a means of holding men accountable and protecting victims. On one hand, we recognized that the system was too slow, too adversarial, too inconsistent, too incident focused, and too unwilling to follow through on its own orders to be of predictable help to victims of battering. On the other hand, we thought that continuing to simply dismiss these cases would only reinforce abusers' notions that they can safely use violence in their intimate relationships.

The DAIP staff asked, "Why should a woman cooperate with a process where there is very little in it for her?" The DAIP tried to argue from the standpoint of the woman: She does not want to testify at a trial that is taking place months after she was beaten; she knows the court will focus on one blow and not all of the abuse she is experiencing; she has nightmares of a courtroom scene in which a defense attorney will subject her to a sophisticated and legalistic version of her abuser's attacks on her, during which she will not be free to argue back; she sees that her abuser has an attorney but she does not; and she knows that none of the results is particularly helpful to her, whether it is a fine, a jail sentence, or an order telling him not to break the law again.

The arguments that ensued could not be reduced to any one or two points, but one important difference between practitioners and activists was that practitioners in the system argued that victims' responses to violence caused the violence to continue, and DAIP staff argued that the state's response to offenders both caused the violence to continue and, in a much broader sense, contributed to batterers' sense of entitlement to use violence in their private, intimate relationships. The DAIP staff shifted the whole discussion about the violence from a focus on types of offenders and victims to a discussion about the broader social implications of the criminal justice system's laissez-faire approach to these cases and the connection between that approach and the prevalence of domestic violence. It should be noted that the DAIP staff argued that the private lives of women are shaped not by the men they marry or live with as much as by the institutions in our society that define and shape intimate relationships.

Advocates from the Women's Coalition (the battered women's shelter) and DAIP first moved to strengthen the protection order process, then pursued a fairly aggressive criminal court intervention process. The civil protection order process was faster, less adversarial, more consistent, and more focused on the pattern of abuse than an incident. Most important, it resulted in practical court-ordered reliefs relevant to the needs of victims, housing, child support, enhanced police protection, and, in Duluth, rehabilitation services for abusers. So we pursued a criminalization path to change the climate of tolerance and create a general deterrence to battering and a civil process to address the immediate needs of victims.

This approach left us with the question of what to do when victims failed to cooperate with our criminalization agenda. We often liken this dilemma to that of civil rights activists trying to desegregate lunch counters, schools, and buses in Jim Crow states. When the first children walked into previously all-White schools, those children did not get a better education. We have all seen news stories of those tense days African American children walked through crowds of screaming, threatening White adults. They entered empty classrooms. The victory was for those who followed. When the civil rights movement used those children to change a basic inequality in society, it secured an agreement from the government to call out the national guard to protect them. The challenge to those of us who argue that we need to criminalize this violence, even when the victim wants us to back off, is to put into place the safeguards equivalent to the national guard's protection of Black children in desegregating Southern schools.

Our solution was to pursue cases even when a victim does not want it. However, we would stop short of endangering a victim or punishing victims for not cooperating with these intervention efforts. The DAIP staff talked about the need for every institution in the community to examine its role in creating a climate in which domestic violence was both normalized and kept private. The DAIP staff saw the legal system as a starting point for community confrontation of domestic violence. Unfortunately, it has failed to expand its institutional reform work to other community institutions (religious, economic, medical, media, education), which in fact have a much more powerful impact on creating social norms than does the reactive institution of criminal law.

We vehemently argued our points about institutional responsibility to confront abusers and our historic duty to criminalize what for centuries has been a problem screened out of the criminal justice system. However, we were also painfully aware of how little the criminal justice system's use of conviction and punishment and rehabilitation had to offer many women who were being beaten. This also has meant that we have had to address the reality that the system's response does not have the same meaning across class, race, and gender lines. We have had the luxury of working in a community where, as these issues and contradictions are raised, key practitioners in the system take them up as legitimate institutional concerns. We have worked to figure out what to do about battered women who use violence, how to build a program that is rooted in a recognition of Native American self-determination and the impact of colonization on Native American family systems, how to design educational programs that respect the culture and personal histories of each man and woman who enter the groups, and how to recognize the many ways that class and gender bias is built into everyday work practices in the criminal justice system.

Changing Institutions

The Duluth model has been hailed as an organizer's miracle. The DAIP staff who present workshops in other cities are constantly asked, "How did you get the police to . . . ? Why did the prosecutors agree to . . . ? How do you get past the secrecy of every agency . . . ? Did you have a coordinating council and who ran it . . . ? How did you involve judges when . . . ?" It is hard to say to what we owe our success in working together. When we all discuss it, we agree that there have been a variety of key factors. Here I would like to just briefly list some of them to help contextualize the discussion on our philosophy or thinking about institutional change. Keep in mind that from 1979 to 1980, there were no police departments in the country that were voluntarily agreeing to an arrest policy. There were no coordinating councils or interagency agreements to bring as examples to agency directors.

What We Did to Create Institutional Change

1. The DAIP staff (project organizers) spent 8 months learning all aspects of the system from practitioners in each of the participating agencies. The project organizers consisted of three women. Shirley Oberg was one of the original organizers of the shelter and well known and respected by all of the agency directors. Her reputation and ability to talk about being abused without being dismissed opened all of the key doors for us. Coral McDonnell had been a volunteer at the shelter. She had considerable experience in office management

and made us look far more professional than we actually were at the time. I was the third, an outsider from Minneapolis whose father was a salesman and mother a Catholic. My specialty was selling guilt. We were funded by several Minnesota foundations to create a model community interagency response to domestic violence cases and had the luxury of a full planning year before we had to produce actual results.

2. Agency directors took a cautious but still open approach to the DAIP staff requests for them to join the intra-agency approach. Each agreed to participate in new procedures if they were approved by their staff attorneys, if all agencies participated, and if the project was time limited and evaluated. Agency directors gave us a rather informal nod to begin talking to agency staff about these cases. This willingness to try something if others joined was not something we as organizers did. I always think that the DAIP was not an organizing miracle as much as the city of Duluth was an organizer's miracle town. The willingness of nine agency directors to simultaneously try something new speaks to an intangible that has always been a part of this project. It was luck, perhaps, that we chose a community such as Duluth to design a model. We chose it because the shelter was interested in the project, the police were open to an arrest policy, and it was smaller than Minneapolis or St. Paul, where there would have been a lot more politics to deal with and a lot more people to bring on board.

3. During the first 4 or 5 months of the project, DAIP staff met with individual police officers and administrators, probation officers, prosecutors, therapists, judges, dispatchers, court clerks, jailers, and defense attorneys to understand from their perspective the following: (a) What would improve the system's response? (b) What kind of resistance would there be to different proposals (i.e., mandatory arrest)? (c) Why would that resistance be there? (d) Who are the key leaders to sell on trying something new? (e) How could proposed changes backfire on the project and on battered women? (f) What kind of training in proposed changes would be effective?

4. These meetings were informally held in coffee shops, over lunch, and in squad cars during ride-a-longs. We got to know how people in the system think about their work; their relationship to cases and other agencies, rules, and regulations; and the issue of violence in families. These informal sessions created a beginning point of dialogue that was later carried into more formal meetings to discuss new policies and protocols.

5. All of the informal meetings with frontline workers gave DAIP project organizers a practical way of approaching agency leaders to begin discussing the design of the new approach. All initial discussions about policies such as mandatory arrest or a no-drop prosecution policy were kept general and focused on what might be accomplished for the agency and for the protection of victims. These discussions focused on what their workers saw as part of the problem. None of the proposals that we began to formulate suggested that there would be absolute policies with no room for exceptions or applying good judgment when special circumstances were present.

6. The DAIP agreed to raise money to pay for all training costs associated with the project and the evaluation.

7. In each of the participating agencies, project organizers found one or more practitioners who were, for different reasons, very active in helping to bring their departments into the project in a positive way. These practitioners often faced a rather cool reception from their coworkers and, in some cases, faced open hostility. They were usually the people the agency administrators appointed to work with us on preparing draft language for a policy. In many ways, our staff became a support system to them.

We took a low-key nonconfrontational approach to policy development (see Chapters 3 and 4 for further discussion). We focused almost exclusively on writing policies and designing training sessions to teach the basics of the new policies and gain practitioner support for the changes in the approach to these cases.

Our Thoughts About Institutional Change

Our thinking in the 1980s was that to use the criminal justice system effectively, we had to identify what was it about this crime and this type of offender that made it difficult to successfully place controls on the offender. Although this is not directly synonymous with getting convictions, it is close to that. We had this idea that a primary objective should be to shift the burden of confrontation of abusers from the victim onto the system. This meant police could no longer ask the victim whether she wanted him arrested, thus our mandatory arrest policy. We had to neutralize the offender's ability to control the process by getting the victim to ask to have the charges dropped, thus the no-drop policy. We wanted judges to sentence offenders to either jail or rehabilitation groups or both and immediately revoke probation when the offender failed to complete rehabilitation groups or reoffended. We needed an arrest policy that based the decision to arrest on the presence of probable cause and the presence of danger to the victim. We needed a quick civil process that overcame the gaps in a divorce action and a criminal action.

Our first decade focused on broad policy issues, networking and developing support systems for victims and rehabilitation programs for offenders. In our second decade, we have deepened our understanding of how institutional practices can marginalize or centralize attention to victim safety. I think it would be fair to say that somewhere down this long road to change we came to the realization that even if we could handpick every police officer and judge and prosecutor, we would still not eliminate the bad case outcomes that continued to occur after we had changed almost every policy. We had attributed the failure of the system to effectively address victim safety to individual attitudes and poor training. We began to see an institutional ideology that was embedded in work practices that standardized practitioners' actions regardless of their personal idiosyncratic work habits or beliefs.

The project was a local project. Case processing routines were established and carried out in a local setting, but these work practices were linked to conceptual practices that were not produced locally. Much of the masking and obscuring of victims' experiences occurred as their experiences were made into cases prepared through a complex set of administrative procedures that made the case something institutionally recognizable and actionable. Beginning with the administrative methods designed to accept a victim's call for help, continuing with the way police officers are institutionally organized to respond to and document an assault call, and ending with the closure of that case weeks or even years later, each practitioner is guided to think and act on cases in ways that are institutionally prescribed yet often appear to be the result of an individual's objective review of the facts.

In the past 5 years, we have made a significant organizing change in how we think about institutional change. In the past, we might have asked, "Why did this practitioner take this action?" Now we ask, "How was this practitioner institutionally organized to take this action?" Instead of seeing actions as the result of what goes on in the head of a judge or probation officer or police officer, we see it as the result of what is going on in the work practices (i.e., forms, rules, regulations, documentary practices, communication networks, technology limitations, insurance rules, etc.). Ways of thinking about the violence are built into those practices. For example, probation officers making sentencing recommendations are guided to think about appropriate sentencing for offenders in domestic violence cases based on the presentence investigation form used in their interviews and presentation to the court. Imagine the difference in thinking that would develop over a 10-year period if we had 20 probation officers use a presentence investigation form that emphasized documenting the pattern of abuse and violence the offender had used in this and past relationships, another 20 officers documenting the offender's criminal and work record, and a third group of officers documenting the conflict in the marriage that preceded the assault in question. To uncover how routine practices tend to compromise or marginalize attention to victim safety, we have developed an institutional audit that is fully described in the manual, *Domestic Violence Safety and Accountability Audit* (Pence & Lizdas, 1998). That process has directed our examination to how texts used in processing cases act to compromise victim safety.

When a woman who has been beaten by her intimate partner dials 911 for help, she activates a complex system of agencies and legal proceedings that constitute the state's legal apparatus of ruling. It is, in turn, linked to other systems of ruling, particularly the mental health and social service systems. These agencies of social control are themselves coordinated and controlled through administrative processes and regulating texts increasingly present in the mundane but vital processes that manage our daily lives. Most activities that occur in the processing of a case are linked to texts. Texts are the primary instruments of implementation and action in this system; therefore, changing the text can change the outcome.

The number 911 is the first in a series of texts that will coordinate, guide, and instruct a number of practitioners who will participate in processing as a criminal assault case a woman's experience of being beaten. The dispatcher who receives the call does not use her own discretion in accomplishing each of the tasks in this highly specialized system. She instead follows a written script in the form of computer screens that mediate the discussion first between the caller and the 911 intake worker and then between the dispatcher and the police officer who will respond to the call. These screens constitute the second text in the management of a domestic assault case by a community's police and court system. They are not, as Smith (1990) notes, "without impetus or power" (p. 122). These texts and the hundreds that will follow are active. They screen, define, prioritize, schedule, highlight, route, mask, and shape.

The woman's actual experiences become a "case" when the dispatcher begins the process of inscription and is institutionally resolved through a series of processes or organizational occasions. Cases move from one occasion to the next through a series of practitioners who do something—take action—and then textually record those things needed to move the case to the next occasion for action. Much of what the practitioner does is guided by texts such as administrative forms, rules and regulations, screening devices, intake forms, and report-writing formats. The text the practitioner produces is designed to hook up and assist the practitioner at the next occasion for institutional action. As such, the text, like the practitioner, is doing something. Much of the ideological work of the system is buried in the text. Therefore, to incorporate a principle such as prioritizing victim safety into the infrastructure of the system, changes must occur at the level of the text.

A case record or file becomes a key organizational element in taking action; it is the institution's representation of the "incident" (here the incident is an assault on a woman) that precipitated the opening of the case. As an institutional representation, it reflects the concerns of the institution. It is like a medical chart telling the reader who did what, when, and for what purpose. Although some organizational occasions are recorded, case files rarely contain verbatim transcripts of what occurred. Instead, they contain documents that are organized to record what of institutional significance occurred at each processing occasion.

Members of the institution are trained to read and write in institutionally recognizable ways. The reader is linked to the writer of a document in such a system not only through the text but through the legal discourse that organizes their professional training. Professionals are trained to translate what they see and hear and gather from the everyday world into professional discourses about that world. The professional discourse in reports and documents appears to be the objective work of an individual responding to a specific set of circumstances, yet this is far from what actually happens. Battered women's lives are twisted into preformulated categories created not in the lived experience but in the professional discourse.

Conclusion

The understanding of how power works through conceptual practices buried in a textually mediated legal system is a key to our current organizing efforts. It will not hold all of the remaining answers to our community's long experiment with reform. The chapters that follow should be read with the understanding that we are committed to a process of change and a focus on safety and accountability. Our goal is to create a different social climate, not to promote certain courses of action.

Note

1. The overall organization is incorporated (1979) as Minnesota Program Development, Inc. (MPDI). The nonspecific name reflects the intentions of its original organizers. We wanted to create a vehicle for ourselves as a group of activists to work on progressive social change projects that focused on the economic, political, and social issues facing women in the state. We imagined ourselves working on a variety of social justice projects, one of which would be confronting violence against women within marriage. At that time, we were also envisioning working on other issues concerning welfare, child custody, housing, credit scams, and a host of issues one or more of us were interested in pursuing. Today, every project of the MPDI is focused on domestic violence. As one board member stated, "When the DAIP thing took off so fast everything else just sort of went on a permanent back burner."

References

Pence, E., & Lizdas, K. (1998). *Domestic violence safety and accountability audit.* Duluth: Minnesota Program Development.

Smith, D. E. (1990). *Texts, facts, and femininity: Exploring the relations of ruling.* New York: Routledge Kegan Paul.

3

Developing Policies
and Protocols

Ellen L. Pence
Coral McDonnell

The Duluth model's major contribution to the national legal reform effort has been its method of negotiating agreements with community agencies that intervene in domestic violence cases. Included in this interagency effort are victim advocates, law enforcement officers and administrators, prosecutors, probation officers, court administrators, mental health providers, policymakers, and, in a limited role, judges. The model focuses on ensuring that practitioners respond to domestic violence cases in a consistent manner and that their response centralizes victim safety.

Although coordination is a method to reach the overall goal of victim safety, it is not in itself the primary goal of the Duluth model. When reform efforts focus on coordinating the system rather than on building safety considerations into the infrastructure, the system could actually become more harmful to victims than the previously unexamined system.

If we measure success by counting increases in arrests, conviction rates, or a reduction of repeat cases entering the system, coordination may seem to be the key to an interagency effort. However, if we use

the criteria of ensuring victim safety, holding offenders appropriately
accountable for their violence, and changing the climate of tolerance
for this type of violence, we see that coordination is merely a means
to far more complex objectives.

Many cities adopt a strict mandatory arrest or a no-drop prosecution policy on domestic violence cases, as if apprehending and convicting batterers is the only goal of intervention. This course of action
is shortsighted and ultimately fails because typically the victim is the
biggest obstacle in convicting the abuser. The victim, who may or may
not be helped by a conviction, is seen as the problem. From there the
reform effort shifts from a critique of the institution's ability to hold
an offender accountable to a critique of the victim. Ineffective intervention strategies and structural problems with the law fade from
view as objects of inquiry.

Examining and amending our policies and procedures to build in
victim safety has been an ongoing process at the Domestic Abuse
Intervention Project (DAIP) in Duluth. In 1981, we negotiated agreements with nine key agencies to simultaneously enact policies direct-
ing practitioners to follow certain procedures when responding to
domestic assault cases. In the nearly two decades since adopting those
policies, we have continued the process of examination and change.

Our primary task in intervening in domestic violence cases is to
transform the way the system is structured to respond to domestic
violence. Although existing procedures may serve the purpose of
processing other misdemeanor crimes, they are often not effective in
domestic violence cases. As noted in Chapter 2, several structural
realities of the criminal justice system make processing domestic
assault cases difficult. Problems with the structure include the slow
processing of cases, victims being placed in an adversarial position to
the offender, practitioners attending simply to single incidents instead
of the overall use of violence, and texts (regulations, forms, procedures, and reports) that are not designed to direct practitioners to give
attention to victim safety and to the collective goal of placing controls
on offenders. Another significant problem in the criminal justice
system is its fragmentation. Each practitioner in the system is highly
specialized and tends to pay attention to his or her own function
rather than to the collective work of the entire process. Dispatchers
or responding law enforcement officers must see the relationship of
their work during the first hour of a case to the work of other
practitioners who will later intervene in the same case. Prosecutors,

sentencing judges, probation officers, rehabilitation specialists, protection order judges, and custody evaluators read initial police reports, looking for guidance on key decisions they must make in a case. Each practitioner needs to see how he or she is linked with others in the system.

Each practitioner is part of an organizational network. For the network to function properly, each player must be consistent in his or her actions and be aware of what others in the system are likely to do in certain circumstances. Although very little of what practitioners do is at their personal discretion, they do have discretion in whether to screen a case out of the system and to determine the appropriate level of intervention. Once those decisions are made, the practitioner typically complies with standardized procedures in processing the case.

For example, once a law enforcement officer decides to arrest a suspect, the procedures for arresting, transporting, booking, and filing a report are routinized. Consistency in carrying out these tasks is ensured through the use of administrative procedures, standardized forms, instructions, training programs, departmental policy or procedural guidelines, and employee supervision. To achieve consistency and attention to safety, institutional procedures must be linked together, and practitioners must be cognizant of the special problems these cases pose. When a practitioner's response is unpredictable, the best policies and procedures can still lead to failure. In designing an effective response, methods must be in place to ensure a high degree of practitioner compliance because for a battered woman, an unpredictable system is like playing Russian roulette—a game with which she is already far too familiar.

Practitioners' actions are restricted by regulations, including federal and state laws, case law, insurance regulations, agency and department policies, and local interagency agreements. These regulations must be scrutinized relative to victim safety and offender accountability objectives. To centralize safety, the response must take into consideration the risk the offender poses to this and other victims. Therefore, a law, a policy, or a procedure must be constructed in a way that allows the practitioner to account for the probability that offenders who are batterers are likely to retaliate against their victims because of actions taken by the state or community. Policies need to account for the likelihood that most offenders will pursue another relationship in the future. The intervention approach must shift the burden of confrontation from the victim to the institution to whatever extent possible and without coercing victims into a certain course of action. Although the approach assumes that most offenders who batter will use coercion and force in any intimate relationship, responses must not be designed under the assumption that all assaults in intimate relationships constitute battering. Not every person who assaults his or her partner is engaging in a ongoing pattern of coercion, intimidation, and violence. To assess risk, the collective work of practitioners must be directed toward understanding the pattern and history of violence as well as the power differences between the victim and the offender. Because it is so important to understand how the violence is being used in a relationship, the task of documenting and assessing for levels of danger must be built into the work routines of practitioners and seen as the collective work of all interveners.

Some Assumptions of Duluth's Reform Efforts

In Duluth, we work to hold batterers accountable. The term *accountability* means to be held responsible for one's actions. This is a long and complicated discussion when used in relation to battering. We can only highlight some of the assumptions we use in the Duluth response to domestic violence cases.

First, we do not assume that all violence is the same. The person who is physically and sexually abused over a period of time and uses illegal violence as a way of stopping the violence is not doing the same thing as the person who continually uses violence to dominate and control a partner. Similarly, a person who engages in abusive behaviors, including grabbing and shoving his or her partner, is not to be treated the same as the person who threatens to kill his partner and uses actions to terrorize her. All of these parties should be held accountable, but the response must attempt to treat similar cases in a similar fashion. Therefore, policies and procedures should help standardize responses while allowing the system to respond to the specifics of a case.

To hold offenders accountable and protect victims, we need to understand how the violence is used by a person and how victims are affected by the violence. Harsh sanctions are not necessary with people who have used minimal force in a relationship, show potential for rehabilitation, and are entering the system for the first time. More jail time does not always mean more justice. On the other hand, we cannot be naive about how dangerous and deceptive many batterers can be. Offenders must be held accountable accordingly.

In Duluth, we assume that most victims of ongoing abuse (intimidation, coercion, and violence) are safer if the state or court has some level of control over the offender. For example, convictions and probation are preferred over deferred prosecutions, and 2 years of probation is recommended when abusers reach a level of abuse that indicates an escalating pattern of violence. Completely dropping a protection order is discouraged if a couple wants to live together again. Dropping the exclusion order but keeping the restraining order gives the system leverage if the abuse resurfaces. Cases are processed so that the system can respond quickly to renewed violence.

We assume that using violence against a child's parent adversely affects the child. Interventions must not pit the interest of the child against the interest of a parent who is an ongoing victim of the violence. We continue to debate the role of the abused parent in providing safety for the children.

Some Rules of Policy Making

In Duluth, policies evolved and developed over a long period of time. The changes and some of the corresponding conflict came in phases, with many inactive periods between the more active periods of reflection and change. Policy making is as much about the process as it is about content. We have learned over the years that the process needs to be inclusive and based on dialogue, not debate. It must also be attentive to practitioners' knowledge, research findings, and experiences of victims. Finally, the process must be open to scrutiny and evaluation. We list here some of the lessons we have learned during the almost two decades of policy development in Duluth.

Mind Your Politics

In the early 1980s, we worked in an atmosphere of distrust, defensiveness, and finger pointing. Shelter advocates challenged agencies and institutions, which often responded with hostility. Battered women's advocates were usually seen as "pushy, single issue, and inherently biased outsiders."

Internal conflicts existed within and among agencies: Police thought prosecutors were dropping the ball, prosecutors pointed to the weak response of judges, judges claimed a lack of appropriate resources for sentencing, and clerks were tired of all the prima donnas in the system. Dispatchers were concerned about a pending decision to move from the police department into a countywide 911 system. Police officers were split internally over the appointment of a new police chief. Although most of these conflicts were not rooted in problems related to domestic violence cases, they were part of the political climate surrounding the domestic violence reform work in process.

Over the years, defensiveness to the criticism from outsiders—in this case, activists in the battered women's movement—has diminished significantly. Today, our system is not perfect; in fact, it is still far from it. But now proposals for solutions are frequently raised by practitioners, rather than exclusively by advocates.

The number one rule of policy making should be that the change must simultaneously deal with domestic violence while considering the political realities of the multiagency response. Community members wishing to initiate successful institutional reforms should anticipate resistance, be inclusive rather than exclusive, and avoid slogans and rhetoric. They should create an atmosphere conducive to dialogue to sustain relationships through the difficult discussions. Advocates must give up the notion that only they care about battered women and that practitioners in the system are personally responsible for failures in the legal system. Practitioners need to give up the myth that they as professionals have been trained to be objective and fair (as opposed to advocates) and recognize that bias is built into their training and discipline. Finally, administrators must prioritize the protection of victims over the protection of the agency.

Assess Current Practices Relative to the
Primary Goals of Intervention

The Duluth model owes much of its progress to the willingness of practitioners and policymakers to work with advocates and activists in the battered women's movement. These practitioners and policymakers relied on battered women's advocates to help identify problems in the system, participate in sessions to develop solutions, and evaluate the impact of new procedures. Visitors to Duluth are amazed at the extent to which agencies have been open to having their handling of cases be scrutinized by others. The attitude among agency directors in Duluth is that such scrutiny improves their services rather than hinders their ability to operate. A good system is refined by scrutiny; an ineffective system is replaced by it.

Initially, shelter workers drew up lists of obstacles that women faced when using the criminal and civil court for protection. These lists shaped the agenda for reform. Most of the reforms that came from the process between 1981 and 1984 were what we might consider macrolevel changes. New policies were implemented in each agency that led to significant change in procedures—for example, dispatching policy required dispatchers to send a squad to all domestic assault–related calls and to give domestics involving assault the highest priority coding. Police policy required officers to make arrests when there was probable cause to believe that a misdemeanor-level domestic assault had taken place that had resulted in an injury to the victim. Police policy also required officers to write a report on every domestic-related call. Probation policy required probation officers to request a revocation hearing if an offender committed another assault on a victim. The agreement with the judiciary made it routine for judges to order presentence investigations on all domestic violence-related offenses, no matter how seemingly minor. The agreement with counseling agencies required that counselors work with offenders in groups or classes and not offer marriage counseling as a method of reducing violence. All of the policies required new methods of documenting cases and sharing information with other practitioners, including victim advocates.

Later policies were altered on a more microlevel as laws changed or experience highlighted problems. We conducted a series of low-budget evaluations of specific aspects of the intervention process. We then used that data, as well as cases in which practitioners or advocates felt the system failed to protect victims, as the source for ongoing refining of policies. From 1984 to 1994, we continued to make revisions but focused more on procedures than major policy changes. For example, criteria were established for police to distinguish between self-defense and assault. A protocol was developed for police clerical staff to provide victim advocacy agencies access to police reports on misdemeanor cases. We developed a curriculum for abuser classes and designed an interagency communication network that eventually became known as the Domestic Abuse Information Network (DAIN), which is described in Chapter 5. We developed a program for victims of ongoing abuse who had been arrested for assaulting their abusers. We opened a visitation center offering supervised visitation and exchange of children for parents in cases in which offenders were using visitation as an opportunity to continue the abuse. Native American activists reviewed each policy for its impact on Native American families and developed separate advocacy services and programming for the community.

In 1995, we began a new process for assessing our practices by employing the research methods of a Canadian sociologist, Dorothy Smith (1990), to investigate how procedures and daily routines in the system affected certain institutional goals (safety, accountability, and changing the climate of tolerance for violence). Based on her work, we developed a method for auditing our system that examined each step of case processing. From that audit, we uncovered many practices in our system that contributed to the inadequate outcome of cases and provided an agenda for change that will take another 5 years to fully implement.

The audit procedure is fully documented in a manual titled *Domestic Violence Safety and Accountability Audit* (Pence & Lizdas, 1998). The audit process involves an interagency team that includes staff from the police department, probation department, prosecutor's office, court administrator's office, and a victim advocate. The team observes each processing point and interviews the practitioners involved. Such an audit provides a community a full picture of where changes need to be made in the rules that guide practitioners' work and the daily routines used to carry out institutional objectives.

Build Practice Into Everyday Work Routines

It is well known that large bureaucracies are coordinated by paperwork. Beginning with 911, most transactions and actions are textually mediated (paper driven). When a 911 call is made, the conversation between the caller and the dispatcher is guided by how the dispatcher is required to respond to and record the call. When a law enforcement officer arrives at the scene, he or she goes through certain steps to determine if an arrest is to be made and documents what happened in the incident. The strategy of reform has shifted over the years from "change the attitude" to "change the text." Simply stated, if you expect a practitioner in a heavily burdened court system to consistently do something, look for something, or think about something, then request the information on the form that the practitioner uses to process the case. Do not leave safety or accountability to the whim, memory, or personal commitment of hundreds of people. During our audit, we found dozens of places in our system in which normal institutional practices failed to account for the safety needs of victims and left prosecutors in a weak position to obtain convictions even in serious cases. The following is an account from one of the workers involved in conducting the audit of our system. It graphically illustrates how a gap in the system is discovered in the audit process.

The Little Green Frog Story

While we were conducting an audit at the jail, a suspect was brought into the jail. I observed the jailer as he told the man to take off his bootlaces, belt, tie, and all the things he could possibly hang himself with. The jailer then told the man to take everything out of his pockets. Items in his pocket included $5.85, a tiny green plastic frog, a small Swiss army knife, a comb, and a few other items. The jailer put all these items in a plastic bag and wrote down everything that he took: the green frog, the Swiss army knife, the $5.85, the belt, and bolero tie. After writing down what had been put in the plastic bag, he told the inmate that he would put the bag in a box behind his desk and that he would get these items when he was released. The jailer then had the inmate sign a paper that stated what items had been taken from him.

You can see that the jailer was making it clear to the suspect that all his stuff was his, no one was going to take it, and that he would get it tomorrow. They documented everything to avoid a dispute later about what the man had with him when he was brought in.

This process is well thought through, particularly in terms of the potential for future lawsuits. That strange thing was that during the time they were going through this process, the guy was very angry and yelling and was threatening his wife, saying, "Someday I'm going to kill that fucking bitch. She knew this would happen. I can't believe this. Every time I walk into the house she tells the kids to dial 911. She'll pay for this!"

Then he was carted off to his cell. I told the jailer that I noticed he had recorded every item that he had taken from the man but I wondered if there were any place he recorded the threats that the man had made against his wife. He said no. I asked if there was a form for recording these kinds of threats. The jailer indicated that they did have an incident form on which they could report threats. I asked to see the form, and the jailer dug around and finally found the form. I asked him why, in this case, he had not recorded the man's threats. He said he was only obligated to report serious threats. I asked him how he knew the difference between a serious threat and a not very serious threat. He said that this guy had been in jail plenty of times and that he always blew off steam like that, so he knew it was not serious. I questioned the jailer more, and he asked me if I worked at a shelter or battered women's program, and I told him that I did. He asked me if women ever came to the shelter and told us that their husband had threatened to kill them. I told him they did. He asked if we called the police and told them that. I said we did. He then asked if we called the police every time a woman told us that her husband had threatened her, and I responded that we did not. He asked when we did call, and I told him we called when it was serious threat. He asked how we knew it was a serious threat. I said, "I just know."

This example helped us see the need to carefully examine what seems to be perfectly adequate procedures. Two major tasks of an audit are to locate where safety and accountability can be built into the system and to translate safety and accountability into concrete practices such as a new jailer form or a new 911 response to a first call for help.

The following is a description of the first 24 hours of processing a misdemeanor domestic assault case in Duluth. Changes that have been built into the infrastructure of the system are in italics.

Victim calls 911 to report that her husband has assaulted her and violated the protection order. He had slapped her and grabbed the keys to her house. He left the house heading toward the east end of town in a blue 1985 Toyota pickup truck. The dispatcher gives the case a *priority call*, dispatching one squad to the house and alerting all other squads to the description of the vehicle and the alleged offender. The dispatcher *directly quotes the woman's* description of the assault on the CAD (computer-aided dispatcher) complaint report form.

Officers respond to the house, conduct an interview *using a checklist format*, ask about *history of prior violence* by the suspect toward her or others, ask about and *document the involvement of children* in the incident and *overall abuse*, give her a *referral card* to the shelter/legal advocacy program, and *file a complete report*.

Two hours later, a second squad car pulls over a 1985 blue Toyota truck and identifies the woman's husband as the driver. After conducting an interview with him, officers determine they have *probable cause to make an arrest and do so*.

When the suspect is booked, he makes several threatening remarks toward the victim, which are recorded on the *jail incident form and turned over to the arraignment court* the next morning. After placing the suspect in his cell, the *jailer calls the shelter* and gives the name, phone number, and address of the alleged victim. The jail *holds the suspect* until arraignment court the next day.

The *shelter sends a trained on-call volunteer advocate* to the house to talk with the woman. The advocate provides advocacy and information on the shelter services, protection orders, and what might happen in court and asks for her permission *to forward information regarding the history of abuse to arraignment court. If the victim gives permission, the advocate fills out a history form and a statement regarding the wishes of the victim regarding full, limited, or no contact with the offender. The advocate also obtains the name of a person who can reach the victim at any time.*

Domestic assault arrest police reports are given *priority by the word-processing department. A copy of each report is distributed to*

the Domestic Abuse Information Network,

the shelter advocate assigned to follow up on the case,

the probation officer and judge at pretrial court,

the court administrator,

the detective bureau for follow-up on enhancing the charges,

the suspect's probation officer (suspect has a previous conviction),

the domestic violence file.

The next morning an employee of the city attorney and probation department prepares a file on the case that includes the arrest report, any past police arrest or investigative reports on this offender, CAD printout reports, a risk assessment form completed with a women's advocate, photos of victim injuries, copies of past and current protection orders, any pending court cases, probation information, past DAIN involvement, any prior victims known, and criminal history to be available in all future considerations of the case by the prosecutor, judge, probation officer, rehabilitation program, and so on.

The suspect is arraigned, and the probation officer appointed to this offender is sent the file to determine if he or she should ask for revocation of probation regarding the previous conviction.

All of these changes are the result of years of modification to the way our courts process these cases. Most changes represent many hours of discussion and debate. Others just seem to happen following one meeting on the subject. Effective policy development is a process that requires a commitment to the long haul.

Beware of Categories

Several problems inherent to generalized policies and regulations often fail to account for the multiple social positions of those to whom the policy is being applied. For example, the arrest of an immigrant man who has recently arrived in this country could have devastating effects on him and his family. The use of a sentencing matrix that bases the decision to incarcerate an offender on past convictions rather than dangerousness to the victim will result in indigent men being sentenced differently for battering than wealthy men. Obviously, the threat of a conviction has a different meaning to men of different social classes and men from communities with different historical relationships to police and the courts.

Generalizing rules and regulations force interveners to apply broadly defined rules to individual cases in which more effective responses could be made by verifying the specifics. Let us use the example of the Minnesota law, which divides assaults into two broad categories—felonies and misdemeanors. An assault becomes a felony if the assailant used a weapon or the assault resulted in permanent bodily harm or a broken bone to the victim. A misdemeanor is a less serious offense and is treated differently in several significant ways; most notably, a misdemeanor carries a lighter sentence. Judges often sentence misdemeanor cases without requesting presentence investigations.

Statutes are a set of generalizing rules that tend to group different situations together and treat them as if they are the same or similar. Let us look at how victim safety was compromised in a case involving a double arrest in one Minnesota community. State intervention is based on the notion that felony assaults (assaults involving the use of a weapon or permanent bodily harm) are more serious assaults than misdemeanor assaults (no weapon and no permanent bodily harm). The following is an excerpt from a police report documenting the arrest of a woman who had been physically and sexually abused by her husband for 7 years.

I asked Diane Winterstein to tell me what occurred, she said her husband Phillip had come home after drinking at the Y&R bar and was becoming very belligerent. She said he told her that people were "reporting on her." I asked what he might have meant by that and she said that he acts like everybody is his personal watch guard over her and that he makes up affairs she was supposed to have and then says his reporters saw her with someone. She went on to say that Phillip started pushing furniture around; I noted that a chair was pushed over in the dining room. She then went into the kitchen and got out a steak knife and threatened to "poke his eyes out" if he didn't leave the house immediately. I asked her if she was in fear of grave bodily harm at this point and she said no, she thought he was going to leave. Then according to Diane he started to call her names like "whore" and "bitch" and "cunt" at which point she lunged at him and "poked him in the right hand with the knife." She said when he saw the blood he started to cry and she called him a "big baby," at which point she says, "he grabbed me by my hair, began pulling me toward the bathroom and kicking me." She stated that he kicked her three or four times in the legs and right hip area. I asked her if there were any bruises. She showed me the area of her right hip which was red and swollen and beginning to bruise. I asked her if he did anything else to assault her and she stated that he threw her up against the wall and told her that this time she had gone too far. I asked her if she had been violent to him in the past and she said that she often threatens him to get him to leave her alone. . . . She said that he slapped her across the face twice and then spit in her face. . . . I conferred briefly with Officer Dickie and a decision was made to arrest both parties. I informed Diane that I was placing her under arrest for 2nd degree assault and took her into custody without incident. Officer Dickie placed Mr. Winterstein under arrest for 5th degree assault (see Officer Dickie's report for more details). . . . Officer O'Keefe took pictures of both parties' injuries. Both refused medical treatment. I placed a kitchen knife shown to me by Diane Winterstein as the one she used to stab her husband into evidence. (Pence, 1996, p. 123)

In this case, Diane Winterstein faced a prison sentence of 10 years. She eventually pled guilty to second-degree assault for "stabbing her husband with a deadly weapon." Because it was her first offense, she spent only 11 days in jail and was ordered to attend classes for offenders. The case against Phillip Winterstein was eventually dropped in exchange for his agreement to cooperate in the prosecution of the more serious case, the felony against Diane Winterstein.

It is the generalizing character of the law that impedes practitioners from intervening in this case in a way that will protect Diane from future assaults. In fact, it is quite possible that she actually has been made more vulnerable to her abuser by this state intervention than had the police never arrived at her door. Yet each practitioner in this case did his or her job.

Reformists must consider these potential problems when attempting to use generalizing rules, policies, laws, and regulations to enhance victim safety. Of course, it would be impossible to manage a large bureaucracy without these generalizing texts. The implementation team must pay close attention to how redrafts of regulatory texts can backfire on certain groups of people. There is no universal battered woman: Race, class, age, and gender positions result in differing impacts of the same treatment.

Use Policies to Control the Screening of Cases

We have had to grapple with the difference between our rhetoric and the realities of people's lives; for example, consider the following:

- Not every case of domestic violence is best resolved in a courtroom.
- Every act of domestic violence does not necessarily lead to a serious attack on a victim.
- When victims call for help, they are not calling to activate a long, hostile criminal proceeding. They are usually calling to make something happen immediately.
- Many individual victims will not be helped by a prosecution.
- Some cases in which an assault did occur are almost unprovable in a courtroom using the standard of proof required in a criminal trial.
- Most offenders who are arrested for assault will not be with the woman they abused after 5 years.
- With no intervention (sanction and or rehabilitation), most offenders will continue to be violent for many years.

Who determines the significance of such "facts"? Should the responding police officer decide which case should end up in a courtroom? If so, should the officer have full or only partial discretion to make that decision? The first question posed by a policy is to the extent to which a practitioner can exercise discretion when a specific course of action has been prescribed. The loss of discretion is the single biggest source of staff resistance to interagency policy development. Policies should not turn practitioners into robots, mechanically applying a few predetermined actions to a case.

Instituting policies such as Duluth's mandatory arrest policy does not mean that officers stop thinking, evaluating, or making judgments. In fact, the opposite is true. The Duluth police policy states that the officer must decide when and if an arrest is appropriate, providing no injury has occurred. If the case has reached a level of violence in which someone has been injured and there is probable cause to believe that the suspect assaulted the alleged victim, the decision on whether to arrest is moot. This policy has increased officers' use of professional judgment and skills in these cases. In the past, if a case was difficult to sort out or the victim was reluctant to proceed with a criminal case, the officer simply advised and left a brief report or possibly no report. Currently, the officer is required to conduct a thorough investigation and question the parties at the scene to determine whether there is probable cause to arrest, to ascertain if any party was using self-defense, to document any action taken, and to gather evidence needed to prosecute these very difficult cases.

Change Takes Time

The changes we discuss here have been in process for almost two decades. Sometimes rigid policies are needed to change long-held beliefs and traditions in an institution. Eventually, the new practice becomes the routine. The policies can begin to give back a degree of discretion that may have been important to limit for the first 5 to 10 years of reform, given the prevailing thinking about the problem.

Staff turnover affects change. For example, in the early 1980s, when we worked with police officers designing new policy, there was considerable resistance to changing long-held practices. Officers were opposed to giving up discretion on when to arrest. Currently, nearly all of the Duluth police officers comply with and are supportive of the arrest policy and report writing guidelines because most of them became police officers after the policy was enacted. They were trained as rookies to use these methods of responding to domestic assault cases. Recently, when we introduced the notion of not making double arrests when there is a primary aggressor and two assailants, officers again resisted. Some of us thought the officers would appreciate the ability to use their discretion to determine which party to arrest, but instead officers argued strenuously for the application of existing arrest criteria in all cases.

Use Policies to Control for Appropriate Levels of Responses

The criminal justice system cannot treat every assault as if it will become life threatening. Policies and protocols must guide practitioners in determining the level of response to cases based on their perception of the level of danger. With few exceptions, every practitioner has her or his own way of prioritizing these cases.

Policies should dictate the basis for which a practitioner should screen a case out of the system, respond as if it were an emergency situation, or take some action in between. Standard response has been established for domestic violence cases for all responders. Procedural checklists of actions to take on all domestic assault–related cases have been developed. For example, we recently developed a method for practitioners (i.e., prosecutors, probation officers, rehabilitation programs) to alert the sheriff's warrants division to cases that do or do not involve an immediate risk to the victims. The DAIN monitors the attendance of all offenders court ordered to nonviolence classes. If an offender fails to attend court-ordered classes and is harassing or threatening the victim, the DAIN asks for a court hearing to find the offender in contempt of court. The sheriff's department is then notified that this is a high-risk situation. If, on the other hand, an offender fails to attend classes and the victim does not know where he is, has not heard from him, and is not aware of his whereabouts, the DAIN notifies the sheriff's department that this is not a high-risk situation. The sheriff's department then prioritizes the first case over the second in determining how aggressively to look to serve someone. This is necessary in situations in which the warrants division is too overburdened with warrants to look for a person beyond two or three attempts.

We have agreed as a matter of principle not to use scales in determining levels of danger and corresponding levels of institutional action. Instead, in cooperation with practitioners, we discuss and think through the types of cases that would constitute a standard, elevated, or emergency response. An example of this is the sentencing recommendation matrix developed by the probation department in consultation with the shelter advocates and the DAIN staff. This matrix shows how probation officers use information gathered in their presentence investigation, which includes a domestic violence supplement form, to make a decision about an appropriate sentence to recommend. The sentencing recommendation matrix is most effective when it is part of a coordinated community response to domestic violence (see Table 3.1).

Table 3.1 Domestic Violence–Related Misdemeanor Sentencing Recommendation Matrix

	Category 1	Category 2	Category 3	Category 4
Offense	The offender commits an offense against the victim, but no evidence suggests that the offender is battering the victim. The offender has no history of battering.	The offender engages in battering behavior against the victim, but there is no indication that the battering is escalating in severity or frequency or that this offender has battered another person.	The offender has established a clear pattern of battering with this or past victims. The PSI indicates the battering will likely continue and possibly escalate in severity and frequency.	The offender's PSI demonstrates that the heightened, obsessive, or unrelenting nature of the battering poses a high risk of serious harm to this or other victims.
History of violence	This category may include offenders who commit an act uncharacteristic of their typical behavior. It may also include victims of battering who use illegal violence or activities to control or stop violence used against them.	This category may include batterers whose histories include using low levels of violence and activities that threaten or intimidate the victim.	This category may include batterers whose histories include multiple domestic violence–related contacts with the police, demonstrated harassing behavior toward the victim, violation of an OFP, or repeated threats or assaults against this or other victims. The victim may be in fear of serious bodily harm.	This category includes offenders with histories similar to those of Category 3 offenders but also may include stalking behavior, threats to seriously harm or kill, use of weapons or threats to do so, and injuries that require medical attention.

(Continued)

Table 3.1 Continued

	Category 1	Category 2	Category 3	Category 4
Considerations	If the offender in this case is experiencing ongoing battering by the person assaulted, the probation officer considers safety measures for both parties. Specialized programming is recommended, and the probation officer does not consider executed jail time unless the assault is severe.	Recommendations focus on victim safety and rehabilitation programming rather than sanctions.	Victim safety recommendations are combined with more sanction-oriented sentencing, such as the maximum probationary period, some executed jail time, and rehabilitation programming.	Recommendations include the strongest victim safety measures possible, including working with child protection on children's safety. A substantial jail term and long-term probation may be combined with programming if the offender is amenable.
Incarceration or other correctional programming	30 days stayed jail	60 days stayed jail	60 days stayed jail, 10 to 30 days executed jail/ 60 to 90 days stayed jail, 20 to 30 days executed jail	60 to 90 days stayed jail, 20 to 30 days executed jail/ 30 days stayed jail, 60 days executed jail, or 90 days straight time
Gross misdemeanor incarceration or other correctional programming	91 to 120 days stayed jail, 0 to 45 days executed jail	91 to 120 days stayed jail, 45 to 120 days executed jail/ 120 to 180 days stayed jail, 120 to 180 days executed jail	120 to 180 days stayed jail, 120 to 180 days executed jail/ 180 to 365 days stayed jail, 180 to 365 days executed jail
Probation duration[a]	1 year	1 year	2 years	2 years

SOURCE: Arrowhead Regional Corrections and Domestic Abuse Intervention Project, Duluth. Reprinted with permission.
NOTE: PSI = Pre-sentence investigation; OFP = Order for protection.
a. Gross misdemeanor convictions routinely receive 2 years of probation.

58

Another example is the development of the emergency response team. In 1996, we organized a process by which any practitioner in the system can call an emergency response team meeting. If a practitioner feels that an offender poses imminent danger to a victim, he or she can call a meeting of all agents or practitioners involved in the case (e.g., child protection worker, police officer, shelter advocate, probation officer). Either a telephone conference call or an emergency meeting takes place to discuss a response to this case. The recent development of guidelines for jailers to use in alerting the shelter and victims about threats made by suspects in custody is another policy-driven procedure.

Use Policies to Link People Together

As explained in Chapter 5, Duluth agencies have entered into a multiagency agreement in regard to sharing information and documenting responsibilities on these cases. Every policy should guide practitioners on how and when to share information. Figure 3.1 illustrates how we conceptualize each practitioner linking to others in the system.

This figure shows how the probation officer gets information from others in the system. A similar chart can be made with each of the other areas as focal points to see how each agency is linked to others in the system.

Provide Training and Follow-Up

When developing procedures for handling cases, we recognize that most practitioners—whether advocates, probation officers, judges, or police officers—are average people. Forms, procedures, screening tools, assessment forms, and curriculums need to be user-friendly. Practitioners should not be overwhelmed trying to decipher what the tools require, or these recording devices will probably be tossed in the wastebasket and people will go back to using easier methods of dealing with the case.

Training on policies should focus on case examples so that practitioners can apply the guidelines or rules. The DAIP has developed a training curriculum for police officers, probation officers, rehabilitation providers, advocates, and other practitioners in the system. All of the training curricula use case examples and apply policy and proce-

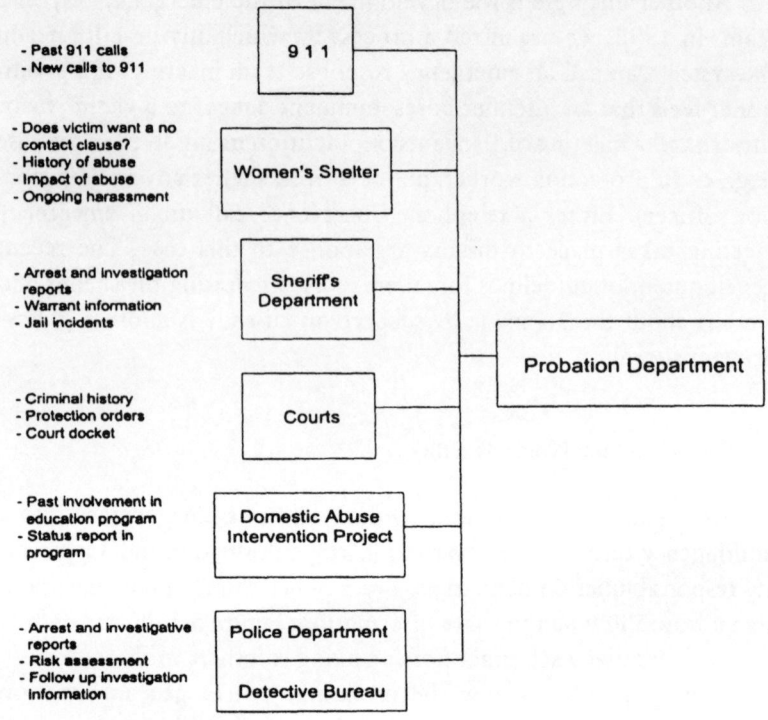

Figure 3.1. Sources of Information for Presentence Investigations

dures to these case examples. For example, in the police training, there are a series of short videos of police officers responding to different cases. Each video is intended to elicit discussion with police officers about a particular aspect of investigating the case, such as identifying the primary aggressor, determining probable cause, distinguishing self-defense from an assault, recording the history of violence, and so on. Each of the training points is centered on actual case studies and practical dilemmas that practitioners face in their everyday work. Similarly, for probation officers, we provide a packet containing 10 cases and ask probation officers to place each of these offenders on the sentencing recommendation matrix. Probation officers then discuss why they placed certain defendants at a level one, two, three, or four on the matrix. In conducting training in this way, we come to an understanding together of how to apply written regulations and rules that we have collectively designed. This style of training has been very effective because it engages practitioners in a process that allows them to understand the intent behind each rule, regulation, and policy, as well as understand the actual requirements on their part. It also leads to discussions that demonstrate how practitioners are linked to others in the system. It helps to identify the problems that practitioners will probably have in applying these procedures and provides them an opportunity to enhance the process by discussing other information or resources needed to carry out a particular policy, regulation, or procedure.[1]

Recognize That Victims and Victim Advocates Are Allies, Not Enemies

It is important to recognize that victim advocates, although they may sometimes seem unreasonable, biased, and maybe even hostile toward the court system, are in fact the most valuable allies that administrators can find if they are truly trying to improve their system's response. Victim advocates are obviously going to be your most vocal critics, but they can tell you where the problems in the system exist. It is important to incorporate ways to listen to the experiences of battered women who have looked for safety and justice from the court system.

In the Duluth system, we have been fortunate to have had a group of battered women who from the beginning volunteered to serve on a policy committee for the shelter and the DAIP. The Battered Women's Advisory Committee (BWAC) consists of 7 to 12 women who have used the system within the previous 4 years. The committee meets six or seven times each year to review and discuss any suggested changes that are being proposed in the system and ask how they believe those changes would have affected them when they were in the process of trying to use the legal system. The committee is made up of women whose class, background, ethnicity, personal history, and experience in the court system differ. Most of the BWAC's meetings center on a 2-hour informal discussion and pizza dinner. Besides this input from victims' perspectives, victim advocates meet on a monthly basis to discuss issues in the legal system and frequently invite supervisors of different agencies to talk about problems in the system. Some of these issues are discussed in Chapter 4 on networking. We believe that without such input from victims and victim advocates, policy reform efforts would not achieve their goal of victim safety as effectively.

Conclusion

We end this discussion on policy making by providing a template we use as the outline for any new policy and a checklist we use when thinking through a policy. This template provides an overview of items that should be covered in a complete policy. It is provided with a warning: If you want practitioners to know what is in a policy, keep it brief and to the point. A policy should have two versions—the practitioner version and administration version. The practitioner version includes I and II. The administration version includes I, II, and III.

    I. The intent and rationale for the policy
    II. Guidelines for processing cases
        (a) what a practitioner should do and under what circumstances
        (b) using procedures, forms, etc.
        (c) what, when, and how information should be shared with others
        (d) applicable laws, definitions, authority
    III. Supervision/monitoring
        (a) how a policy will be monitored by an agency
        (b) steps to ensure compliance
        (c) record sharing for external monitoring (how, with whom)

The following checklist can help policymakers examine how a policy will organize workers to think about and act on the unique features of criminal cases:

- Focus on changing the institution, not the victim
- Balance between the need to standardize and the need to be attentive to the particulars of a case
- Focus on building cooperative relationships
- Focus on practices, not people
- Recognize that nobody owns the whole truth
- Build in methods of ensuring compliance with procedures in policy
- Link practitioners to those beyond the next worker in the system
- Account for the offender's level of danger
- Assume that a victim will be vulnerable to consequences if she or he participates in confronting the offender
- Assume that the offender is likely to batter in future relationships
- Document the pattern and history of abuse when and wherever possible

- Account for how:
  - categories help and hinder the understanding of a case
  - practitioners will get around the intent of the policy
  - offenders will get around the intent of the policy
  - the policy or response will be used against victims of battering
  - different levels of dangerousness and risk require different levels of response
  - punishment or sanction will have an impact on the offender
  - rehabilitation or programming could be used against the victim
  - victims use violence against their abusers
  - slowness will affect victim safety
  - children are affected by violence
  - offenders could use children to control victims
  - institutions send double messages about children's exposure to violence
- Determine who needs information, when, and how they will get it
- Distinguish between differing impacts of intervention depending on the social status of victim or offender
- Put it on the form—do not rely on memory
- Develop standardizing procedures that focus on safety (i.e., matrix, police report form, control log, dispatching screen)
- Do not expect practitioners to be robots
- Provide training that focuses on why and how to carry out new practices by using case studies
- Focus the assessment of institutions on what frames a practitioner's response:
  - rules and regulations
  - administrative forms and procedures
  - resources and technology
  - linkages to others in the system
  - training and ways of thinking
- Make sure the policy covers the following:
  - what to do under specified circumstances
  - guidelines to put cases into appropriate levels of response
  - methods to ensure practitioner compliance (tracking)
  - guidelines for making exceptions to the policy
  - how to document actions
  - how and with whom to share information on a case

If the policy is for the greater good, then it should be carried out in ways that protect the individual victim as much as possible.

Note

1. For information about any of the Domestic Abuse Intervention Project training programs, call or write the National Training Project, 206 West Fourth Street, Duluth, MN 55806; phone: (218) 722-2781.

References

Pence, E. (1996). *Safety of battered women in a textually mediated legal system*. Unpublished doctoral dissertation, University of Toronto, Canada.

Pence, E., & Lizdas, K. (1998). *Domestic violence safety and accountability audit*. Duluth: Minnesota Program Development.

Smith, D. E. (1990). *Texts, facts and femininity: Exploring the relations of rulings*. New York: Routledge Kegan Paul.

4

Enhancing Networking Among Service Providers

Elements of Successful Coordination Strategies

Denise Gamache

Mary Asmus

Despite years of advocacy efforts in communities across the country, the high degree of fragmentation within the justice system continues to result in serious harm to victims of domestic violence. A recent tragedy in Minneapolis is a case in point. In September 1997, a 48-year-old woman, Ilka Mondane, was shot and murdered by her ex-husband. The previous month, Douglas Mondane shot Ilka's current boyfriend in the foot. On September 5, he pled guilty to the felony-level gun charge. He requested a conditional release that was denied, but his bail was lowered so he could be released and get married while awaiting his formal sentencing, scheduled for the end of October. Court records show the county prosecutor did not object to the request. At the time, the court also knew that, in 1995, Mondane had been convicted of robbery in a neighboring county. Mondane posted bail the day it was reduced. Then, police presented another case to the county attorney's office involving an allegation of domestic abuse on August 5, and an order for protection against him issued in 1994 also surfaced. Both cases involved women other than Ilka Mondane (Zack, 1997a, 1997b). The August case involved an allegation that Mondane had threatened his 32-year-old girlfriend by holding a gun to her head, then grabbed her by the throat and said, "You won't be with anybody else" (Powell, 1997, p. 1). Three weeks later, Mondane shot his ex-wife, a few days after they had been officially divorced. The judge who released Mondane commented in the local paper, "If I had known anything about a prior domestic threat, I wouldn't have even thought about reducing bail. To me, [the gun conviction] looked like an isolated kind of event . . . and I honestly didn't think he'd make the $5,000 bail" (deFiebre, 1997, p. 3). The head prosecutor was quoted as stating that it was not unusual for prosecutors to lack information on a case at the bail hearing. "The system we are provided with doesn't get the right information to police, prosecutors, the courts and probation officers in a timely fashion" (Adams, 1997, p. 1).

Seeking to address this problem, many communities have significantly improved the level of communication and coordination among the agencies intervening in domestic violence cases. Different approaches to networking have been developed by projects across the country, and much has been learned about the benefits and problems associated with each strategy. This chapter will discuss the approaches used by the Duluth Domestic Abuse Intervention Project (DAIP) and attempt to identify key elements of successful networking strategies currently implemented around the country.

DAIP's Networking Strategy

When the DAIP project was initiated, its organizers approached law enforcement agencies, the prosecutor's office, court personnel, local social services, and the women's shelter to propose that the DAIP assume the task of coordinating the response to domestic assault cases from initial police intervention through the end of the court's jurisdiction over the case. It is important to stress that the DAIP defined coordination as a dynamic process that went beyond the improvement of communication or case handling within current policies and procedures. The DAIP also proposed to assume the tasks of evaluating the impact of the entire coordinated response and guiding the development of solutions to identified problems. In effect, the DAIP provided the community with staff and resources devoted exclusively to the analysis and reform of the total justice system response to domestic violence cases. This provided the cooperating agencies with new and critical feedback about their work that was not previously available. Although the leadership of each agency may have had measures in place to evaluate their own workers' compliance with internal policies, the resulting impact of their joint efforts and its consequences for victims were not really known. The DAIP organizers felt strongly that the unique nature of the relationship between victims and perpetrators in domestic violence crimes, particularly the abuser's unusual access to the victim and the victim's vulnerability to continued violence, required that the results of the coordinated system be evaluated and reformed from the perspective of their impact on victim safety.

In addition to working with each agency to develop interlocking policies that would improve the consistency of the overall response (as described in Chapter 3), the project initiated various strategies that increased communication among the agencies to accomplish several goals: (a) to improve decision making on individual cases by enhancing the quality of case information available to the intervening agencies, (b) to initiate critical analysis of the combined justice system response to domestic violence cases by providing information on case outcomes and victim satisfaction to all intervening agencies, and (c) to develop and implement solutions to systemic problems by engaging the intervening agencies in problem-solving efforts. The methods used to coordinate the project in the early years still form the basis of the DAIP's approach to networking today.

To maintain its focus on the victim's safety, the DAIP organizers first established a cooperative agreement with the local shelter, the only other advocacy program at the time, and involved shelter advocates in their organizing activities. The fact that the key DAIP organizers were former advocates facilitated this agreement, which remains in effect today. However, since then, additional advocacy programs have been created, so for the past 3 years, a monthly meeting of all women's advocates has been held to maximize their input into the DAIP system's change efforts.

The DAIP organizers learned during the initial negotiations with other agency leaders that each was less defensive and more willing to honestly discuss problems in his or her own agency and the system as a whole when met with individually and privately. Building on this experience, the organizers avoided convening large groups of agency representatives and continued to meet with individuals or in small groups to identify problems and develop solutions. The DAIP became the hub for interagency communication and the catalyst of problem-solving activities. In time, as linkages between personnel in different agencies were established, more communication occurred directly. However, some justice professionals in Duluth would argue that there are advantages in maintaining an outside group to take on certain issues, even when direct communication is quite extensive. It is some-times politically difficult for a representative from one agency in the justice system to directly confront problems with another agency, as each must operate daily within existing power relationships in the justice system. The existence of the DAIP provides practitioners with a way to raise sensitive issues that they do not feel comfortable tackling directly. Over the years, the DAIP staff have devised various strategies to confirm the problem referred to them and bring this information to the attention of the appropriate agencies for resolu-tion. Some examples are discussed later in this section.

To obtain broad participation in the project, the DAIP organizers initially contacted agency leaders to obtain a general commitment to cooperate in this experimental approach. Recognizing that agency heads typically have limited time to devote to any one project and are not necessarily aware of day-to-day practice, the DAIP organizers requested that an appropriate staff person be appointed to serve as the agency's representative to the project, someone who was likely to be interested in this issue or held a position within the agency that was relevant to this effort. The DAIP staff relied on lots of informal dialogue with line staff to gain insight into the actual practices of the intervening agencies and to understand their perspective on the prob-lems associated with the handling of domestic violence cases. Soon after the project began and the new agency policies were adopted, the DAIP initiated a networking group that continues to meet today. To improve ongoing communication on case handling and to better understand the impact of the new interagency policies on individuals, a bimonthly "brown bag lunch" was convened with representatives from the probation office, women's advocates, the DAIP, and the men's group facilitators. (Batterers' educational groups were an inno-vation that the DAIP introduced as part of the project, and three local mental health agencies also agreed to initiate them.) These practitioners are uniquely positioned to follow the victims and offenders after the case reaches sentencing. This group trained together to develop a common philosophical approach and continuously reexamines their shared perspective as, over time, experiences with individual cases force all of the cooperating agencies to acknowledge problems with existing policies and revise their approach. As these issues arise, representatives from the appropriate agencies will be invited to attend and participate in the discussions. The group is particularly sensitive to victim safety issues during the probationary period and may signal others in the justice system when risky situations arise.

Once the agency policies were implemented, the DAIP organized quarterly interagency meetings involving the heads or designated representatives of the probation office, the city prosecutor's office, the mental health agencies, the shelter, and the judges. The purpose of these sessions was to keep the leadership informed of the project's activities and results. Issues that required policy-level changes were presented for discussion. During the first years, some problems were identified and discussed at these meetings, but it was not the ideal vehicle for identifying less obvious problems in the system that were better uncovered in the brown bag lunches and a series of project evaluations (see Pence & Lizdas, 1998). As successful experience with the coordination effort built and the usefulness of the interagency meetings faded, they dwindled to once a year. The DAIP now uses the meetings in the same manner as its other networking activities. Interagency meetings are convened when the issue to be discussed and resolved involves the agencies at the policy-making level of decision making. For example, after several years of dormancy, members of the interagency meeting were recently very active in the development of new interagency agreements on data sharing required by the adoption of a computer network that linked the cooperating agencies for the first time.

To summarize, systemic problems, whether identified by justice practitioners or advocates, are discussed with the DAIP staff who assist in developing different strategies to address different problems. Typically, the staff will gather any further information needed to ascertain the exact nature of the problem. Case files for a period of time may be reviewed, or interviews with relevant practitioners or affected victims may be conducted to clarify the issues involved. Staff then bring together representatives from the appropriate agencies to discuss the data and develop solutions that are implemented and evaluated. This approach allows problems to be discussed initially in a nonpublic setting, decreasing the defensiveness of the agency involved and facilitating openness to change. If the issue cannot be resolved without major policy changes, a proposal is developed and brought to the appropriate agency leaders for their review and approval. Depending on the issue, this process has taken weeks and, in some complex cases, more than a year. Despite the conflicts and tensions that are inherent in these types of negotiations, a high level of trust has been established among the cooperating agencies as they built a history of mutually satisfactory outcomes and successful reforms. As a result, communication among the partners is now quite frequent and open. Within the guidelines of the interagency agreements, each agency allows an incredible level of access to information and scrutiny of their practice, to a degree that is often remarked on by visitors. This trust level has facilitated the development of increasingly sophisticated networking processes that address highly complex issues related to the justice response to domestic violence. Some examples from the DAIP's history illustrate how the coordination process has operated and developed over time.

One of the innovations incorporated into the project at its inception was the development of batterers' education groups, which were offered as an alternative sanction in sentences of misdemeanor offenders. The groups were also available as a remedy that could be ordered by the civil court in protection order proceedings. Soon, the members of the brown bag lunch groups were faced with the dilemma of how to handle reports of repeated violence made by the men in the groups that were not reported by the victims. How should these probation violations be handled? Should the abuser automatically be dismissed from the program? Should the victim's wishes on the matter be taken into account? How could an abuser be held accountable for this violence in a way that safeguarded the victim's safety? After much discussion, the group agreed that incidents involving injury should always be reported to the probation officer to hold the offender accountable. If after contacting the victim, the group facilitator found that the incident did not result in injury and it was not in the best interest of the victim, he or she could discuss the case at the next brown bag lunch, which could decide not to report. The probation officer would impose some type of sanction but would decide these on a case-by-case basis, depending on the circumstances. For example, after talking with the victim, the probation officer might order the offender to serve a few days in jail but allow this done on weekends to permit the offender to retain his job if this would adversely affect the family. The initial agreement not to report some offenses was quite controversial, with the group split almost equally on this approach. A few years later, the policy was altered to require reports of "all acts of violence" with one exception. Contact by an advocate with the victim was required before a report was made, and if the victim, advocate, or counselor believed that reporting the act would place the victim in danger, the matter was referred to the brown bag members who formulated an appropriate recommendation to the probation officer. The evolution of this policy provides a good illustration of the ongoing struggle to centralize the goal of victim safety while attempting to achieve the project's other goals of offender accountability and deterrence of violence in the community.

A more recent example deals with the issue of women who had been arrested for assaults on partners who had previously assaulted them. During a period of a few months, it appeared to the advocates that an unusually high number of women had been arrested, and their concerns were brought to the DAIP through the Women's Advocates meeting. The arrest of victims has a serious effect on victim safety. If victims are arrested inappropriately, their right to defend themselves is compromised, as well as their willingness to call for police assistance if beaten again. For these reasons, it was important to gain an accurate understanding of why these arrests had occurred. The police department agreed to pull the 12 cases from that period, and the appropriate supervisor reviewed them with the responding officers. The advocates also gathered information from the women involved. The DAIP staff, local advocates, and the supervisor then met to review the cases. The group agreed that the majority of arrests had been properly executed according to the existing arrest policy. This swift and open response effectively answered the advocates' concerns and prompted them to shift their attention to the arrest policy itself.

Over the past couple years, the community has been involved in a major rethinking of the criminal justice approach to cases involving victims of battering who use violence themselves. This initiative illustrates the exceptional level of coordination and trust that exists among the Duluth partners. As the issue of the arrests of victims was discussed informally, the concern about justice and safety for these women was shared by many practitioners. Police officers felt badly when arresting a victim whom they knew was responding to repeated abuse. The prosecutor's office questioned the impact of proceeding with these cases and wondered if they should be handled differently from other domestic assaults. The DAIP women's group facilitators were struggling with how to best work with the women court ordered to their groups. At an informal lunch of prosecutors, police officers, probation officers, and advocates, the group was asked to identify a past case of this type that had been handled properly according to existing policies but that had resulted in an outcome that they felt created a worse situation for the victim. Everyone could think of at least one case, but the group was stymied about how best to solve the problem.

The prosecutor's office and the DAIP staff together developed a strategy to engage the agencies in addressing this issue. Taking advantage of the Violence Against Women Act funds administered by the state, the prosecutor's office submitted a proposal for the project that included cooperative agreements from the police department, the probation office, the shelter, Mending the Sacred Hoop (Native American services organized by the DAIP), and the DAIP outlining their roles. The proposal was funded, and a networking group composed of two representatives from each agency was instituted with a meeting convened every other week. For the first 7 months, the group struggled to define this complex issue because little published research was available to guide decisions on how best to respond. The DAIP devoted other financial resources to conducting a series of interviews with women who had been arrested in Duluth and in other communities in which a sister project operated. The networking group invited additional staff members to assist in discussions of various nuances of these situations, such as when alcoholism is an additional factor in the case.

When the group was able to articulate some of the key controversies that were impeding their progress, they held a large meeting of approximately 50 police officers, prosecutors, court administrators, probation officers, and advocates. The participants were assigned to multidisciplinary groups and asked to consider sample cases that raised the particular dilemmas stumping the networking group. Although many issues remained unresolved, the meeting reaffirmed the fact that all agencies were willing to consider alternatives to their existing policies. Over the next 9 months, the networking group developed and revised a series of proposals for a new coordinated approach to these cases. Debate was extraordinarily heated and difficult, but eventually the group agreed to experiment with new case disposition guidelines. The prosecutor conducted additional meetings with a few individuals at a time to hammer out details. Several different prosecution and probation guidelines were written and scrapped, until consensus was finally reached on an approach to try as long as everyone agreed to modify or halt the project should the planned evaluation uncover problems. The newly titled *Crossroads Program* is intended to provide victims of domestic abuse who are charged with criminal offenses against their partners an opportunity to address their use of violence within the larger context of their victimization. It seeks to hold participants accountable without invoking the full ramifications of the criminal court process and provides guidelines for prosecutors to defer charges on the successful completion of certain conditions. The program is outlined in several documents: (a) a statement of philosophy that explains the program's intent; (b) a memorandum of understanding signed by the city attorney's office, the probation department, the shelter, and the DAIP that details each of their agreed responsibilities; (c) evaluation guidelines for probation officers and prosecutors on how to determine eligibility for the program; (d) prosecution guidelines that set requirements for the case to be considered for deferral; and (e) an application form. The program was initiated in December 1997, and the networking group is currently finalizing plans for its evaluation.

Other chapters in this book describe the networking that produced a new sentencing matrix, the Domestic Abuse Information Network (DAIN) interagency agreements on data sharing, the emergency response team, and the visitation center. All of these examples demonstrate the flexibility and sophistication of the DAIP's coordination model, its ability to design innovative approaches to complex issues and implement real reforms in the community, and its ability to persuade the intervening agencies to centralize victim safety as the guiding principle of their policies and practice.

Key Elements of Successful Networking on Domestic Violence Cases

Greater coordination among community agencies is a concept that has been embraced and encouraged by several national organizations—notably, the National Council of Juvenile and Family Court Judges, the American Prosecutor's Research Institute, the American Bar Association, and the American Medical Association. All of these organizations have urged the formation of "coordinating councils," an approach that differs from that of the DAIP in many ways. To compare this model with the DAIP's approach, it is important to clarify what is meant by the term. In this chapter, *coordinating council* denotes any model in which a committee is created to lead the coordinating effort. The membership consists of representatives—usually leaders at a policy-making level—from agencies, departments, and community groups dealing with domestic violence. Its stated purpose is to increase communication and improve coordination among the member agencies so that incidents of domestic violence are reduced and prevented. Within this broad goal, a range of activities are planned. Most large councils eventually develop a system of subcommittees to accomplish their work. Leadership of the council varies but is often a judge or prosecutor and sometimes the head of a local organization or governmental unit. Councils often focus on coordinating the justice system response with social services to victims, batterers, and their families. However, in many jurisdictions, the council has defined its role as much broader and concerns itself with the entire community response to domestic violence, including representatives from medical facilities, public schools, public health nurses, religious institutions, and local businesses. Although some states have also set up coordinating bodies to guide statewide plans, this discussion relates more to coordination issues on the local level.

Several points distinguish the coordinating council model from the DAIP approach: There is not an external monitoring agency focused on institutional advocacy guiding the process, the council model emphasizes the participation and leadership of personnel at the policy-making level of institutions, and the recommended council structure does not necessarily facilitate ways to overcome the existing power dynamics in the criminal justice system that can impede the work of the council. Over the past years, different communities have experienced varying levels of success when adopting either networking model. An analysis of the key elements of successful coordination efforts provides important guidance for communities that are initiating coordination efforts or those attempting to revive an ailing or ineffective project.

The Stated Goal of the Coordinating Effort Centralizes
Victim Safety and Protection

Because the DAIP has always considered battered women to be its primary constituency, its coordination efforts have been directed toward the goal of victim safety. Proposed changes or additions to the justice system response were examined as to their contribution to this end. The key question that advocates repeatedly posed was, "How does this practice improve or impair a victim's protection and safety?"

The importance of maintaining a commitment to this priority is clear when conflicting goals arise in discussions of proposed reforms. For example, a local coordinating council was considering a proposal from the court administrator, who was responsible for assisting victims in writing up protection orders. She was concerned that the criminal acts described in the orders, some of which were extremely serious, were not often being charged in criminal court. She proposed that procedures be implemented to automatically refer the protection order forms to the appropriate police department so they could initiate charges based on the information on criminal acts contained in the orders. Her intent was to hold these abusers accountable for their criminal acts, a common goal of coordination efforts. However, in discussing the idea, the former victims and advocates on the council were unanimous in arguing that this change could be harmful to victims in several ways. Victims choose not to pursue criminal charges for different reasons, but often they feel that this process may endanger them. The protection order process allows victims different remedies from those available in the criminal courts, such as removal of the abuser from the home or temporary custody arrangements. A victim who feels that these remedies are more helpful to her should be allowed to seek them without being forced into other legal proceedings that she is not interested in pursuing. Most important, many felt that this change would keep women from applying for protection orders, thus blocking access to a significant legal option. The council's priority on victim safety led them to reject the proposal. Similar concerns are present in the current debate over the public policy in some states that requires mandatory reporting by medical personnel of patients who disclose domestic assaults. Should patients be thrust into the legal system when seeking medical aid, even when they do not wish to involve the criminal courts? Will this practice keep women from obtaining critical medical attention and further endanger their lives? Only recently have studies been initiated to evaluate the impact of this policy on victims of domestic violence.

Another example highlights the difficulty of adhering to this priority, even when all parties share a strong commitment to it. The DAIP's experience with the development of a domestic violence prosecution policy has been a struggle to safeguard victim safety in a context of ambiguous circumstances and conflicting goals. In its original interagency agreement, the city prosecutor's policy was to vigorously pursue domestic assault cases, to subpoena victims to appear, and to proceed to trial if necessary. Cases were not dismissed unless evidence was so lacking that the prosecutor felt it was impossible to proceed. Victims were subpoenaed and sometimes forced to testify, but they were not punished if they altered their testimony or failed to appear in court. The theory behind this approach was that the state was trying to shift the burden of confronting the abuser from the shoulders of the victim. The state understood that the victim's relationship with the abuser resulted in her reluctance to participate in the process. However, to place sanctions on the abuser that would aim to deter future violence, the prosecutor proceeded with the case. After several years, the prosecutor and advocates expressed concern about the policy's impact on the safety of reluctant victims and the sense that the trials were revictimizing the victims. Since the policy had been implemented, guilty pleas had decreased and the defense bar brought more cases to trial. The prosecutor found that these trials were often lost or, if won, felt like hollow victories if the victim was so anguished by the proceedings. After many discussions about these concerns, the policy was shifted, and the prosecutor's office was more willing to negotiate pleas to lesser charges or possibly dismiss a case if a victim clearly desired it. However, experience with this policy resulted in the belief that the new approach also was compromising victim safety. If the reluctance of a victim stemmed from the abuser's control over her outside of the court, the dismissal only reinforced his sense of power by rewarding his ability to escape sanctions by manipulating her and the courts. The prosecutor began to see repeat offenders enter the courts and felt that the justice system lacked any controls over their behavior. Again, the prosecutor, advocates, and the DAIP staff reviewed the policy and sought ways to sanction the abuser but safeguard the victim from retaliation. The prosecutor refocused his or her trial strategy on proving the case without the victim's testimony, which led to a new cooperative training effort with the police department that enhanced police investigation and evidence gathering in ways that strengthened the prosecutor's ability to try the case. As a result, more trials were successful, and the prosecutor's ability to obtain guilty pleas and spare the victim from court proceedings was improved.

In some of the articles about coordinating councils, the first step of organizing a council is described as "decide on a common goal." However, without a clear commitment to the priority of victim safety, it is more likely that the council will propose changes in policy that cause additional problems for victims or actually endanger them. It is important that coordination not be seen as an end in itself but as a means to achieve the overall goal. For example, in response to internal case-processing concerns, a local coordinating council recommended changes to the court calendar that sped up the processing of misdemeanor cases. As a result, a large number of victims failed to appear at hearings, and record numbers of cases were dismissed. The shortened time frame made it impossible for court staff and advocates to contact or work with victims. Although the calendar change solved a court personnel problem, the failure to evaluate the proposal from the viewpoint of its impact on victims had serious negative consequences.

In addition, the institutions represented on the council have roles and interests in the justice system that can sometimes compete with the priority of victim safety. A prosecutor who puts a high priority on obtaining convictions may seek to institute policies that punish victims who refuse to cooperate. A police department may resist enforcing violations of protection orders if it takes the view that the victims are to blame for the offenders' return to the residence. Projects such as the DAIP and early coordinating committees or task forces were organized by advocates or practitioners who already had a strong commitment to victims. The "core group" kept the priority of victim safety clearly in focus as it involved others in its work or established a formal council structure. However, with the promotion of the coordinating council model around the country, a formal council structure may be adopted as a starting point for coordination efforts, rather than having formed organically over time. The resulting group often lacks a shared understanding of domestic violence and a core group that will maintain a focus on victim safety as the cornerstone of the project. One of the most difficult challenges for these councils is the development of a shared philosophical base that centralizes victim safety and maintains this priority over time.

The centralization of victim safety is ensured through the composition of the coordinating body and by instituting various means by which activities are evaluated from this perspective. To repeat an important concept noted in the previous chapter: Without some kind of significant input from victim advocates and victims in this process, the outcome of the justice reform effort is unlikely to actually centralize issues of victim safety. The involvement of these two groups is invaluable to a coordination effort because they have firsthand knowledge of the handling of the case from police intervention through probation in criminal court and through related proceedings in civil court, unlike justice system practitioners who must pass cases along to the next intervening agency in the system. Advocates often have the best opportunity to gather information on the overall impact of the system's intervention on victims. Successful coordination efforts using different structures, such as Duluth, San Diego, Pittsburgh, and Seattle, have been inclusive in their approach and actively sought the participation of numbers of advocates and victims.

The composition of the coordinating body should facilitate the participation of all existing advocacy programs in a community. In Duluth, the DAIP staff and shelter advocates are involved in all coordination activities. In San Diego, the large domestic violence council has numerous representatives from the local advocacy programs who are also active on all of its subcommittees. The Los Angeles County Domestic Violence Council also has taken a unique approach to this issue. Half of the council's membership comprises representatives from the relevant city and county departments who have contact with domestic violence victims, and half of the members represent advocacy programs and shelters. In addition, battered women's agencies are represented by two voting representatives, and public agencies have only one. In a statement explaining their structure, Alana Bowman (1993), then council chair, wrote,

> Until the Council created this bold structure, battered women and
> their advocates were too frequently outnumbered during policy meet-
> ings in which one or two advocates met with many representatives

from government agencies. . . . Without this commitment to strong
representation by domestic violence programs, county agencies can
numerically overwhelm the true experts on the Council, those community-based agencies whose sole purpose is to represent battered
women's interests. When only a single shelter exists in a county, that
single representative voice can easily become viewed as just another
member of the Council, and the focus can become diffused, addressing instead other agency priorities. The concerns of battered women's
representatives can become just one of the voices on the panel, rather
than the necessary controlling force. . . . This distinction is important
and should become the model for all proposed domestic violence
coordinating agencies which may be created. (p. 1)

Too many communities have instituted councils that exclude significant input from advocates or victims. The example of the court
calendar fiasco cited earlier was a decision of a council that had been
constituted to deliberately exclude all but one advocacy group in its
large metropolitan area. In addition, the inclusion of all groups serving
victims increases the input of racial or ethnic minorities within a community and other groups who have particular issues related to their
treatment by the justice system, such as gays and lesbians or immigrant
and refugee women. This is not to say that victim advocates do not
also propose ideas that are misguided or that they should not be challenged by justice system practitioners. However, the deliberate limitation of this input raises the likelihood that reforms will fail to account
for the safety of all victims in a community.

It also must be acknowledged that not all advocacy programs in
local communities are prepared to assume the key role that is necessary for coordination to be effective. Some have limited experience in
community organizing or working with the justice system in their
community; many lack the resources that would allow them to devote
staff to this function. Once a coordination council is established, the
time required to participate effectively sometimes has overwhelmed
small advocacy programs, leaving the governmental agencies frustrated by their absence. As communities develop coordination plans
and apply for additional financial resources, it is important that funds
be designated to local advocacy programs so that they can hire staff
capable of fulfilling these coordinating functions. With the additional
funds now available through the Violence Against Women Act to
support collaborative initiatives, communities have a unique opportunity to improve the effectiveness of their coordination efforts, regard-

less of the model they have adopted, by supporting the expansion of their local advocacy programs.

In addition to the meaningful inclusion of victim advocates, the coordinating body should institute ways to actively gather feedback from victims to monitor the impact of their activities on victim safety. As previously described, the DAIP has conducted a series of evaluations that survey victims about their experiences with each intervening agency. After the results are written up, the women are invited to discuss their views on what the data really mean and how the project could resolve the problems that have been identified. The DAIP also maintains an advisory group of victims who have been through the courts and convenes meetings a few times a year to discuss each new idea for reform. An overwhelmingly negative reaction from this group will effectively veto a proposal, and alternative solutions will be pursued.

The coordinating body takes account of the existing power dynamics in the justice system and the community when developing decision-making procedures and strategies for resolving problems and conflicts. As described in the examples previously cited, the DAIP customizes its coordination efforts to fit the issue under consideration. A major reason for this approach is an acknowledgment of the power dynamics and politics operating within the justice system and the community at large. In the early development of the project, it became clear to the staff that discussions were more open and honest, with much less defensiveness when conducted in private meetings with an agency or with only the agencies involved in the problem. In more public forums, agency staff tended to defend their practices or personnel and avoid any detailed discussion of possible problems. The power relationships within the justice system also impeded honest interchanges. The police department deflected any suggestion that they were not conducting good investigations in front of the prosecutor or judge. Due to the adversarial nature of the justice system, the prosecutor's office avoided discussion of their protocols when defense attorneys were present. Advocates and practitioners found it difficult to discuss problems with the judiciary when they were likely to appear before the same judges on individual cases. Therefore, large public meetings with all of the cooperating agencies were reserved for keeping agency leaders informed about the impact of the coordinated response and more general discussion of their views on future project activities. Later, in-depth discussions of these plans were held in more informal settings with the individual leaders of the affected agencies.

A coordinating council often duplicates the makeup of the justice system and the existing power relationships. The meetings are public, with many councils now including other community institutions outside of the justice system. This structure presents serious impediments to open discussion. Time for in-depth analysis is often limited. Difficult issues or conflicts are unlikely to surface in this type of public forum unless organizers develop additional strategies to identify and resolve them. In fact, a common complaint about councils is that they have tended to stagnate after the more obvious coordination problems have been resolved. Several large councils, such as the Domestic Violence Council in San Diego, have assigned the bulk of their work to subcommittees composed of advocates and related practitioners who are able to work out conflicts without involving the entire body or to prepare proposals for the full council. Clearly, staff from the concerned agencies need to be involved in a decision that affects their work, and others should be involved when it becomes clear that they are affected or that the strategy for solving the problem involves them. A flexible approach, employing a variety of customized and timely problem-solving strategies, is an important element of successful coordination efforts.

Another way to improve effectiveness is to maximize the participation of middle managers and frontline workers in problem-solving discussions. Although the participation of agency leaders has the advantage of engaging the staff who have the power to adopt policy changes, leaders may lack information on the day-to-day experiences of the agency, unlike the staff who directly handle these cases. When analyzing the actual practices in an agency, this is precisely the level of information needed. Here again, power dynamics have to be respected. Putting line staff into discussion groups with their own supervisors can stifle their willingness to openly discuss internal problems or disagree publicly with their supervisor's views.

Last, additional questions have been raised about the participation of judges on coordinating councils. This has been encouraged for different reasons: Judges have a unique perspective on the ways courts operate, control how parties have access to judicial intervention, and play a major role in holding offenders accountable by imposing sanctions or controls on their behavior. Some judges have also acknowledged that they as a group are in need of education on domestic violence. In Santa Clara, the judges claimed that by their participation, they learned a great deal about the different ways that domestic violence cases are processed through the court system and made significant administrative changes as a result (Edwards, 1992). However, these benefits are counterbalanced by concerns about separation of powers and the impact of participation on judicial impartiality.

An incident from a local judge-led council illustrates this point. All council members had been asked to prepare recommendations for any changes in the handling of domestic violence cases that they felt would improve the system. At the meeting, the public defender's office suggested that police should photograph not only the victim's injuries but also take photos of others at the scene. As council chair, the judge facilitated and participated in the subsequent discussion of this proposed change of police procedures on the gathering of evidence. The prosecutor and police officers present grasped immediately that the public defender would use these materials to attempt to attack their cases. The proposal was ultimately not supported, but the discussion was uncomfortable. Whereas the defense attorney and prosecutor have clear roles as advocates in the system, the judge's role is designed to be impartial. This incident caused some members of the council to ponder the issue of the judge's participation: Should judges participate in setting police policy when they may be asked to rule on evidence that arises from that policy? Should they participate in setting policies for prosecutors or defense attorneys? Could the perception arise that a judge's decision in an individual case was prejudiced by his or her public agreement with the manner in which the case was presented to the court? Was it appropriate for the judicial branch of government to be involved in setting policies of the executive branch? In this situation, these concerns were exacerbated by a lack of clear decision-making procedures for the council. The judge had convened the council and acted as chair; no further discussion of how decisions would be reached had occurred. This omission resulted in the appearance that the judge was in a position of authority over other council members, even if this was not intended.

In a model such as the DAIP, these concerns have not arisen because the judges are not asked to be involved in the policy making of other agencies. They have been invited and have attended educational training sessions on domestic violence and related issues. They have attended informational meetings about the project's progress or evaluation results, which provided the victims' perspective on the impact of the combined intervention. Staff have met with judges to address issues related to court procedures that were important to the coordinated case response, such as their initial agreement to order presentence investigations for all misdemeanor domestic crimes, not a standard practice at that time. The DAIP approach preserves judicial impartiality and sidesteps separation of powers issues.

In discussions of these issues around the country, a range of opinions have been expressed. At least one judiciary ethics committee (Judicial Qualifications Commission, 1995) has issued an opinion defining some limitations on judicial participation in certain aspects of the work of state commissions and local task forces. Certainly, further debate and guidance on this topic are needed. In the meantime, it would probably be wise for councils that include judges to discuss this issue and formulate their own guidelines about limitations on judicial participation, if the group feels they are warranted. Clear definitions of the council's mission and the adoption of democratic decision-making procedures also can facilitate the open participation of all members of the council.

The cooperating agencies agree to exchange information that not only improves the response to individual cases but also allows the coordinating body to monitor adherence to interagency agreements and evaluate the impact of the coordinated effort. To reduce fragmentation in the response to individual domestic violence cases, most coordination efforts institute new ways to communicate vital case information to each professional intervening in the case. The lack of these linkages is often one of the most obvious problems in the justice system response. In the early stages of many coordination efforts, attention has focused on the development of new sources of case information, such as reports provided by advocates with the victim's permission and on the improvement of data exchange among the intervening agencies, such as the inclusion of civil court data on existing protection orders in the case file of a defendant appearing in criminal court. Data privacy laws must be taken into account when proposing new data exchanges, but most communities find it possible to introduce many improvements fully within these guidelines.

Increasingly, data exchanges are being facilitated by the computerization of databases and the introduction of computer networks, but many improvements can be accomplished manually with the dedication of resources to the task. For example, in Duluth, the protection order files are located in the same building as the probation office, yet for years, neither probation officers, prosecutors, nor judges were routinely checking these files before making decisions in criminal domestic assault cases. Once this problem was identified, funds were raised to allow the police department to contract with the DAIP for a staff position whose role was to ensure that information from this source and others is routinely included in each case file and provided to all of the intervening agencies in accordance with interagency agreements on data sharing. Only recently has this information exchange been computerized.

However, to evaluate the effectiveness of these and all other changes instituted as part of a coordinated effort, the coordinating body must be able to monitor the actual compliance of the cooperating agencies with the protocols they have adopted. Lacking this information, conclusions cannot be accurately drawn about the success or failures resulting from the effort. Without access to police reports, how can a coordinating body be assured that arrest policies are being implemented properly? If a probation department has agreed that certain actions by offenders should result in violations of probation that are reported to the court, how can the coordinating body ascertain that this is happening without access to probation records? To be able to demonstrate its success, a coordinating body must be able to identify the information necessary to monitor and evaluate its progress. Then, it must obtain agreements to provide access to this information from the cooperating agencies. A clear plan for how the evaluative information will be relayed to the agencies and how it will be shared with the public facilitates the process of negotiating these agreements.

Over time, normal institutional processes, such as staff turnover, can erode compliance with agency policies. It is important to continue to randomly assess performance so that any resulting problems can be identified and resolved. At a recent conference, one of the authors heard Casey Gwinn, the San Diego city attorney who has been an active member of the city's Domestic Violence Coordinating Council, speak of the need for his city to review accountability to written policies and revitalize its response. Over the past 2 years, the DAIP has developed and used a method of institutional analysis, titled a "safety and accountability audit," to examine all agency practices in depth. The audit team of advocates and justice professionals observed and interviewed workers in each agency and randomly surveyed case records as to their compliance with agency policies. They developed more than 60 recommendations for additional changes to agency practices, even after 18 years of successful collaboration and reform. For communities to continue to make in-depth improvements in the justice response to domestic violence cases, each cooperating agency needs to subject its practices to the scrutiny of its partners and to participate fully in the discussion of how problems can be resolved.

The coordination role is assumed by persons who possess exceptional negotiation skills and who are able to devote the time and resources necessary to adequately fulfill these responsibilities. Successful coordination efforts of either model have been initiated by extraordinary individuals with exceptional organizational and leadership skills. These leaders, whether justice practitioners or advocates, have possessed key qualities needed to build a successful collaboration: strong analytical and problem-solving skills, highly developed interpersonal skills, exceptional ability to negotiate agreements and resolve conflicts with diverse groups of people, and a passionate commitment to this work. When communities adopt a council structure with appointed members, the resulting group may or may not include individuals with these skills.

This problem may be remedied to some degree if skilled staff can be employed to implement the coordinating effort. Some communities effectively use subcommittees to enable greater participation of community members in the actual coordination effort, another strategy that increases involvement by people committed to this issue. An organization attempting to adopt the DAIP's networking approach also needs to hire community organizers of this type. Although some individuals just seem blessed with these qualities, it is also true that most of us can improve our abilities in these areas with effective training. However, the education of many justice professionals and advocates prepares them only to fulfill their individual roles in the system and may not necessarily provide them with the skills needed to lead successful collaborations. Communities that intend to shift their entire justice response to a more open, collaborative process must plan to provide training in collaboration skills to the staff charged with this task.

The success of both coordination models has been greatly facilitated by the availability of adequate numbers of staff who are able to devote their time to coordination activities rather than other agency functions. Although initial efforts may succeed with the participating agencies donating staff time, it becomes increasingly difficult to sustain these activities or initiate the monitoring or evaluations necessary to measure the impact of the project without additional resources. Although it is true that many of the policy changes enacted by these projects may not entail additional expenditures, the communication and time necessary to identify issues and create these solutions do. Currently, available federal funding can assist local communities in supporting the additional staff needed to organize effective coordination efforts.

Conclusion

There is no question that greater coordination among intervening agencies will help prevent tragedies such as the death of Ilka Mondane. The challenge to our communities is to create and maintain coordination efforts that effectively result in desirable and predictable outcomes for victims, such as greater access to civil and criminal court remedies that increase her protection, more effective confrontation and control of the abuser by the justice system and by the community at large, and greater access to community resources that provide tangible support as she attempts to plan for the future.

The coordinating council model has been heavily promoted to the extent that advocates and justice professionals have sometimes concluded that they cannot address fragmentation issues unless a formal council is established. However, for all the reasons discussed earlier, the adoption of a council structure should not be viewed as the solution to coordination problems. Although some communities are developmentally ready to formalize existing cooperative relationships, in too many communities, much energy has been wasted in repeated attempts to bring everyone to the table in the face of considerable resistance from a number of key players in the system. Instead, a more effective strategy would devote these scarce resources to the building of linkages among those agencies willing to initiate collaborative problem-solving efforts and later use these successes to persuade other agencies to participate. The creation of some type of coordinating structure alone, whether a council model or the DAIP approach, will accomplish little unless the cooperating agencies are willing to hold themselves accountable not only to each other but ultimately to the victims in their community. This commitment is best demonstrated through the active monitoring of compliance with interagency agreements and the ongoing evaluation of reforms from a perspective of their impact on the safety, autonomy, and agency of domestic violence victims.

References

Adams, J. (1997, October 10). Man free on bail is charged in killing, judge and prosecutor learned of new assault allegations against suspect after bail was reduced. *Minneapolis Star Tribune*, p. 1.

Bowman, A. (1993). *Structuring county domestic violence councils*. Unpublished manuscript.

deFiebre, C. (1997, October 3). House to review criminal-release practices: "We want to do what it takes to keep our streets and peoples safe," said Rep Joe Mullery, DFL-Minneapolis, who will lead the panel. *Minneapolis Star Tribune*, p. 3.

Edwards, L. P. (1992). Reducing family violence: The role of the family violence council. *Juvenile & Family Court Journal, 43*(3), 1-18.

Judicial Qualifications Commission. (1995). JQC Opinion No. 201, issued by the Georgia JQC, Suite 206, 77 E. Crossville Road, Roswell, GA 30075.

Pence, E., & Lizdas, K. (1998). *Domestic violence safety and accountability audit*. Duluth: Minnesota Program Development.

Powell, J. (1997, September 30). Woman slain by man free on bail, police say prison term was coming. *Minneapolis Star Tribune*, p. 1.

Zack, M. (1997a, October 31). Man, fiancee indicted in death of ex-wife. *Minneapolis Star Tribune*, p. 1.

Zack, M. (1997b, December 9). Plea withdrawn in gun-possession case. *Minneapolis Star Tribune*, p. 3.

5

Building Monitoring and Tracking Systems

Dennis R. Falk
Nancy Helgeson

This chapter provides a description of monitoring and tracking systems (hereafter referred to as tracking systems) as they relate to responding to domestic violence, drawing heavily on the experience of developing and maintaining a system in Duluth, Minnesota. The philosophy underlying a tracking system is described, followed by a description of tracking systems in general. Our experience in Duluth is emphasized, describing the historical background and current system, followed by a description of benefits and problems based on our experience. The final section, which focuses on what we have learned from developing the Duluth tracking system, includes guidelines for others to follow if they want to take advantage of our experience.

This chapter primarily relates to experiences with a tracking system in one community and therefore does not include references to literature on what has been undertaken elsewhere. Although tracking systems are used elsewhere in criminal justice systems (Hamilton, 1991; "System Improves," 1997), limited resources on tracking systems related to domestic violence are difficult to obtain (Nova Scotia Family Violence Tracking Project, 1995). This chapter will incorporate other writing undertaken at the Domestic Abuse Intervention

89

Project (DAIP) in Duluth by Barnes (1996) but will not cite that work on an ongoing basis.

Philosophy for Monitoring and Tracking Systems: Monitoring as a Form of Accountability

Safety for women must be at the core of all activities in responding to situations in which domestic violence has occurred. For decades, women's safety has been jeopardized in part because knowledge of violence remained in the home. By maintaining secrecy about domestic violence, batterers were able to maintain control over their victims. Thus, women continued to be battered because those members of the community who could intervene either did not have information about the offenses or were drawn into the thinking that public intervention was not warranted.

As shelters opened across the country, women were given a vehicle in which to break the silence and to report domestic violence. When they do so, a specialized and fragmented legal service system responds to these reports. Operators at 911, police officers, court advocates, prosecutors, judges, probation officers, and rehabilitation class facilitators may all become involved in a single case. Each component of this community response collects some information about the case as they encounter the victim or the batterer, and each component requires information to do its job effectively.

A new kind of silence is rooted in the institutional methods of processing these cases. No person follows a case from the 911 call through the literally dozens of steps that are involved in processing a misdemeanor or felony assault case. The court file stands in for a voice. What practitioners record on forms, in reports, or in computer terminals becomes the documented case. A tracking system is not simply a vehicle to monitor a case from one point of institutional action to the next. It is a method of coordinating what gets documented, who sees it, and, to some extent, how it is to be interpreted.

The appropriate flow of information among practitioners can promote women's safety in two ways. First, by sharing relevant information among various practitioners, the offender can be held accountable. If it is known that the offender has been involved in other violent relationships or if the violence is escalating, the court system and rehabilitation program can take this information into account and respond appropriately. If the risk to a woman is known to be higher, the system can take additional steps to provide protection.

A second way that information can promote women's safety is to hold the criminal justice system that responds to the violence accountable. When a pattern of cases "slipping between the cracks" becomes evident, the component of the system (agency) responsible for the slipping can be brought into compliance with community intervention standards. By addressing problems of the system, it is more likely that interventions in domestic violence will be effective, leading to increased safety for women.

The primary purpose of a monitoring and tracking system is thus to promote women's safety by sharing information among practitioners in a way that will hold individual offenders accountable and maintain accountability among various agencies in the criminal justice system that responds to domestic violence. The remainder of this chapter will describe interagency tracking systems in general and, specifically, the developing system in Duluth. Examples of using information at the micro- and macrolevel will be provided, and lessons from the experience in Duluth will be shared.

Interagency Tracking Systems

General Description

In general, a tracking system records relevant information about a particular case as the persons involved move between various individuals and agencies that attempt to respond to the problem that is present. For domestic abuse cases, the tracking system will follow the victim and offender from the time of initial contact with a 911 operator or police through the shelter, jail, and court system and into the rehabilitation classes, probation offices, and beyond. At each step along the way, (a) relevant information must be obtained and submitted in a consistent form; (b) this information must be received, organized, and stored; and (c) needed information must be retrieved and provided to those who need it in a timely manner. These three aspects of tracking systems are described more fully below, along with criteria for an effective tracking system.

Obtaining Relevant Information

An essential process in a tracking system is to obtain information that is institutionally relevant, reliable, and valid while reflecting what is actually going on. One function of developing a tracking system is to redefine what information is helpful to various components of the system. In each setting (e.g., 911, police, women's advocates) from which information is obtained, a staff member must provide relevant information on victims and offenders. In addition, practitioners at different agencies must have similar ways of reading and interpreting information.

As suggested earlier, three criteria are paramount in obtaining data. First, the data must be collected consistently. New victims and offenders are constantly coming into the system, and information must be routinely gathered by intervening agencies. As we will see, those persons running the tracking system must regularly seek information from the agencies to tangibly indicate the importance of this activity.

A second criterion related to obtaining data is that information must be accurate. People providing data must work with common definitions so the information coming into the tracking system is reliable. When prosecutors and judges make decisions that dramatically affect people's lives based on information provided at this point, it is essential that the data provided be accurate.

Finally, the information must reflect the experiences of the people involved and not be so transformed by the need to make it institutionally readable that it no longer tells us what is happening.

Receiving, Organizing, and Storing Information

Those persons who maintain the tracking system will receive significant amounts of information from several different agencies in the community. A system must be developed that can receive this information and organize it in a logical manner. In addition, the information must be stored for later use. It is possible to organize information in paper format and develop an elaborate filing system to fulfill this function. The volume of information in most communities and recent advances in technology point to using a computer database to provide the receiving, organizing, and storing function.

Two important considerations for receiving, organizing, and storing information are security and confidentiality. Information received on paper must be stored in a secure place, usually a locked file cabinet in a secure room. Data in a computerized database should be backed up regularly, with at least one copy stored at a site away from the computer. Confidentiality means making sure that only public information is available widely. For example, most information collected by a women's advocacy group should be held out of a tracking system, and information about a denied order for protection should not be available to an offender. Confidentiality is sometimes essential to a woman's safety.

Providing Information to Those Who Need It

Various components of the system that respond to domestic violence require information in a timely manner if they are to make effective use of it. Prosecutors need information to determine charges, appropriate plea agreements, and the strength of their case. Probation officers conducting presentence investigations need to know the history and severity of abuse the offender has used toward the victim and others, and judges require information on the potential dangerousness of an offender before setting bail or sentencing an offender. A tracking system must be able to provide timely, focused reports to those who need the information.

In addition to timely information, a tracking system must provide reports that are actionable and comprehensible to those receiving them. Different agencies in the legal system use different terms for similar phenomena. Reports must use language that is understandable to the receiving agency, sometimes requiring a translation of sorts from the information received from the providing agency. At the same time, institutional language can act to misrepresent what we might call the lived experience. For example, the legal system typically divides criminal acts into level of crimes—misdemeanor, gross misdemeanor, or felony. Reading an institutional record of an assault, we would conclude that a felony assault was more dangerous or serious than a misdemeanor even though that might not be the case. A single blow to the face can cause a broken nose (a felony in Minnesota), but if a man grabbed his wife by the hair, pulled her to the ground, kicked her several times, twisted her arm behind her back, and spit on her (as a recent police report documented), he will be charged with a misdemeanor (Minnesota assault statutes). Building a tracking system that documents what is going on in domestic cases inevitably means changing almost every form used to process a case.

Summary

A tracking system involves three important processes. First, data must be obtained from agencies that possess relevant information. Second, the information obtained must be received, organized, and stored. Third, relevant, focused information must be provided to each component of the system responding to domestic violence that has need of data. Criteria for a tracking system include that information must be (a) accurate, (b) consistently collected, (c) stored in a secure place, (d) confidential, (e) available in a timely manner, and (f) reportable in a comprehensible format.

History of Duluth's Monitoring and Tracking System

The action phase of the DAIP began in March 1981, when Duluth police officers began an experiment in which 50% of the officers used their discretion in making an arrest in a domestic dispute and 50% followed a mandatory arrest policy. This experiment lasted for 6 months, and a follow-up study indicated that mandatory arrests, followed by court-ordered groups, led to more positive outcomes (Novak & Galaway, 1983). In mid-1982, mandatory arrest was instituted as a universal policy by the Duluth police department.

At the same time that more arrests were occurring, a women's advocate began to follow up on arrests to offer immediate advocacy to victims. The advocate followed individual cases through the court and kept track of these activities on a huge chart on the wall, recording each new step with a marker. After a period of time, she would type a letter to the arresting officer (keeping a carbon copy for her records) describing what had happened to both the victim and the offender.

The process of collecting and recording the information on these arrests became overwhelming, and this initial tracking was dropped for a while. It then became evident that some cases were slipping through the cracks, and a new tracking system was developed.

The new system began when a DAIP employee began keeping separate sheets of paper for arrests, arraignment, jury pretrial, trial, sentencing, and probation for each month. This worker would then check to see if arrests in one month were followed by the appropriate steps in subsequent months. The separate sheets of paper provided thorough information, but tracking individual victims and batterers proved cumbersome. A new process was developed whereby each step following an individual arrest appeared on a single form. The single form provided an easy means to track individual cases but reduced the amount of information that could be maintained.

The first attempt to develop a computerized tracking system occurred in 1993. A DAIP team developed an extensive list of information that might be helpful to maintain, and the bookkeeper began to enter this information into a Paradox database. Because she never had the time to devote to completing a program and entering data, this effort was abandoned. A File Express database was used successfully to monitor attendance and other aspects of batterers' involvement in the DAIP program. These efforts were inadequate but still allowed DAIP staff to bring the majority of problem cases to interagency meetings for discussion and spot many problematic trends in the system. These early efforts helped the DAIP establish a role as information coordinators, demonstrate the usefulness of sharing information, and successfully argue for a more comprehensive system to be developed.

Current Duluth Monitoring and Tracking System

In 1995, the DAIP received funds from the Centers for Disease Control and Prevention to enhance the community's response to domestic assault cases. Part of that grant involved formalizing the tracking system and hiring consultants with computer programming experience to design a database that would serve as the hub of all the interagency information-sharing need in a coordinated response to cases. The project was named the Domestic Abuse Information Network (DAIN) to get interagency buy in and set it apart from any one agency.

The database application selected was dBase, and the appropriate fields (variables) on which to collect data were identified among DAIP staff and representatives from human service agencies involved in domestic violence cases. The information required from each agency was identified, and the information needed by each agency was considered. A formal memorandum of understanding was developed between the DAIP and each agency that would provide and receive information.

DAIN consists of three integrated components. The first component involves the process of collecting information related to domestic violence. The second component includes storing and selectively retrieving relevant information from that which is provided. The final

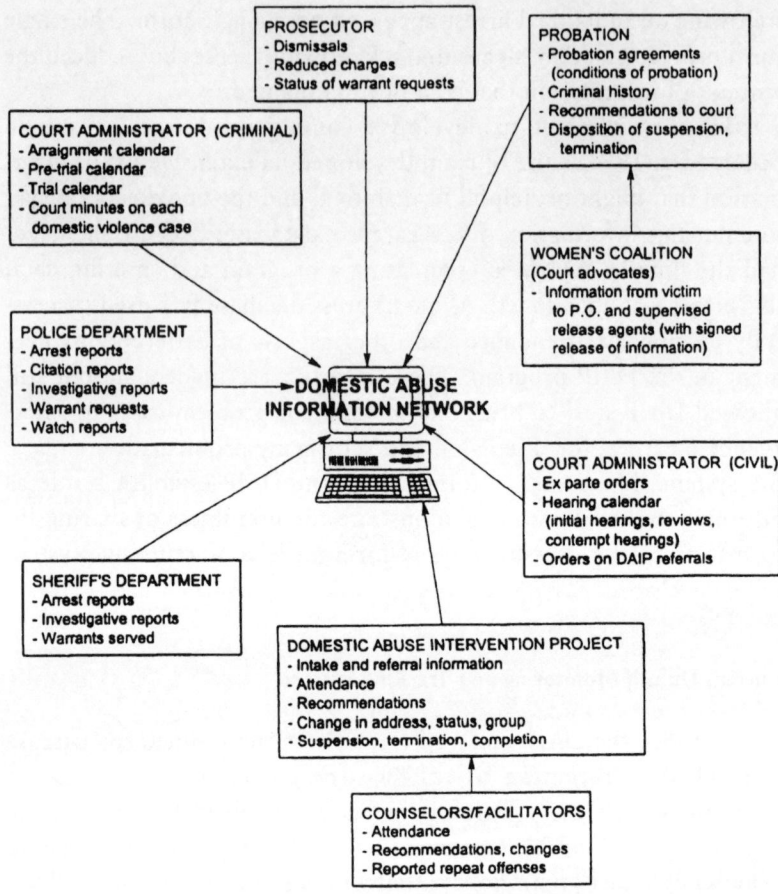

Figure 5.1. Collecting Information

component is reporting relevant information to those who need it in the system that responds to domestic violence. Each of these compo nents will be described more fully later.

Collecting Information for DAIN

The collecting information component involves obtaining consistent information from the various agencies that are involved with domestic violence cases. Figure 5.1 graphically describes the sources and types of information collected from various entities. As examples from this figure, the police department provides information from arrest reports, citation reports, investigative reports, and other information available to them. The probation office provides information on probation agreements, criminal history, recommendations to the court, and dispositions. Figure 5.1 also indicates the type of information provided by other agencies.

Storing, Organizing, and Retrieving Information

The storage and retrieval component of DAIN is visually represented in Figure 5.2, which reflects the DAIN database structure. This component is actually composed of six interrelated databases, with domestic abuse incidents at the center. Other databases focus on information about (a) the abuser, (b) the victim, (c) criminal court, (d) civil court, and (e) the DAIP.

Consistently entering the data into a database is an important aspect of this component. For example, a field may be present for indicating whether children were present during the domestic violence incident. If a police report indicated that children were sleeping in a bedroom, a protocol would need to be provided to determine if this situation should be reflected as children being present.

Because of the complexity of the information involved in the tracking system, a relational database (in this case, dBase, which is being changed to Access) is used to store, organize, and retrieve data. This database has the capability of identifying other domestic violence events in which an offender has been involved and can monitor the abuser's involvement in the men's group in the DAIP. Progress on orders for protection, prosecution, program involvement, and probation can all be monitored on an ongoing basis.

Reporting Relevant Information

The third component of DAIN, reporting relevant information, is graphically represented in Figure 5.3. This figure indicates that the same agencies that provide information to DAIN also receive reports back from DAIN. For example, the court advocates from the women's coalition receive information on police and civil and criminal court activity, and the criminal court receives data on police activity, civil court activity, and time frames in disposition.

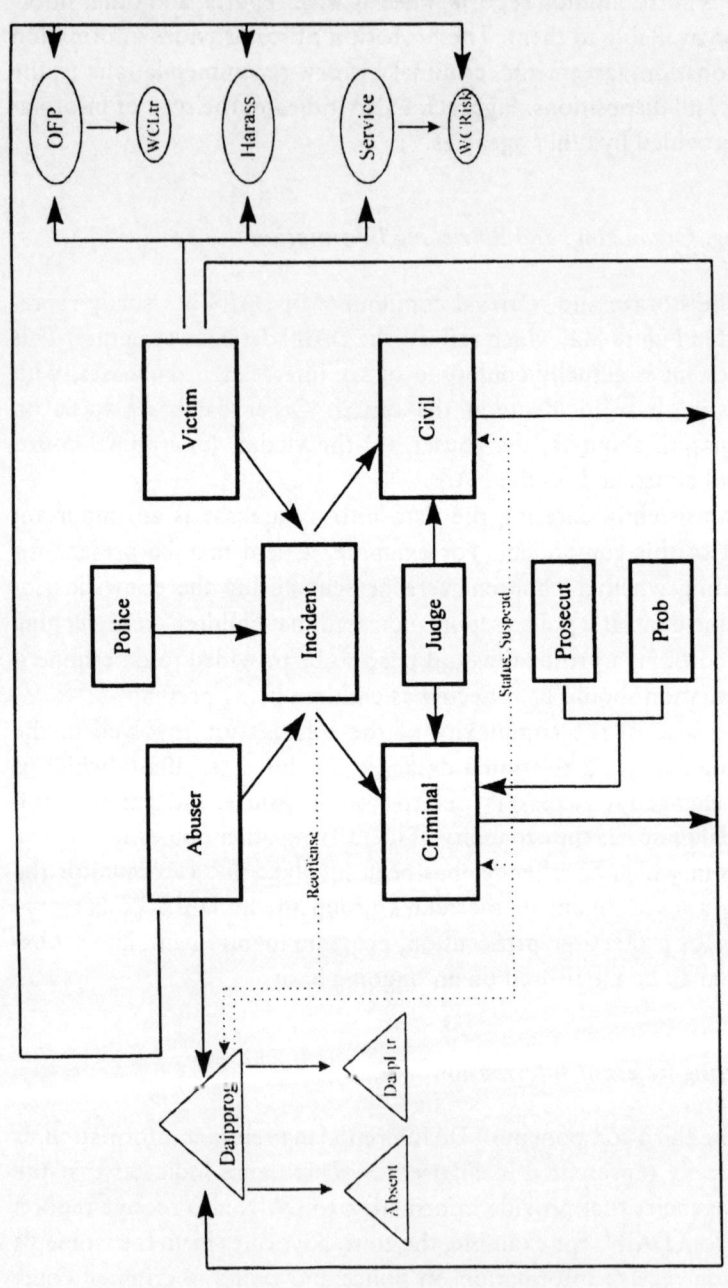

Figure 5.2. DAIN Database Structure

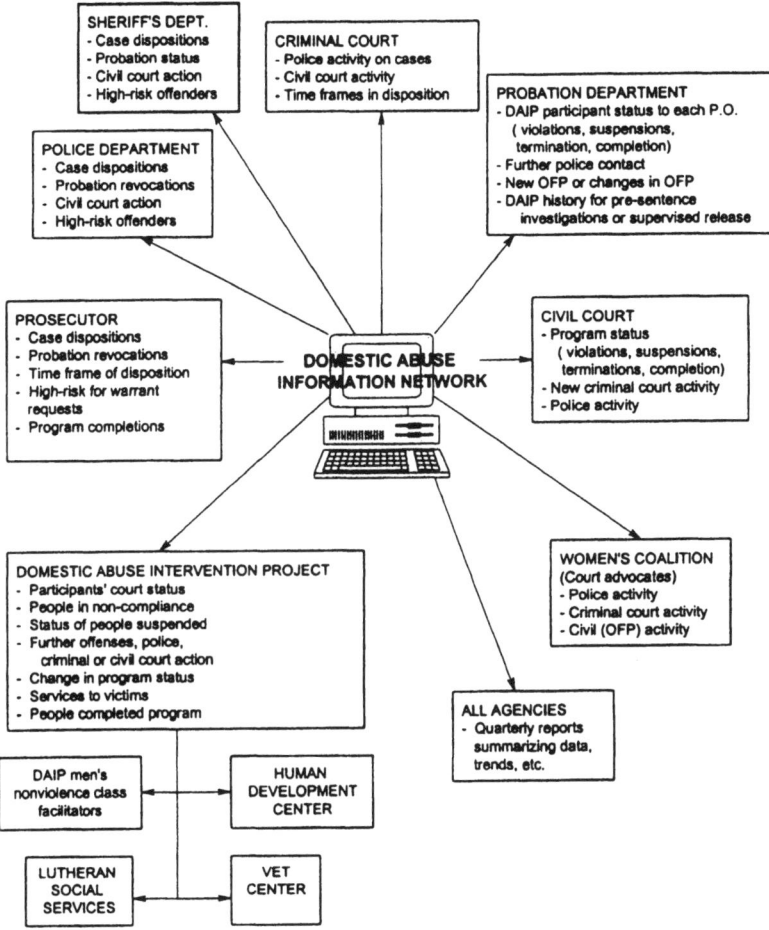

Figure 5.3. Distributing Information and Reports

Benefits of Tracking Systems

A number of benefits can be derived from an effective tracking system. These benefits include (a) increasing attention to victim safety by ensuring that practitioners take action based on what information is in fact institutionally available and giving practitioners at critical points of intervention information about the whole case, not simply a single incident; (b) holding individual workers accountable; (c) holding individual offenders accountable to court orders; (d) identifying cases slipping between the cracks; (e) recognizing problems of procedures that work against victim safety; (f) revealing patterns of possible bias; and (g) providing information for program evaluation and planning. Each of these potential benefits will be described more fully below.

Increasing Attention to Victim Safety

If an officer responds to a call and does not know the alleged offender is on probation for a previous assault or the judge sets bail based on the officer's report on a single incident, even though there is a file cabinet in the same building with four other police reports on domestic abuse by that offender, the system cannot adequately protect victims. Similarly, other examples of the importance of this awareness include a jailer who has no place to record a threat made by a suspect to get back at a woman while he is being booked, children who are at the center of a particularly violent assault but no one follows up on their needs, or an officer who responds to a call and the alleged offender has smashed his car into his ex-wife's bedroom window—the suspect is on probation, but the probation officer never sees the investigative report. All of these occasions existed in Duluth quite a few years ago. None of them does now. Safety is linked to what people know about the overall case and when they know it.

Holding Individual Practitioners Accountable

Individual practitioners are guided to attend to relevant information because they are required to provide this information to the tracking system. Individual practitioners also can be held accountable to effectively fulfill their role because a tracking system can follow victims, abusers, and activities related to an individual practitioner. The tracking system can indicate if a police officer is filing reports, whether a prosecutor is appropriately charging cases, or if the men's program coordinator and probation officer are following through on their responsibilities. In one local case, one offender had three separate charges of violating orders for protection and two charges of fifth-degree domestic assault; the offender was able to plead to a single driving under intoxication charge and a single fifth-degree domestic violence charge, with subsequent sentences being served concurrently. The tracking system brought this situation to light.

Holding Individual Offenders Accountable

Smooth flow of information provided by a tracking and monitoring system can hold individual offenders accountable. In general, if practitioners in one part of the system know the responsibilities and limitations imposed on an offender by another part of the system, these practitioners are better able to hold the offender accountable. Examples in Duluth include men's program staff being aware that one offender with an order for protection stipulating no contact was in fact in contact with his partner and that another offender with a probation stipulation of no drinking came to a group meeting with alcohol on his breath. Both of these offenders subsequently served jail time. In addition, attendance in the men's program is closely monitored, with the probation officer being notified if excessive absences occur.

Identifying Cases Slipping Between the Cracks

In a complex system such as the one that responds to domestic violence, it is possible for cases to slip between the cracks unless someone is monitoring the progress. It is important for the system to follow through on cases, or those who are thorough in the earlier phases of intervention, such as police officers, may come to believe that their work can be in vain. In one local case, a report of a woman being assaulted was received, but a hearing was postponed and the case had not made it to court in 3 months. The tracking system picked up this delay, and it was discovered that the defendant worked at the courthouse, which may have contributed to the delay. The case came to court shortly thereafter. Each month DAIN produces a report of which offenders are not in compliance with their probation conditions, the name of their probation officer, and the date and kind of action taken by the probation officer.

Revealing Problems of Procedures That
Work Against Victim Safety

By monitoring the nature and timing of activities in the system responding to domestic violence, a tracking system can reveal problems that could reduce victim safety. If a court case takes too long, an offender could "work on" the victim to minimize consequences. If probation officers do not receive information from the victim, critical data related to a presentence investigation may not be available. An examination of information-related practices and procedures with victim safety in mind can identify shortcomings that can then be addressed.

Recognizing Patterns of Possible Bias

Bias in various parts of the system responding to domestic violence may be based on race, class, gender, sexual orientation, ethnic origin, or age. These patterns of bias may be very difficult to detect without systematically collecting and examining information. With a tracking system, it is possible to identify how individuals providing service respond to different types of people and monitor these responses for possible bias. The tracking system can monitor sentencing patterns by race, gender, and, in some cases, economic status. It can also look for differences in time periods. For example, DAIN frequently notes significant changes in numbers of arrests, protection orders issued, cases dismissed, or any significant change that is then examined to determine if a problem exists.

Providing Information for Program Evaluation and Planning

A tracking system can be used to provide selected information that can be useful for program evaluation and planning. Information on services provided can be used to assess program implementation, and information on outcomes can be included in the analysis of goal attainment. Identification of problems in the system responding to domestic violence can serve as a basis for planning program and system changes that will address these problems.

In Duluth, information from DAIN is being used to determine if a coordinated community response is being implemented as intended and is achieving goals of reduced recidivism for offenders, as well as increased safety and well-being for victims. Problems related to the transfer of information between agencies has resulted in interagency response teams being developed to coordinate a response to dangerous situations involving domestic violence.

Barriers and Problems

"Anything that can go wrong will go wrong." Murphy is alive and well and spends a fair amount of his time dogging tracking systems. To implement DAIN, a DAIP staff member, fully versed in how the legal system processed cases and how the shelter and DAIP worked, was selected as the DAIN coordinator. Like many DAIP staff, she was familiar with word-processing programs but not database programs. The DAIP hired computer programming consultants from the local university to develop the databases for the DAIN system. These consultants were unfamiliar with the criminal justice system. The task of creating DAIN became increasingly difficult because of the number of agencies involved, ongoing requests for different information from the system, and a computer program that was not user-friendly for DAIP staff. The results were predictable but nonetheless painful for everyone involved.

Some of the barriers and problems that have affected DAIN include (a) difficulties getting information from the agencies, (b) problems getting and keeping people involved, (c) increased workload, (d) computer and technology problems, (e) the complexity of the information system, and (f) not having the required skills available at the proper time.

Difficulties Getting the Information

Initially, administrators from various agencies and organizations agreed to provide certain types of information to DAIN from their agencies, and formal memorandums of understanding were drawn up with these administrators. Unfortunately, the staff of the agencies knew very little about the agreements and were often uninformed as to the type of information that was to be provided and the purpose of forwarding this information. Many practitioners were resistant to giving information to DAIN because it was not a court agency. It was seen as a special interest group, and allowing an outside agency to play this role would open Pandora's box to all kinds of special interest groups demanding such extensive access to court records. Many staff members were not trained on how they would benefit from the system, and their fears that it would create work but no significant help were confirmed in our first 2 years of computer problems. Practitioners required to contribute information did not always have a broad perspective on the tracking system and were therefore unclear on what information to provide or unmotivated to provide any data at all. Because of these narrow perspectives, the quantity and quality of the information collected early in the development of DAIN were limited.

Problems Getting and Keeping People Involved

Related to the difficulties described earlier, it is hard to get all of the people who need to provide information involved in the process. Each officer, court administrator, probation officer, court advocate, and a variety of others involved with domestic violence cases must provide accurate information on a consistent basis for the tracking system to work, and it is most difficult to get literally hundreds of people from very different settings to all fill their roles in making the tracking system work. In addition, once people are "on board," some staff will leave and new staff will need to be trained. Although a tracking system is based on information, the information is only as accurate and complete as the people involved make it. But a bureaucracy's most significant feature is its structural capacity to get many workers to follow routines that guarantee at least some level of consistent documentation. Once a change is built into the regular institutional record-keeping system, this problem diminishes.

Increased Workload for Agency Staff

Collecting and reporting information for a tracking system most often involves extra work for the staff in large institutions, like the court system. It is already an overburdened system. Thus, providing information to a tracking system may be viewed as a burden and not receive a warm reception, resulting in yet another reason why the quality and quantity of information available may suffer. Practitioners must see the value of the system early and get results.

Computer and Technology Problems

"To err is human; to really botch things, use a computer." The problems and barriers described earlier all relate to human factors, but the computers and other technology involved in a tracking system can really mess things up. In Duluth, a faulty hard drive led to mysterious crashes and lost data over a period of several months before the source of the problem was identified. Compatibility with different agencies was lost as some switched to Windows 95 and others remained with DOS. Irregular power outages in the old building in which the main computer is housed resulted in lost data on several occasions. The dBase system proved very user-unfriendly.

Complexity of the Information System

When a number of agencies all request a variety of information from a tracking system, the scope of the database to enter, organize, store, and retrieve the resulting plethora of data can become so complex as to be difficult to understand and nearly unmanageable. In addition, agency programs and demands from the environment change, resulting in changes in one part of the database that require changes in other parts. In putting DAIN together, we failed to set a priority early on and fully think through what each agency needed to enhance its ability to intervene.

The DAIN system in Duluth includes six main interrelated data-bases and more than 500 fields of information. More than 70 reports can be generated. The men's program added a new program, which required an additional set of attendance records to be kept. New requests for reports and changes in reporting needs, including from the funding agency, have further complicated the system. We think one or maybe two people fully comprehend the tracking system and how to use it.

Not Having the Required Skills Available
at the Proper Time

A variety of skills are required to develop and maintain a tracking system. A person at the administrative level needs to negotiate with other administrators to develop interagency agreements, and at least one staff member working with the tracking system must develop relationships with staff members at agencies providing information. At least one computer programmer must be available to set up the database, maintain it, troubleshoot, and generate the reports required by various agencies. Our coordinator has overcome the problems of resistance to the system by talking regularly to key people in each agency that participates and by making sure agencies are kept informed of significant changes on cases. Agency administrators can decide to join the interagency effort, but the leaders in the trenches always set the tone for how an agency will or will not cooperate with a venture such as this.

In a small organization coordinating a tracking system, having a key person unavailable at a crucial time can provide significant problems. If the administrator is out of town when conflict among agencies is occurring, the coalition on which the tracking system is based may deteriorate. If the staff member is on vacation, some information may not get collected in a timely way and therefore not be available when it would most be needed. The programmer may be on a military leave when an important new request for information is received, but no one else knows how to conduct the query to obtain that information. Each of these examples has occurred in Duluth.

Using Information at the Microlevel and Macrolevel

Information available from a tracking and monitoring system can be used at both the microlevel and macrolevel. The microlevel refers to a system's activities at the individual worker or small work group level. The macrolevel refers to a system's activities at the level of the organization, community, or larger system level. General implications and examples of using a tracking system at both these levels are described below.

Microlevel: General Implications and Examples

General Microlevel Implications

In general, a tracking system can provide individual practitioners and staff supervisors with information about the nature of the domestic violence cases they have in their caseloads and the type of actions taken in these cases. The tracking system can list a caseload for each practitioner, including the current status of each case and the actions that have been taken by the practitioner. The system can similarly list the caseloads and actions for all members of staff, enabling a supervisor to examine the characteristics of the clients with whom the staff is interacting and the nature of the activities of the group. Examples of making use of this information are described below.

Microlevel Examples

In one dramatic incident, the tracking system indicated that one batterer had violated an order for protection on four separate occasions and had subsequently received a stalking arrest. Because different police officers had filed these incidents, each was unaware of the other incidents. When tracking system workers became aware of this situation, the victim was contacted, and with the help of several agencies, she took steps to avoid the offender. He tried to find her just prior to taking his own life. She will never know, but had she not left as suddenly as she did, she would very likely have been killed.

Another microexample involved the regularity with which individual probation officers were referring offenders to the men's groups in the DAIP. The tracking system indicated that one newer probation officer was not referring offenders to the men's group, which was the current policy for the type of domestic violence cases the worker was seeing. The men's group coordinator set up a meeting with this new worker and resolved the problem.

In a final example, a female offender had been found guilty of assault on her partner and referred to the DAIP women's program. The women's program coordinator discovered that the woman's partner had been in the DAIP men's program three times after assaulting previous victims. She did not give the information to the court. As a result, the woman's case was reexamined and her sentence reduced.

Macrolevel: General Implications and Examples

General Macrolevel Implications

By keeping track of all domestic violence cases that are reported in a community, various trends in the response to these cases can be identified. Reports can be generated to determine if policies are being followed and if there are trends in the procedures and practices undertaken or in the outcomes of cases involving domestic violence. Specific examples of making use of this type of information are described below.

Macrolevel Examples

An example of monitoring whether a policy was being followed occurred recently when probation officers were to initiate a new risk assessment procedure and make sentencing recommendations for offenders based on a matrix that indicated how dangerous an offender might be. A report from the tracking system indicated that probation officers were rating a disproportionate number of cases at the least dangerous level, and some of these ratings were inconsistent with facts of the case. The tracking system does not always say why a problem exists. It indicates that a problem may exist. In this case, a follow-up meeting with the probation department uncovered several causes for the mislabeling of cases.

A number of reports have examined decisions by prosecutors and the courts. In examining data from the city attorney's office, the number and percentage of cases that were pled down have been examined for trends over time. The number of ex parte cases that came to court, the number of orders for protection issued, and the number of times the offender was not ordered to a rehabilitation program have all been examined. When data indicate that a particular policy is not being followed in the best interest of victim safety, these data are shared with the appropriate group, and changes in practice or policy are negotiated with the supervisors and staff. The use of the tracking system for evaluation purposes is further discussed in Chapter 9.

Lessons From Duluth

During the 15 years that some sort of tracking has occurred in Duluth, particularly since the computer-based DAIN system has been developed, a number of key lessons have emerged. These lessons are described below in hopes that other communities can gain from our experience.

A Key Person Must Hold the Center

A strong individual must be available to make connections with all the agencies involved in the tracking and monitoring system and to maintain relations with these agencies over time. This individual must articulate the "big picture" of what the tracking system is about and encourage key individuals and organizations to buy into the tracking system concept. This person must also be available to troubleshoot and resolve conflicts when disagreements arise, which they inevitably will.

Build Ongoing Relationships at All Levels of the Organizations

A project that involves the degree of cooperation required of a tracking system must be based on strong ongoing personal relationships, or its chances of success will be limited. People at all levels of the organizations will need to relate to one another—directors must talk with directors from other organizations, supervisors must communicate with other supervisors, and staff must relate to staff from other agencies. These relationships will form a basis for developing a tracking system and, more importantly, for maintaining the system over a period of time when difficulties will arise.

Focus on Positive Outcomes/Potential Benefits

Developing a tracking system requires a significant investment of time, energy, money, and other resources. If it is to succeed, everyone involved needs to focus on the positive outcomes and potential benefits that can result from the tracking system. At the broadest level, the superordinate goal of safety and well-being for women is at the core of DAIN. Each agency is motivated by this important goal. In addition, each organization is motivated by the anticipation that the information provided by DAIN will help the organization and its staff do their job better. The potential benefits should be identified early and serve as a basis for all steps in the development and implementation of the tracking system.

Promote a Sense of Ownership at All Levels of the Organizations

Workers at all levels of each organization must buy into the purpose and the activities of the tracking system. The tracking system will require extra work for those involved, and unless they have a sense of ownership in the system, they will not be motivated to contribute effectively to making the system work. DAIP has provided lunches for key staff and scheduled meetings to clarify the purpose and potential benefits of the tracking system. Each person involved in providing information to the system receives reports that are relevant to them. Through verbal reinforcement and praise and an occasional bag of candy or bars, the ongoing message to everyone involved in the system is that they are important to making the tracking system work and consequently in helping the agencies to function more effectively and promoting safety and well-being for women.

Select a Name That Is Inclusive

The name that is selected for the tracking and monitoring system is significant. *Tracking* and *monitoring* do not have positive connotations and should therefore be left out of the name. The name should be descriptive and without gender bias but should not be so long as to be difficult to use. The Domestic Abuse Information Network (DAIN) was selected in Duluth because the full name is descriptive and without bias, and the initials provide an easy shorthand for regular conversation.

Create a Team With Relevant Skills and Knowledge

A variety of skills and knowledge are required to develop and maintain an effective tracking and monitoring system. An administrator (see above) must relate to heads of other organizations, articulate the importance of the project, and mobilize a variety of people to take appropriate action. Staff must know a complex system responding to domestic violence and must relate to other staff from a variety of organizations. Someone must attend to public relations and fund raising. Programmers must develop and maintain a suitable computer database, and staff must collect and enter the data on an ongoing basis. Collectively, this group, along with numerous agency representatives, needs to conceptualize what the tracking system will be able to do and how to create that system.

There are two aspects of creating a suitable team. First, individuals with the requisite skills must be identified and brought together. Second, these individuals must develop trust and cohesion among themselves that will sustain them through a long and demanding process of developing and maintaining the tracking system. This team-building process will be an important investment in helping the project succeed.

Keep the System Simple

A tracking and monitoring system that tries to be all things to all people and organizations can become so complex as to become unwieldy. This situation has developed, to an extent, in Duluth. A complicated computer database is attempting to generate too many reports on too much data to too many people. We are currently trying to prioritize and simplify the system. If we were starting from scratch, we would do it differently. Because others may be starting from the beginning in the future, they could follow the process described immediately below.

Engage in a Process That Begins With the End in Mind and Builds on That Foundation

Step 1: Identify the information that each agency needs in a report they would receive. Meet with representatives of each agency to determine the information that they would need from other agencies to improve their response to domestic violence. Consistent with the need to keep the tracking system simple, emphasize that only information that is absolutely needed should be identified, not what someone might want. For each bit of data that is requested, ask the representatives to describe how they would use the information and what difference it would make to have the information. If agencies list large amounts of information that they believe they need, ask them to prioritize the list. Keep expectations realistic at this point.

Step 2: Build a data dictionary by identifying the information each agency will need to contribute. Once the needed information is listed, determine how that information could be most efficiently obtained. This step involves identifying the needed information that each agency could provide. Ask the representatives of the agency, both at the administrative and staff level, how difficult it will be to provide these data.

Step 3: Design the database, selecting appropriate hardware and software. Enlist the help of a knowledgeable programmer to review the available hardware and software that can receive and organize the data and can generate reports containing the information needed. Select a database that is user-friendly, and choose hardware that will be compatible at various agencies that will be involved. Make sure that a person who is not a programmer can create simple reports.

Step 4: Enter 100 fictional cases and generate reports based on these data. Once the database is set up, enter 100 fictional cases that are representative of those that will ultimately be in the real system. Generate reports on these data and provide it to the intended information users who originally identified the information that they would need. Confirm that all of the information that is present in the report is actually useful, and make sure that no essential information is missing. Make modifications in the system as needed.

Step 5: Develop a memorandum of understanding with each organization. Based on the trial runs with fictional data, develop a memorandum of understanding with each organization involved in the system. Clearly specify who will supply what information from each organization, and append a copy of the type of report that the agency will receive. Address issues of the frequency of provision of information and reports of confidentiality.

Step 6: Debug the system prior to providing the initial reports. Begin collecting authentic data and enter them into the database. Then generate reports and examine them carefully for accuracy. After internal examination, ask a trusted representative from each organization to provide a preliminary review of the reports that are to be distributed. In each review, look for any data that could be inaccurate.

Step 7: Implement the system with the agencies. Once the system is debugged, continue entering information and begin providing regular reports to the agencies. Meet with administrators and staff from each agency to clarify the meaning of the reports and to confirm their utility.

Step 8: Conduct ongoing quality control checks on the information provided. Periodically check the accuracy of the information coming into the system by providing summaries of that data to representatives of the organization providing that information. When reports are provided to an agency, check to make sure that the information provided is clear and complete. Discuss the implications of the reports with representatives of the agency.

Conclusion

The secrecy that once surrounded domestic violence is breaking down, but communication among various components of the human service system responding to domestic violence must be enhanced if their response is to be effective. Monitoring and tracking systems have the potential to share relevant information about domestic violence and to help agencies to work together more effectively. A specialized and fragmented system must come together to address the needs of victims of domestic violence.

Tracking systems must be organized to obtain consistent and accurate data, to store and organize that data in a secure and confidential manner, and to generate reports that are timely and easily understood. The experience of DAIN in Duluth, Minnesota, demonstrates many potential benefits of tracking systems but also documents the barriers and problems that exist. Lessons from Duluth's experience can provide guidelines for implementing monitoring and tracking systems elsewhere as part of a coordinated community response to promote the safety and well-being of women.

References

Barnes, G. (1996). *Tracking the criminal justice system response to domestic violence.* Duluth, MN: Domestic Abuse Intervention Project.

Hamilton, T. S. (1991). Developing an automated evidence tracking system. *The Police Chief, 58,* 146-149.

Novak, S., & Galaway, B. (1983). *Domestic abuse intervention project: Final report.* Unpublished manuscript, University of Minnesota, Duluth.

Nova Scotia Family Violence Tracking Project. (1995). *The repines of the justice system to family violence in Nova Scotia.* Halifax: Solicitor General Canada.

System improves sheriff's department's tracking. (1997). *American City and County, 112,* 32.

6

Advocacy for Battered Women

Implications for a Coordinated Community Response

Melanie F. Shepard

Community intervention projects that focus on institutional reform should not be initiated without an infrastructure of community services in place to provide support to battered women. If these services are not available, a community intervention project must ensure that they are in place before initiating institutional reforms. Creating and maintaining a supportive infrastructure requires collaborative efforts among many community agencies that share mutual goals. Advocates for battered women are the stewards of this infrastructure as they direct, guide, and support battered women while confronting and challenging obstacles to their safety. Because there are excellent resources already available, these services will be discussed only briefly.[1]

AUTHOR'S NOTE: This chapter is based on group discussions with Jill Abernathy, Marilu Johnson, Michelle Lebeau, Tina Olson, Ellen Pence, Madeline Tjaden, and Vicki Ybanez.

The main purpose of this chapter is to reflect on the role of domestic violence advocates within a coordinated community response and the unintended consequences that institutional reforms may have on the safety of battered women.

Essential Services for Battered Women

A supportive infrastructure is a network of community services that are designed to assist battered women in meeting their needs. The essential services that must be in place before or as part of an interagency effort to address domestic violence are emergency housing, confidential victim-directed court advocacy, support and education groups, and financial assistance to enable women to live separate from their abusers. Without these essential services, battered women may be placed in greater danger when the criminal justice system responds to the offender's violence.

Emergency Housing

Emergency housing has been recognized as a critical service for battered women since the beginning of the battered women's movement in the 1970s. Despite all the reforms that have taken place to improve the response of the criminal justice system, many women continue to need protection 24 hours a day and a safe place to plan for their future. The Women's Coalition in Duluth operates a shelter that provides emergency housing, advocacy, and support for women and children. Shelter advocates provide women the information needed to make choices about their future and assist them in obtaining the necessary resources. In a study of women in Texas shelters, the services obtained by women during their shelter stay were important to gaining safety and independence. Gondolf and Fisher (1988) found that "women are more likely not to return to the batterer if they have child care, transportation, and income available and have obtained a variety of shelter services" (p. 93). A recent survey of battered women's experiences with different components of a coordinated community response in Duluth found that next to having an order for protection, shelter services were perceived by battered women as being the most helpful (Shepard, 1997).

Legal Advocacy

In Duluth, court advocates from the Women's Coalition work with more than 90% of the women who obtain civil protection orders by helping them to complete forms and obtain temporary orders and by accompanying them to hearings. Because changes in police and prosecution polices were made to strengthen the protection order process, the number of protection orders has increased threefold (Pence, 1996).

When an offender is arrested, the jail contacts an on-call advocate so that the abused woman can be visited. Advocates also review police reports in which arrests were not made and initiate contacts with women who may be in need of advocacy services. This move to reach out to battered women who have not requested shelter or other assistance has marked a shift in the role of advocates. On-call advocates have become a part of the institutionalized response to domestic violence by routinely initiating contact with battered women and by providing information to the criminal justice system when the woman give permission to do so.

In Duluth, court advocates and on-call advocates are housed in a separate building from shelter advocates. Although they are all part of the same organization (the Women's Coalition), they focus on different aspects of advocacy. The Domestic Abuse Intervention Project (DAIP) also provides advocacy to women whose partners have entered the men's program.

Although advocates can help women understand the criminal justice process, they are in the difficult position of not being able to guarantee the outcome. Having confidential, victim-directed, court advocacy available for women is different from having a victim witness worker in the system. An advocate focuses on the needs of the woman, which may or may not include having the case prosecuted. A victim witness worker works with the woman to facilitate institutional goals, which may not always coincide with her wishes and interests.

Groups

Groups for battered women are a vital community resource. When we asked a group of Duluth advocates what made the biggest change in battered women's lives, they unanimously responded, "women's groups!" In Duluth, battered women are offered several types of groups run by the shelter and the DAIP. Neighborhood-based educational groups teach women about all forms of battering and the impact of battering on them and their children. They learn that it is the community's responsibility to hold abusers accountable for their behavior. Support groups also are offered to assist women in making decisions and dealing with crises in their lives. The agenda of these self-help groups is set by those who attend. At the DAIP, women's groups are offered to women whose partners or former partners are under court order to attend the men's groups. They learn about the men's educational curriculum and are assisted with exploring their options. A group designed to support and educate Native American women whose partners are in the men's program is also available.

In the past, a women's social action group provided a vehicle for women to address social and institutional practices that contribute to violence against women. Although this group is no longer active, Duluth offers women other avenues for social justice work. Forming coalitions in the community among organizations concerned with similar issues can strengthen the supportive community infrastructure and empower battered women. For example, tenants unions, welfare rights organizations, and women's groups can work together on issues of common concern.

Financial Resources

Access to financial resources is critical for battered women seeking to live separately from an abusive partner. Advocates can assist women in negotiating the welfare system and provide information about education and employment options. Women who have experienced domestic violence are more likely to have experienced unemployment and to have lower personal incomes than those who have not (Lloyd, 1997). When battered women are employed, their work performance is impaired by the ongoing abuse they experience, resulting in absenteeism and tardiness (Shepard & Pence, 1988). The achievement of economic self-sufficiency is vital for women who are dependent on an abusive partner for income. Women often need a variety of community services to assist them in achieving economic self-sufficiency, such as child care, medical care, transitional housing, and counseling. Advocates play an important role in making connections with community resources and facilitating access to them for battered women.

Unintended Consequences of Reform Efforts:
A Conversation With Victim Advocates

The role of advocates in Duluth has changed over the past 20 years, particularly since the DAIP emerged on the scene in the early 1980s. To reflect on these changes, two group discussions took place with seven seasoned advocates from the Duluth community, including advocates from the DAIP, the Women's Coalition, and transitional housing programs. Our conversation focused on issues for advocates to consider when a community intervention project is being developed and unintended consequences of reform efforts. Although this discussion of unintended consequences is not to meant to discourage others from following the path of reform, it is meant to caution advocates to think through all the twists and turns of legal reform efforts. As might be expected, there often was not consensus on issues the group discussed. What follows are paraphrased excerpts of our conversation as we reflected on the past 20 years of advocacy in Duluth.

On the Change in Advocates' Roles

Several themes emerged as we discussed changes in advocates' roles: Responsibilities have become more narrowly delineated and institutionalized; the community has developed more negativity about the shelter, which can discourage women from seeking services; advocates work with more women who have not sought their services and who may not want or be ready for help that advocates can provide; and new advocates do not always share a common bond and purpose with advocates who have been a part of the battered women's movement since its beginning. It is important that advocates be closely involved with community intervention projects in developing a coordinated community response. However, they need to maintain their separateness and unique role in the community. The following are paraphrased comments of what the advocates said.

It's not as easy to do advocacy as it was 20 years ago.

It is not so clearly us and them anymore. Our programs have become institutionalized. The criminal justice system is now seen as working with us.

Advocacy changed when the Women's Coalition shifted from being shelter advocates to including a legal advocacy unit and being part of a community intervention project. Some of the staff who worked everyday in the shelter were all of sudden assigned to do only legal advocacy; it was a radical shift which created a bit of class division between advocates who worked in the criminal justice system and those that worked in the shelter.

Women used to come to us for services. With the switch, we were going out to women, and that changed things too.

We were going to women's houses without being invited.

The uncomfortable part is that I am caught between advocating for women and being part of a system. That's the difficult part for me because I'm doing both things at the same time. I'm on call to keep me focused on the women, yet I work for an agency that creates and helps to change the institutional practices.

There's this negativity that's been going around in the community; actually, it is on a national level too. It became okay to get really verbal, and there have been hurt feelings and so you get to where you feel a little on edge, a little unsure of what you are coming up against. You've got new people doing this work and we don't have the same common bond or reason why we all came into doing this work. Some people do advocacy because it is a job, and others have a long history of doing advocacy as part of a broader social movement. There's no connection or trust built between the two groups.

On the Focus on Criminal Justice Reform

The group of advocates examined whether the focus on criminal justice reform was the right path to have taken. Advocates have argued for policy reforms (e.g., prosecution of cases) only to turn around and ask for exceptions for individual battered women. The criminal justice process does not always effectively address the individual needs of women and does not work well for many. Although concern was expressed that the battered women's movement may have been co-opted by the system, the advocates recognized that substantial progress had been made.

I think it is hard to say whether or not it was a mistake to focus on the legal system. Twenty years ago, we starting out with nothing. We basically started putting women up in our homes. And then the shelters and hotlines evolved. We wanted the police to arrest and they were saying, "Okay, we'll give you this, but you give a little bit here too." At the time it didn't seem like a lot. There's things that maybe we shouldn't have given up, and there's things that maybe we shouldn't have done. Now reflecting back, we're saying that everything wasn't great 20 years ago, but everything isn't great today either.

The legal system was so screwed up to begin with. It's racist, homophobic, sexist, it's all those things. So we're looking at a system that is inherently screwed up.

When we make domestic violence into a crime, it has to be proved beyond a reasonable doubt that this guy beat up this woman on this day.

When it is prosecuted as a crime, the victim can be forced to do things she doesn't want to do.

When it works [the criminal justice system], it works really well. Personally, I wouldn't say it was a mistake to criminalize domestic violence. We all know of situations where it worked really well and changed women's lives.

I've always thought that it is rare that women want to testify. They don't want their husband to be convicted. Advocates pushed for prosecution, not battered women. A women may look back and think he should have been convicted, but not when she is in it. We've been the ones to push women into the system. It doesn't work for individual women a lot of times. But on the other hand, we're trying to make this larger social, historical move to say that men who beat women up should be brought to court.

I think there's always a plan, and I think the system knows the best way to kill a radical, potentially revolutionary movement is to make it part of the system. When the shelters started getting money, that's when we became institutionalized. And when we became institutionalized, that's when we adopted all of these policies and we became mandatory reporters, and we did all of these things that, in reflection, I don't know that I would have chosen that route. Because I think we gave up a lot from doing that. I think that some of the things that we were pushing for 20 years ago have gone by the wayside.

I don't accept that if you look over the past 20 years that there isn't
a fairly radical change that's happened. For centuries women would
go to police or sheriffs or magistrates and not be helped. Now the
state actually steps in.

On Harm to Battered Women

The advocates agreed that the criminal justice system is far more
protective of women than it was prior to the development of a
coordinated community response. However, the group thought that
it was important to convey a warning that criminal justice reform
efforts frequently have negative consequences for battered women.
Women are more likely to be arrested for using violence (see Chapter
10), forced to testify in court against their will (see Chapter 3), and
have experienced unwelcome intrusion into their lives by child protection and other community agencies (see Chapter 8). The advocates
weighed the cost and benefits to women of legal reforms and did not
always reach the same conclusions.

Battered women are getting arrested when they act in self-defense.

Women are forced to participate in the criminal justice system when
they don't want to. In some communities, they are forced to testify
against the batterer.

Other systems are pushed into her life (e.g., child protection and
guardians ad litem).

Battered women are mandated to groups. Not in Duluth, but in some
communities they can be mandated to support groups whether they
want to attend or not. They end up being blamed for not getting out
of the relationship.

I think the problem is that the criminal justice system wants to say
that the battered women who use violence are doing the same thing
as the men who are beating them up. They are not making the distinction. The legal system just wants to look at the incident and say
it's the same. We want to contexualize the violence. I think they want
to equate these two uses of violence as being the same thing. It makes
us [advocates] act like women don't use violence, when we know they
do. We say things like 90% of batterers are men, but we don't ever
really get into the fact that most women who are being battered are

using some violence back, because of the way they turn it around and say women are battering too. That's the biggest problem with the criminal justice system; it does not allow you to deal with something in its context. It washes out everything and deals with this incident and previous convictions. A woman who's been convicted two or three times becomes a big problem to them. A guy who has never been convicted before is not seen as being a problem to the state.

The new issue is what do we do with women who are mandated to our groups, and who are on probation, and one of their conditions is to abstain from alcohol. Do we report it when they do not or don't we? Do we treat them differently than we treat men in groups? And we do treat them differently. But there's a reason why we do. You cannot convince someone in the courthouse that we should be treating it differently. You can't convince people that this woman hitting a guy and getting convicted of it is not the same as his beating the shit out of her for 10 years. If we say, "We're not going to do it," they say, "Well, you're biased." They threaten to refer them elsewhere for services.

On the Relative Importance of Individual Advocacy and Institutional Advocacy

The group of advocates differed on the relative merits of individual advocacy and institutional advocacy, although the group agreed that both played an essential role in a coordinated community response. Concern was expressed that shelter advocates and court advocates not be swallowed up by community intervention projects and lose their capacity to promote institutional change. Maintaining a partnership between the shelter and court advocates and staff at the community intervention project needs ongoing attention.

When the DAIP started, there was a shift from the shelter doing systems [institutional] advocacy and individual advocacy to the shelter doing mostly individual advocacy and the DAIP doing mostly systems advocacy. The shelter ends up less vital in a lot of ways as it became service oriented. We set it up so that we would meet together and look at the issues and the DAIP would follow up on them. I think shelter advocates ended up getting the message that they should focus on services and that when there was a problem, they should bring it to DAIP to follow up on.

The other question is, "So we set up all these really good women's groups and then women come to them and their individual lives are changed, but who gives a shit if 200 women have a change in their life?" The question is are we doing anything that makes it so women get beat up less? If you criminalize it and say to men, "You don't get to do this, and being a husband doesn't give you a right to beat women," then in the long run, women are not going to be subjected to violence in their marriages. If we took this all away and we said let's focus all our energy on women's groups, will it make any difference? Women will come in and have a different consciousness. But will it make any difference in how marriage is seen in society and women's and men's ability to use violence?

I don't think you could change the lives of 200 women without changing the community around them. I go to my own experience. I went through education groups, and that was really life changing for me. And it changed the way I interact with my children. It changes the way I interact with my friends, and it kind of just keeps going from there. And so women are going through educational groups, and their consciousness changes; they're impacting people around them. The kind of change we would like to see will take a long time because of how screwed up our society is. But it has its affects, in small ways. It circles around those women.

What's important about being part of this movement or being an advocate is that individual shift I see in women.

There's always the question, "Does this individual service that you provide this woman, which might be kind of a feminist consciousness raising, in isolation of something else, do any good?" I believe a little bit of the ripple theory, but not very much. I think that unless you organize to change the institutions that shape people's lives, substantial change will not occur. I think the weakness of what we've done is that we focused only on the legal system. If we had tried to do more of a multi-institutional approach dealing with the religious institution, social services, and the legal institution, it would have been better. We've just focused on the criminal justice system.

But it's also more than ripple effect. We just got done talking about women getting out there and engaging in social action. And so that's part of it. There's the impact of the quiet kind of personal way that you interact. But then there's the bigger piece where women get out there.

Conclusion

The voices of these advocates as they reflect on 20 years of the battered women's movement remind us that, as we pursue reforms and adopt new strategies, careful attention must be given to what the unintended consequences of our efforts might be. Readers are encouraged to find ways to avoid some of these unintended consequences in their own work. Although we cannot forsee them all, we can anticipate many.

Note

1. For information about advocacy programs for battered women, contact the National Resource Center for Domestic Violence at 1-800-537-2238.

References

Gondolf, E., & Fisher, R. (1988). *Battered women as survivors: An alternative to learned helplessness.* Toronto: D. C. Heath.

Lloyd, S. (1997). The effects of domestic violence on women's employment. *Law and Policy, 19*(2), 139-167.

Pence, E. (1996). *Coordinated community response to domestic assault cases: A guide to policy development.* Duluth, MN: Domestic Abuse Intervention Project.

Shepard, M. (1997, June). *Battered women's experiences with a coordinated community response.* Paper presented at the Fifth International Family Violence Research Conference, Durham, NH.

Shepard, M., & Pence, E. (1988). The effect of battering on the employment status of women. *Afflia, 3*(2), 55-61.

7

Batterer Intervention Programs

The Past, and Future Prospects

Fernando Mederos

This chapter focuses on what to do with the offender once he is court mandated to attend a batterer intervention program within the context of a coordinated community response system. The editors have requested that academic citations be minimized in the interest of emphasizing a thoughtful and nontechnical dialogue about different aspects of the coordinated community response to domestic violence. Readers who wish to explore the literature about men who batter and domestic violence can consult Aldarondo (1999); Edleson and Tolman (1992); Gondolf (1993); Holtzworth-Munroe, Smutzler, and Bates (1997); Holtzworth-Munroe, Smutzler, and Sandin (1997); and Holtzworth-Munroe, Bates, Smutzler, and Sandin (1997). In this chapter, the following questions will be considered:

- What is the focus and the purpose of batterer intervention programs?
- What are the basic tasks of batterer intervention programs?

- What differentiates the Duluth curriculum from other intervention models?
- What tasks do we need to give more attention to in batterer intervention programs?
- What challenges does this field face in the coming years?

The Focus of Batterer Intervention Programs

Battering was not an acknowledged problem in the mental health profession before the battered women's movement in the early 1970s. Wife assault was trivialized whenever it was noted in the literature. It was considered that the real problem was either that the man was reactively lashing out against a spouse who was verbally aggressive or domineering (castrating) or that the spouse provoked the violence due to her own masochistic character. In either case, marital relations were shrouded in a veil of privacy that was supposed to protect domestic relations from public intrusion. Keeping the family intact took precedence over other concerns. The mental health establishment simply reflected the attitudes of other social institutions such as the police, the judicial system, and the medical and religious establishments. The only exception to the silence about marital relations was in marital counseling and family therapy, in which many battered women came with their (usually reluctant) spouses to seek help. These encounters were often disastrous. Marriage counselors were trained to help couples communicate and negotiate better; family therapists were encouraged to look at family processes as circular and were guided by the belief in therapeutic neutrality—the importance of avoiding labeling and blame in the clinical encounter. Family therapists and marriage counselors were not prepared to give an unequivocal message that violence is not justified and that physical abuse constitutes a fundamental violation of family relations. In practical terms, this led to many situations in which battered women were taught to use "I" statements and not keep secrets, which resulted in many retaliatory assaults by physically abusive partners. In other instances, therapists refused to address violent behavior as a primary issue, believing that the circular processes in the relationship were at the root of the batterer's violence. Ironically, the therapeutic traditions of family therapy and marital therapy emerged as progressive efforts to concentrate on function in reaction to psychoanalytic approaches that relied heavily on long-term treatment intended to undo deep-rooted psychopathology. Yet their approach left them conceptually and strategically unable to cope with marital violence.

Although clinicians such as Ganley (1981) visualized and implemented perceptive treatment with physically abusive men, this work did not become widely adopted as the standard in mental health treatment of offenders, perhaps because it departed so strongly from then-established practices. Profeminist batterer intervention programs were developed in an attempt to address these conceptual blinders and to make stopping violent behavior a central concern. Early programs such as Emerge and Raven rejected a mental health perspective and centered their work on male resocialization toward equality and toward having the aggressor take responsibility for his behavior. Despite the layers of denial, minimization, and victim blaming in which violent conduct is usually shrouded, physical abuse was demystified as an instrumental or purposeful activity.

However, stopping violence was not the sole focus of profeminist batterer intervention programs. Activists had listened closely to women's accounts of battering relationships and learned that women had to cope not just with violent incidents but with a pervasive climate of intimidation. Men who batter use a variety of behaviors—ranging from subtle looks and changes in tone of voice to constant rage and screaming and throwing things—to evoke and maintain a climate of fear and threat and to get their way in many situations. In addition, battered women reported equally pervasive patterns of psychological abuse, such as constant criticism, ridicule, jealous accusations and monitoring, inability to tolerate disagreement, undermining a mother's authority with children, withholding affection, and being ignored. Psychological abuse isolates victims of violence, erodes their self-esteem, and tends to make them more susceptible to external control. The climate of intimidation, with the always present threat of violence, pressures many women to become less assertive and to hold back in many ways with their partners as a means of self-protection.

Accordingly, activists redefined battering as an ongoing pattern of coercive control that includes both intimidation and psychological abuse and is reinforced and maintained through the use of violence. The focus of treatment expanded beyond teaching men to stop violence to helping them end the ongoing pattern of coercive control (i.e., a series of actions whose goal is to control some aspect of their partner's conduct).

The Primary Tasks of
Batterer Intervention Programs

By the mid-1970s, pioneering programs such as Raven, the Domestic Abuse Project, and Emerge had developed group counseling models to educate men and help them change their behavior. These programs focused on reframing violent acts as examples of controlling behaviors rather than as impulsive or random eruptions of violence. They also developed a common framework for counseling physically abusive men: (a) examining belief systems that underlie abusive conduct, (b) identifying and defining controlling behaviors, (c) developing awareness of the effects of violence, (d) teaching and practicing alternatives to controlling behaviors, and (e) maintaining contact with victims of violence to ascertain the offender's level of violence and to provide referrals and support to battered women. These programs were effective at holding men responsible for their abusive behavior, and they reversed the victim-blaming stance of many other practitioners. Another significant departure from customary mental health practice was that group participants were offered sharply curtailed confidentiality. As a condition for participation, programs required broad permission to communicate with partners and, if necessary, with the courts. However, program participation was voluntary and attendance was poor. Also, the lack of systematic involvement by the courts and other social institutions meant that there was little external reinforcement and pressure for men to remain nonviolent. If men stopped attending groups, there were no consequences. To some degree, these voluntary group models carried some of the same limitations of mental health approaches in that their work was limited to the offender and his spouse.

The Duluth Model

The Duluth model came about later (1980-1981) and took a different course. Instead of being freestanding programs, the Duluth batterer intervention groups were situated in a community-wide framework of institutions that held physically abusive men accountable and provided safety for victims of violence and their children. Being part of the coordinated community response system in Duluth meant that physically abusive men were arrested, tried, and given the option of serving their sentence or being placed on probation with strict conditions of refraining from further violence and attending a mandatory batterer intervention program. Within this system, a court-mandated offender knows that the probation department will monitor his attendance and maintain contact with his spouse, the prosecutors, the mental health center, and other agencies involved in the coordinated community response effort. Men's group leaders in the Duluth model are taught from the beginning that their work is not limited to their encounter with the physically abusive men or with their partners. Ensuring accountability for physically abusive men by providing information to spouses, probation departments, and other agencies is one of their fundamental responsibilities.

The Duluth model also took a different course with respect to counseling men who batter. Activists had noticed that physically abusive men had belief systems that justified or excused their abusive conduct. Other programs had identified some elements of traditional masculinity as the fundamental source of beliefs that justify abusive behavior. Some approaches focused on patriarchal male privilege; others emphasized the importance of male socialization in childhood as the formative influence. The developers of the Duluth model were influenced by Paulo Freire, a Brazilian educator who had pioneered participatory literacy education programs for landless peasants in his country. Freire (1970) felt that Western society is profoundly permeated by hierarchical or authoritarian relationships in which one person or group establishes dominance over others and maintains it through oppressive control and through promulgating belief systems that support asymmetrical power relationships. These belief systems are usually deeply enshrined in hierarchical arrangements. The oppressors and the oppressed both affirm doctrines that rationalize their positions, and both parties come to believe or internalize these doctrines. Ultimately, both come to be entrapped by similar beliefs, although the oppressed are more decisively disadvantaged. Freire found that landless peasants saw themselves as incapable of learning and could see no other future for themselves except for endless toil. They saw their situation as a part of nature rather than as a result of complex and mutable historical forces. These beliefs limited their interest in learning to read. Believing that change was not possible and that their circumstances just reflected the way things are, they were not motivated to change. If alternatives are not believed to exist, they cannot be envisioned. Freire devised a group discussion model called reflective and critical dialogue to help people in such situations develop an analytical dialogue to understand how their circumstances are part of history and culture rather than immutable parts of nature.

Ellen Pence and Michael Paymar (1990, 1993), the developers of the Duluth model of batterer intervention, adapted this process to men who batter. Freire's (1970) work gave them the basis for launching what could be called a cultural offensive on domestic violence. In their view, physically abusive men have belief systems that legitimize and obscure their abusive behavior in various ways. These can include (a) *dogma,* unshakable and unquestionable beliefs that come from the Bible or some other authoritative source; (b) a *given,* an unchanging part of nature that stems from our genetic heritage or our hormonal makeup; or (c) an element of *masculinity*—something that is believed to be an inherent and indivisible part of male identity and cannot be discarded without undoing or destroying masculinity. Applying the critical-reflective dialogue to these beliefs helps men see their ideas as parts of culture rather than nature and their resulting behaviors as choices rather than unavoidable responses. In practice, this is not an intellectual process but a simple and consistent strategy of questioning ideas about themselves and about women that men present as absolute truths. This process is reinforced through the use of 13 videotapes illustrating vignettes of typical abusive behaviors by men of their partners.

After watching these realistic video scenes, group participants are asked the following: What was the man's goal? What beliefs does he have that justify his behavior? What impact did the man's conduct have on his partner? On himself? On other family members? Through analyzing and discussing the behavior of men like themselves, group participants begin to experience what they and others do as a result of choice and of beliefs that can be changed rather than as inevitable, "natural" events. The dialogic process, which is described here in highly abbreviated form, sidesteps much direct confrontation with the men. Group members are seen not as demonic beings out to inflict pain and suffering but as people who are acting from a set of beliefs that are harmful and make stable and loving relationships impossible. Furthermore, this process defuses confrontation even more by acknowledging that men's beliefs originate from their social environment. It is not as if abusive men are bad people who invented these ideas by themselves. Yet at the same time, group participants are held responsible for perpetuating the belief systems and the harmful behaviors that sound acceptable once one has certain ideas.

The development of the video vignettes was another illustration of the cultural campaign against domestic violence. Two hundred battered women attended 30 focus group sessions in Duluth in 1984. Their descriptions of the abusive incidents that they had undergone with their spouses were translated into the vignettes. The women's descriptions of abusive incidents also were used to develop the Power and Control Wheel (see the Appendix; Pence & Paymar, 1990, 1993), which systematically illustrates the primary abusive behaviors experienced by women living with men who batter. In a sense, the process involved a methodical investigation of many dimensions of abuse in battering relationships in American culture. Consequently, many men spontaneously state that seeing the videos is like watching themselves in action.

There were other examples of Pence and Paymar's (1990, 1993) cultural methodology. Rather than focus the change process on personality development, remedying developmental deficits, or some other familiar psychological construct, they chose a basic European American value—equality—as the ideal toward which men were encouraged to strive. Equality is a central espoused value in American culture; it is "espoused" because it is a resonant motif in American culture, but like many such cherished ideals, it is often not followed in practice. Nevertheless, it is an effective goal for many European American group participants. It is a principle that they can readily recognize; with some reluctance, they can come to acknowledge a contradiction between some of their general beliefs and their beliefs and practices with women. The Duluth model also linked this ideal to a series of discussions in which men are asked to envision or define nonabusive ways of relating. Among these are the following: What is nonviolent behavior? How can you help someone feel safe? What is respect? How do you show respect? What is supportive behavior? How do you demonstrate support? What is fair negotiation? How do you do it? What is shared responsibility? These envisioning exercises are complemented with concrete instruction in interpersonal skills, such as negotiation, fair fighting, making amends, time-outs, and use of the Equality Wheel (Pence & Paymar, 1990, 1993), which illustrates the behavioral basis for egalitarian relationships.

Thus, as a man progresses through this 27-week curriculum, he views videos that illustrate different forms of abuse, engages in a reflective critical dialogue about the men who appear in the videos, engages in a similar critical and reflective dialogue about examples of his own abusive behavior, collaboratively develops interpretations of nonabusive behaviors, and is exposed to specific behavioral skills that he can use to resolve problems without violence and coercive control. Finally, he is asked to relive his own abusive incidents through detailed role-plays and to attempt to resolve the original situations without abuse. Through this final "task," he can explore the difference between what he believes he has learned and what he is actually able to do.

This program offers a comprehensive culturally based opportunity for men to change. Because it is a curriculum and presents 27 fairly detailed lesson plans, it can be easily adopted by community activists who obtain the requisite training. In fact, it is the most widely used approach to undoing men's abuse of women.

As we turn to controversies in the field and future developments, it is important to remember that the Duluth model began with an instructional methodology developed for oppressed Latinos, which was altered for European American physically abusive men. Freire's (1970) transformative cultural methodology is widely adaptable; it does not single out male supremacy as the sole source of oppressive conduct and beliefs. It is based on the observation that there is a generic but avoidable tendency for human beings to establish hierarchical and oppressive relationships. Pence and her colleagues in Duluth have used Freire's methodology to develop curricula for Native Americans and for people in gay and lesbian relationships.

Controversies and Future Developments in the Field

In this section, we discuss topics that are relevant to the Duluth curriculum and broader concerns that deal with batterer intervention programs in general: What is missing in batterer intervention programs? What challenges does this field face in the coming years? Perhaps the best starting point is to revisit the origins of the Duluth model and other profeminist batterer intervention programs. In 1997, Jacqueline Campbell, a leading domestic violence researcher, characterized these programs as an attempt to create a "firewall" against therapeutic practices that at best ignored the asymmetrical and gendered power arrangements of battering relationships or at worst endangered battered women and colluded with abusive men. This firewall was successfully built. Many of the approaches that were developed to work with physically abusive men focus on accountability and stopping violent and coercive behavior. In many states, police were directed to actively pursue and arrest men who violated protective orders. They also were required to arrest offenders when responding to domestic disturbance calls based on probable cause that abuse occurred rather than on the basis of having directly witnessed an assault. Some prosecutors adopted "no-drop" policies regarding cases of domestic violence, pursuing prosecution of offenders based on evidence collected at the time of arrest, instead of depending on victims to testify against defendants. These proarrest and proprosecution policies were complemented by a more proactive judiciary response to domestic violence and by probation practices that monitored offenders actively and mandated them to attend treatment as a condition of probation. Specialized domestic violence units were created in district attorneys' offices and within probation departments. Domestic violence "courts" that develop special expertise and sensitivity about protecting victims of abuse and holding perpetrators accountable also have multiplied. More than 30 states have created strict standards for batterer intervention programs. These standards usually mandate group counseling approaches that focus on stopping violent and coercive behavior and exclude marital counseling or family therapy as acceptable remedies for court-mandated offenders. State-approved batterer intervention programs are generally required to establish contact with victims of violence and to warn them of threatening conduct by perpetrators. Programs also are required to provide information to probation departments about further assaultive or harassing behavior by group participants and about offenders' attendance and compliance with program standards. Many offenders who have failed to attend treatment, reassaulted their partners, or violated other probation requirements have been compelled to serve their jail sentences. This marks the development of a community response to physically abusive men, although in most jurisdictions, it is not yet a coordinated approach.

By achieving such success, this movement enshrined both the negative and positive aspects of what began as a very creative and flexible effort to hold men accountable into somewhat rigid beliefs and practices about intervention with men who batter. In fact, the aversion to approaches that do not focus on accountability has crystallized into a fear that to focus on other issues with batterers means a wholesale abandonment of concern for safety for battered women and for holding offenders responsible for their conduct. For example,

Pence and Paymar (1993) acknowledge that more than half of program participants have problems with excessive drinking or drug use, and in this they are ahead of many of their peers. Yet given the prevalence of substance abuse problems among physically abusive men, it would make sense to spend two or more sessions examining beliefs and practices about substance abuse and its effects, as well as to promulgate standards for effective concurrent substance abuse treatment for program participants. The Alcoholics Anonymous (AA) and substance abuse recovery communities have had an admittedly problematic relationship with the battered women's movement because of attempts to apply concepts such as enabling and codependency to battered women. There were also clashes when people in this community blamed substance abuse for men's violence, when many substance abusers are clearly not violent and many substance abusers are violent when sober. Yet they may have an important point when they insist that treatment for substance abusers must be intensive and long lasting. Duluth is experimenting with groups for physically abusive substance abusers, but carefully thought-out concurrent treatment for substance abuse is a rarity rather than the rule in the batterer intervention establishment. Neither battered women nor offenders may be served well by this lack.

Another example of enshrining early blind spots into rigid standards of practice is the fact that programs are structured with the assumption that all offenders are similar psychologically or that psychological differences between physically abusive men are not significant when it comes to appropriate intervention. Recent research seems to suggest that different types of batterers benefit from somewhat different approaches in treatment (Saunders, 1996). Even if one does not want to credit this research, activists have known for a long time that some men are more dangerous (although this is not to claim that we can detect all the men who are extremely dangerous). It is not difficult to identify many of the men who appear more lethal and are less tractable to our intervention strategies, yet our well-founded distrust of mental health approaches has meant that little experimentation has occurred with this segment of the population of physically abusive men. Although incarceration may be the best solution, it is particularly difficult to achieve this with many of these exceptionally frightening men. Their partners recant or are often unwilling to testify out of their realistic fear of retaliation. Is it correct to assume, as we did originally, that mental health group work has nothing to offer to accountable intervention with men who batter? Some sex offender treatment models regularly combine psychodynamic group work with strict accountability and detailed, lifelong safety plans with some success. Saunders's (1996) research suggests that some offenders may do better in such treatment approaches. This is not to argue that activists ought to indiscriminately adopt other treatment models, but we should explore what they have to offer and bring our specialized and indispensable knowledge about safety and accountability into other arenas. Offenders and battered women may be better served by this.

It also can be argued that the goals of accountable treatment may be too narrow. As we saw earlier, most programs focus on having men accept responsibility for abusive and violent behavior and on learning alternative relationship skills. The Duluth model takes this further by presenting the ideal of equality as a culturally resonant goal for European Americans. Yet few programs have explored men's ideals of manhood and masculinity to help them develop new, nonabusive models of manhood that are congruent with their cultural backgrounds. This is a conscious goal for men of color counseling other men of color, and Williams (1992, 1999) and Carrillo and Tello (1999) are making important contributions in this area with African American and Latino men, but their work is an exception in a field that has largely ignored the renewal of masculinity for European American men. Perhaps this deficiency is due to the previously mentioned fear that if we take on other tasks in batterer intervention programs, we will abandon concern for safety and accountability. In addition, there may be other good reasons for our having missed this potentially productive avenue to help men change. In our work, we repeatedly come face-to-face with many men's persistent cruelty toward women and children. After years of this work, it has been easy for many of us to see all aspects of masculine traditions as beyond redemption. After all, very little of our past history is free of patriarchal influences. Yet it is possible to find men in our past who were rooted in their culture but who were not abusive or controlling with their families. There are examples of respect, love, responsibility, hard work, and fairness that we can recover and use to help men in the present to renew traditions in a way that makes sense to them within their cultural mainstreams. The tendency to turn away from all aspects of traditional masculinity also has contributed to limiting the potential for the men's antiviolence movement to develop a broader constituency among men in general. To fail to pursue this avenue may not serve the cause of giving offenders the best tools for long-term change. It also marginalizes batterer intervention programs.

One of the most severe challenges to the protective firewall and its insistence on men-only groups that focus exclusively on halting violent and abusive behavior is arising from the domestic violence research establishment. Some (not all, by far) researchers are targeting state standards for batterer intervention programs as unjustifiably restrictive and not based on empirical findings. Their campaign is based on recent research that has compared couples counseling or couples counseling groups for moderately violent and non-substance-abusing batterers with men-only groups, which found that there were no significant differences in treatment outcome. Other research compares some men's groups of different durations (3 months, 6 months, and 9 months) and finds no significant differences in treatment outcome depending on the length of treatment (Gondolf, 1997). Furthermore, the initial results of a large study conducted by the San Diego Navy study (Dunford, 1997) find no difference in outcome between men-only groups, couples groups, and no-treatment groups, except for monthly stern warnings from officers about the negative consequences of continued physical abuse (although the interpretation of preliminary results is questioned because of the low numbers of women who actually attended the couples groups). If carried forward, this challenge will have considerable impact within the judicial system and could weaken or roll back some of the accountable state standards for batterer intervention programs.

At one level, this research is important and needs to be scrutinized carefully. However, there are some shortcomings to the position that research-based opponents to state standards have adopted. Many of the studies they cite are based on 6- to 12-month follow-up evaluations based on spouses' reports. They tend to report dramatic improvements in violence cessation within these brief time spans, yet earlier work by Shepard (1992) and Bodnarchuk, Kropp, Ogloff, Hart, and Dutton (1995) suggests that after longer time spans, the effects of treatment wane rapidly (although Bodnarchuk et al. found a significant long-term difference in the frequency of assault for men who had completed treatment as compared to those who had not participated in treatment). A further problem is that many of the same researchers who oppose the state standards also champion marital counseling for moderately violent men who are not substance abusers.

Yet those of us who are engaged in direct work with physically abusive men know that it is often impossible to determine whether men are drinking or using drugs at the time of referral or for some time thereafter. Police reports may not be available, clients minimize their problems, and partners may have fled. It is frequently impossible to make a definitive determination about substance abuse until months have passed. Likewise, determining who is a moderately violent batterer is very difficult. If information is available, it is easy to identify severely violent men. However, there are many men who minimize their violence quite plausibly and whose partners corroborate their accounts only to call the program months later and tell an entirely different and quite lethal story. It is not realistic to expect to make valid determinations about substance abuse and levels of violence and to engage in potentially dangerous interventions based on the present information-gathering capacity of programs in the field.

Furthermore, many researchers who oppose state standards view wife beating as a strictly clinical problem. They construct the response to battering in terms of developing accurate diagnoses and implementing appropriately targeted treatments; they tend to view regular sharing of information with court officials about program participants strictly as a violation of confidentiality. The notion of reporting a man who reassaults his partner so that he will be arrested seems to be alien to them. In all fairness, these are mental health practitioners who have learned much about assessing and working with men who batter. Furthermore, some have learned much about working with men who batter and their spouses in conjoint therapy, but they have not grasped the fact that domestic violence is now considered no different than other forms of violence. Physical abuse of a partner has important clinical dimensions, but it has been recategorized definitively as criminal behavior, not unlike bank robbery or physical assault of strangers. As we have seen, this categorization was brought about by the battered women's movement—the activists who made intervention with men a social priority as part of an overall attempt to attend to the safety of battered women. This movement has made this issue stand out in the political arena and has obtained resources, including research funding, for work in this area.

Ultimately, it is critical for the activist community and for researchers opposed to state standards to make sustained efforts to engage in serious dialogue and to develop collaborative research efforts. Activists need to scrutinize the work of researchers to see whether there is useful knowledge that can broaden our work (there is). There is deep mistrust and bitter feelings on both sides, and both sides feel entirely justified in their positions. These two camps can harm each other severely, but they also can help each other enormously. It is useful to recognize that some of the distrust stems from structural obstacles inherent to research design (Gondolf, Yllö, & Campbell, 1997). On the other hand, researchers need to understand the social and judicial context of batterer intervention. In the struggle to introduce and test new methodologies and ways of intervening with men who batter, there should be a comprehensive concern for battered women's safety as well as a capacity to integrate new treatment approaches with the coordinated community response.

However, a good argument can be made that the research enterprise is essential for the activist community. Activists also need to pose questions for researchers that are germane to our work. Research in the following areas would benefit intervention with men who batter enormously:

1. Long-term treatment outcome research that compares different lengths of treatment and different treatment models for different types of offenders. This includes more research on developing and researching models of accountable intervention for different types of physically abusive men.

2. Long-term treatment outcome research that compares different intensities or types of coordinated community response for perpetrators and their victims. In other words, what multi-institutional (judicial system, probation, batterer intervention program, battered women's shelters, to name a few) coordination practices have the most impact on the reincidence of violence or the frequency of recidivism of violent assaults against partners? What type of coordinated community response system creates more safety for battered women? Does it make a difference whether probation focuses on monitoring the perpetrator or whether it also focuses strongly on outreach to the victim?

3. Are there effective means of rapidly assessing substance abuse among perpetrators? What are the best measures for the concurrent treatment of substance abuse and domestic violence? Are different levels of concurrent substance abuse treatment advisable for different levels of substance abuse involvement?

4. Similarly, are there effective means of assessing levels of dangerousness for physically abusive men? In field conditions, program staff have limited time, limited information from the courts and the police, and limited access to the victim, yet batterer intervention programs can have an extraordinary influence on probation's level of monitoring of an offender. In addition, their efforts can result in the revocation of probation for certain offenders, so research into this issue is critical.

It is easy to imagine that many researchers would look at these questions with dismay and skepticism. The funding needed to investigate these questions in field conditions is not available, and most researchers are forced to respond to funding levels and research priorities established by federal agencies. The activist community may have to use its political influence to facilitate the most useful types of research.

Other problems and challenges for the field of batterer intervention go beyond the rigidities that were integrated dogmatically in the initial establishment of this movement. It is clear that few culturally and racially specific models have been developed for counseling African American, Latino, and Asian American men. Physically abusive men from these cultures explain and contextualize their abusive behavior in different ways, and their sense of manhood differs from that of European Americans. There are some exceptional developments. Ramirez has translated the MANALIVE program into Spanish (Ramirez & Sinclair, 1991). He has used this model in the United States and has taken it to Mexico and other locations in Central America. As mentioned earlier, Williams (1992, 1999) and Carrillo and Tello (1999) are doing pioneering work that attempts to incorporate and transform traditional models of masculinity into batterer intervention programs, and the Domestic Abuse Intervention Project in Duluth has developed a curriculum for Native American men (Balzer, James, LaPrairie, & Olson, 1994). To be fair, many agencies offer batterer intervention programs in Spanish, many have groups that preponderantly serve African American men, and some even have specialized groups for Asian Americans, but specialization of treatment modalities and content is usually left to on-site staff to do as best as they can. Consequently, these efforts have suffered from the general lack of resources in the field, from the isolation of many practitioners of color, and from a lack of a sufficient allocation of resources by the larger batterer intervention programs. Admittedly, the latter point can be seen as an example of asking the poor to give what they do not have. Yet the sizable and well-established batterer intervention agencies can help racially and culturally specialized programs to develop: They can provide fund-raising support for practitioners of color who may want to develop specialized programs, they can make it a point to recruit and train such practitioners, and they can provide sufficient (although limited) financial support for people of color to meet, share information, and advance each other's work.

This work is hampered by the need to carry out more research to further explore the intersection of race, ethnicity, and class with wife assault (Moore, 1997; Ptacek, 1997; Ritchie, 1996). In general, higher rates of domestic violence are often reported for African American and Latino populations as compared to European Americans. In addition, lower levels of income are correlated with higher levels of spousal violence. At the same time, the critical variables that may predispose a man to domestic violence—usually referred to as the risk markers—seem to differ across cultures. A clearer understanding of the relationship between the rates of domestic violence, socioeconomic levels, and race/ethnicity is critical both for batterer intervention programs and for targeting support for battered women. If culture is a major risk factor in violence, it makes sense to focus on developing racially and ethnically competent batterer intervention programs. If low-income levels are a more significant risk marker for wife assaults, then providing services that mitigate poverty for battered women (shelter, financial assistance, transitional housing) and for men who batter (education to promote employment) becomes more important.

However, we must still ask if there is a higher level of physical abuse of women of color within their own communities. African Americans, Latinos, Asian Americans, and Native Americans are all oppressed groups who are disproportionately disadvantaged with respect to income and educational levels. Higher levels of spousal abuse may be one outgrowth of this unfortunate intersection of class and racial or ethnic oppression. On the other hand, culture may play a role in how men respond to economic, racial, and ethnic oppression. The only large-scale study of Hispanics and domestic violence (Kaufman Kantor, Jasinski, & Aldarondo, 1994) found that rates of violence varied significantly among Puerto Ricans, Mexican Americans, and Cuban Americans, suggesting that cultural differences in the predisposition to domestic violence need to be explored. Ptacek (1997) theorizes that researchers and activists fear that studies exploring race, ethnicity, and class as factors underlying higher rates of domestic violence may be used as ammunition in classist and racist attacks on communities of color. This may have inhibited a more objective scrutiny of this area. To the extent that this has happened, battered women of color may have been deprived of more focused intervention and support.

The link between race, ethnicity, and domestic violence also raises questions about the coordinated community response model. If either low-income levels or race/ethnicity predispose some men toward violent behavior, and our response is to create a system in which incarceration is a very likely outcome for men of color who are physically abusive, this is a highly problematic response in a social environment that already overly criminalizes men of color. Do we need to think more carefully of community interventions that are educational and cultural—of integrating discussions and awareness of domestic violence in community settings such as schools, churches, social service agencies, and similar sites—rather than marginalizing those discourses to shelters and batterer intervention programs? Almeida (1994; see also Almeida & Bograd, 1991; Sykes Wylie, 1996) has developed batterer intervention programs that integrate a high level of public community involvement that point to some possibilities to addressing these issues.

The emergence of lesbian and gay battering as an issue (Renzetti, 1992, 1997) poses another challenge for the profeminist batterer intervention field. There is much new research in this area, including surveys indicating that the rate of domestic violence is similar to or higher in the gay and lesbian communities than in the heterosexual community. These survey results should be interpreted with care because the sample groups were not randomly selected (nonrandom surveys may be representative of a segment of a population rather than the whole population; their results can be strongly skewed). However, it may be reasonable to assume that battering occurs at a significant level in gay and lesbian populations. What sort of challenges does this pose? At one level, activists who believe that patriarchal values are the fundamental impulse behind male battering and that these values produce elevated levels of male violence are challenged to accept that women or gay men can have a significant level of violence directed at intimates. Does this mean that the almost 20 years of experience with physically abusive men has led to erroneous conclusions about the role of parts of traditional masculinity in explaining male violence with spouses? A more realistic view is that male dominance is but one potent reinforcer of a more basic hierarchical and authoritarian tendency that pervades our culture and that many people embody. As Freire (1970) and the earlier school of critical theorists noted, authoritarian and hierarchical relationships are a powerful undercurrent in Western culture. Human beings can find justificatory rationales other than gender for engaging in coercive control and violence with intimates. Male dominance is a central focus in counseling men who batter because it has a cultural base that normalizes coercive control for men with women, but it is not the only basis for such attitudes and practices. In any relationship, a combination of a person's belief in the right to control and punish another, along with developmental deficits that limit empathy and increasing stress and frustration, can combine to produce coercive control and violence. Thus, it should not be surprising that battering relationships can occur in an infinite number of ways in intimate and private relationships. In some instances, culture may potentiate domestic violence; in other instances, it may be a personal feeling of superiority, stress, or a power asymmetry (parent-child relationships, adult child–aged parent, etc.). Our experience with men who batter should make clear that not all people who have the "upper hand" in asymmetrical relationships move toward coercive control; conversely, not all people will attempt to establish dominance and control when they have an asymmetrical relationship.

Another formidable challenge is the lack of public funding for batterer intervention programs. This is ironic given that the preponderance of men mandated to attend intervention programs are either low income or indigent. Yet in most states, clients have to pay for services out of pocket, and higher fees are charged to those few who can pay more. Although well-managed programs have managed to survive and grow, this lack probably has restricted the resources of many existing programs and made it more difficult for inner-city and rural agencies that serve people of color and low-income populations to establish batterer intervention programs. These agencies rarely have a surplus that can be used for start-up costs and for the lengthy training and ongoing supervision that help trainees to understand the intricacies of holding men accountable compassionately and of participating responsibly in the coordinated community response effort. Consequently, many communities are underserved or are served by agencies that provide services only to those who can pay. Restricted resources also have made it easier for many agencies to avoid participating in the coordinated community response because it is a time-consuming activity that does not bring in income. If community-based agencies had lower barriers to becoming involved in batterer intervention programs, a rich process of adapting programs to varied cultural experiences would ensue. This can happen only with difficulty now.

Finally, it should be mentioned that the lack of funding has limited the capacity of batterer intervention programs to consolidate their alliance with probation departments. Faced with the task of compelling low-income men to pay for treatment and the lack of programs in poorer communities, many probation officers have come to view mandatory attendance in programs as another unfunded mandate. And this has proven fertile ground for group participants' complaints, escalating a climate of hostility and mistrust.

Conclusion

The overarching intent of this chapter is to promote a searching and reflective exploration for activist-practitioners about our work and its meaning. As we have seen, batterer intervention programs have been institutionalized in many states through standards that certify programs as eligible to accept court-mandated referrals and through practices such as mandatory arrest and prosecution of physically abusive men that ensure large numbers of referrals. Yet it can be argued that these programs are the most vulnerable component of the coordinated community response to domestic violence. Many factors contribute to this vulnerability—our own unrealistically high expectations about treatment outcome, the fact that intervention programs were generally not provided public funding, the culturally and therapeutically limited scope of the programs, the insufficient focus on confounding issues such as substance abuse, and research that has often been of limited relevance to field conditions. These structural conditions make the resolution of these problems difficult: Our clients are court-mandated and do not go on to advocate for the importance of our services or of funding for these programs; the judicial system is justifiably confused about the impact of treatment and uncomfortable about compelling many men who are indigent or low income to pay for treatment; the battered women's movement has been ambivalent about the benefits of such programs for battered women and concerned about competition for public funding in a fiscally conservative environment; communities of color view the arrest of men as an extension of the criminalization of men of color in European American society; and the psychology/psychotherapy establishment will compete for another treatment population and may militate against accountable state standards. In other words, accountable batterer intervention programs have restricted resources, major challenges, and a very narrow constituency.

To overcome these obstacles, the activist batterer intervention establishment will have to expand its resources, probably by consolidating its alliances with the battered women's movement. This movement provided the original impetus to develop the batterer intervention field well in advance of the research establishment or of the professional mental health disciplines. The battered women's movement remains the most important lobby for creating, defining, and protecting the regulatory and legislative framework that created the coordinated community response and court-mandated batterer intervention programs. However, as mentioned earlier, much ambivalence exists about the value of such programs and about the wisdom of allocating funding for them. Yet the restricted funding means that many programs will remain in a survival mode—they will continue to be marginalized, will be unable to have much impact in communities of color, and will have a very difficult time mounting a creative response to many of the challenges that we have reviewed. They also will have a very difficult time reformulating their message of respect and responsibility for men in a way that will help them expand their constituency among men in general. This probably will leave the field open to traditional mental health agencies that will tend to focus on "billable" activities and minimize their participation in the coordinated community response.

The basis of the alliance between the battered women's movement and activist batterer intervention programs is not well defined. Activists will need to engage in a sustained dialogue with the battered women's movement about the value of batterer intervention programs. First, are these programs important for battered women's safety? Do they produce worthwhile effects on men's behavior and affect victim safety? The outcome research about batterer intervention programs indicates that when men attend these programs, there is a strong short-term gain in women's safety and a smaller but highly significant long-term gain in the lower frequency of assaults by men who remain violent. In addition, more focused interventions with substance-abusing offenders and highly dangerous abusers also may bring about a further reduction in the social damage caused by men who batter. Also, accountable batterer intervention programs may play an important advocacy role within the judicial system on behalf of women's safety and for holding offenders accountable. Furthermore, to decline to maintain these programs may relinquish the field of intervention with physically abusive men and the resulting influence in sentencing and case disposition to professional disciplines such as psychology. On the other hand, another position to be considered in this dialogue is whether it makes sense to simply increase the intensity of all other aspects of the coordinated community response—such as increased monitoring of offenders, maximizing the judicial system's supportive interventions for battered women, more funding for shelters, community domestic violence roundtables, public education about domestic violence, and so on—rather than "divert" resources to programs for offenders. If funding for programs becomes a possibility, limited subsidies to ensure the provision of services for indigent or very low-income men may be a reasonable solution. This may make a significant difference in enabling programs to provide services, participate fully in the coordinated community response, and have some leftover capacity to innovate.

Moreover, the indispensable safety and accountability features of batterer intervention programs should be defined in these discussions. Can state standards be made more flexible without compromising safety for victims or accountability for physically abusive men? Achieving consensus about this issue is a critical precursor to enabling responsible experimentation and change in batterer intervention programs. Tasks such as integrating concurrent substance abuse interventions, developing specialized treatment formats for different or more dangerous offenders, and developing culturally competent programs that diverge even more strongly from existing Eurocentric models will be facilitated if we have a clearer vision of the indispensable safety features of programs. The goal can be to create a more flexible framework within which experimentation on program design can occur safely. For example, it is probably essential that programs provide group participants restricted confidentiality so that the partners and the courts can be notified about offenders' compliance with program requirements such as attendance, that some provision be made for communication with partners, and that men address responsibility for abuse and following a safety plan as primary goals. Yet it should be possible, for instance, to incorporate a few sessions of sustained work on substance abuse, not as a way of diverting attention from the imperative to change violent and coercive conduct but as a means of addressing an issue that very frequently sabotages the offender's capacity for change. Again, instead of a firewall, we can have a strong, flexible structure that never loses sight of women's safety or of holding men accountable for their behavior while opening as many routes as possible for offenders to reach these goals. A potential by-product of this dialogue with the battered women's movement is to establish the basis to move beyond a somewhat unclear alliance to a partnership based on clearly articulated mutual interests and lasting commitments.

Finally, the goal of further expanding the constituency of batterer intervention programs can become a transformative experience. We should not stop at worthy objectives such as enabling safe programmatic change, obtaining reasonable funding, or perfecting the coordinated community response. I suggest that we consider further dissolving the boundaries between batterer intervention programs and the communities they serve. This is a common thread running through the intervention models of Almeida and Bograd (1991), Carrillo and Goubaud-Reyna (1999), and Sinclair (1989). In the first of these models, nonviolent men participate in batterer intervention groups as critical links of accountability and responsibility between group participants and their communities; in the next model, religious and spiritual practices that recapture messages of liberation and connection from Native American and Hispanic culture are brought into the project of change in batterer intervention groups; and in the last model, physically abusive men are organized as activist-missionaries of nonviolence who take their message and experience into the wider community.

Pence and Paymar (1990, 1993) took the extraordinary step of making offender accountability a community goal through the collaboration of many agencies in the task. They broke the mold of separation that is inherent in many mental health services and located the change process in a system of social accountability. These other pioneers further break the isolation of the change and accountability process, enhance community, and enroll the wider society into the process. If we did, in fact, assume that the fundamental message of batterer intervention programs was too alien to many forms of traditional masculinity, the work of these pioneers shows the promise of remedying this tragic oversight.

References

Aldarondo, E. (1999). Perpetrators of domestic violence. In A. Bellack & M. Hersen (Eds.), *Comprehensive clinical psychology* (pp. 243-269). New York: Pergammon.

Almeida, R. (Ed.). (1994). *Expansions of feminist family therapy through diversity.* Binghamton, NY: Haworth.

Almeida, R., & Bograd, M. (1991). Sponsorship: Men holding men accountable for violence. In M. Bograd (Ed.), *Feminist approaches for treating men in family therapy* (pp. 243-259). Binghamton, NY: Haworth.

Balzer, R., James, G., LaPrairie, L., & Olson, T. (1994). *Mending the sacred hoop.* (Available from Minnesota Program Development, 206 West Fourth Street, Duluth, MN 55806)

Bodnarchuk, M., Kropp, P. R., Ogloff, J. R. P., Hart, S. D., & Dutton, D. G. (1995). *Predicting cessation of intimate assaultiveness after group treatment.* (Available from British Columbia Institute on Family Violence, Suite 290, 601 West Cordova Street, Vancouver, BC, Canada V6B 101)

Carrillo, R., & Goubaud-Reyna, R. (1999). Clinical treatment of Latino domestic violence offenders. In R. Carrillo & J. Tello (Eds.), *Family violence and men of color: Healing the wounded male spirit* (pp. 53-73). New York: Springer.

Carrillo, R., & Tello, J. (Eds.). (1999). *Family violence and men of color: Healing the wounded male spirit.* New York: Springer.

Dunford, F. W. (1997, June). *Partner abuse: An experimental comparison of interventions for Navy couples: Research design and preliminary findings of the San Diego Navy Experiment.* Paper presented at the Fifth International Family Violence Research Conference, Durham, NH.

Edleson, J. L., & Tolman, R. M. (1992). *Intervention for men who batter: An ecological approach.* Newbury Park, CA: Sage.

Freire, P. (1970). *Pedgagy of the oppressed.* New York: Herder and Herder.

Ganley, A. (1981). *Court mandated treatment for men who batter.* Washington, DC: Center for Women Policy Studies.

Gondolf, E. (1993). Treating the batterer. In M. Hansen & M. Harway (Eds.), *Battering and family therapy: A feminist perspective* (pp. 105-118). Newbury Park, CA: Sage.

Gondolf, E. (1997, June). *A comparison of four batterer intervention systems: Do court-referral, program length, and services matter?* Paper presented at the Fifth International Family Violence Conference, University of New Hampshire, Durham, NH.

Gondolf, E., Yllö, K., & Campbell, J. (1997). Collaboration between researchers and advocates. In G. Kantor Kaufman & J. L. Jasinski (Eds.), *Out of the darkness: Contemporary perspectives on family violence* (pp. 255-267). Thousand Oaks, CA: Sage.

Holtzworth-Munroe, A., Bates, L., Smutzler, N., & Sandin, S. (1997). A brief review of the research on husband violence: Part I. Maritally violent versus nonviolent men. *Aggression and Violent Behavior: A Review Journal, 2*(1), 65-99.

Holtzworth-Munroe, A., Smutzler, N., & Bates, L. (1997). A brief review of the research on husband violence: Part III. Sociodemographic factors, relationship factors and differing consequences of husband to wife violence. *Aggression and Violent Behavior: A Review Journal,* 2(3), 285-307.

Holtzworth-Munroe, A., Smutzler, N., & Sandin, S. (1997). A brief review of the research on husband violence: Part II. The psychological effects of husband violence on battered women and their children. *Aggression and Violent Behavior: A Review Journal,* 2(2), 179-213.

Kaufman Kantor, G., Jasinski, J. L., & Aldarondo, E. (1994). Sociocultural status and incidence of marital violence in Hispanic families. *Violence and Victims,* 9(3), 207-222.

Moore, A. (1997). Intimate violence: Does socioeconomic status matter? In A. Cascarelli (Ed.), *Violence between intimate partners: Patterns, causes and effects* (pp. 90-100). Boston: Allyn & Bacon.

Pence, E., & Paymar, M. (1990). *Power and control: Tactics of men who batter: An educational curriculum* (Rev. ed.). (Available from Minnesota Program Development, 206 West Fourth Street, Duluth, MN 55806)

Pence, E., & Paymar, M. (1993). *Education groups for men who batter: The Duluth model.* New York: Springer.

Ptacek, J. (1997, June). *Political moves: Class, race, and research on women battering.* Paper presented at the Fifth International Family Violence Conference, University of New Hampshire, Durham, NH.

Ramirez, A., & Sinclair, H. (1991). *MANALIVE: Programas de Intervencion de Abogacia Responsable para el Hombre Violento.* (Available from MANALIVE Training Programs for Men, 345 Johnstone Drive, San Rafael, CA 94903)

Renzetti, C. (1992). *Violent betrayal: Partner abuse in lesbian relationships.* Newbury Park, CA: Sage.

Renzetti, C. (1997). Violence and abuse among same-sex couples. In A. Cascarelli (Ed.), *Violence between intimate partners: Patterns, causes and effects* (pp. 70-89). Upper Saddle River, NJ: Prentice Hall.

Ritchie, B. (1996). *Compelled to crime: The gender entrapment of battered black women.* New York: Routledge Kegan Paul.

Saunders, D. (1996). Feminist-cognitive-behavioral and process-psychodynamic treatments for men who batter: Interaction of abuser traits and treatment models. *Violence and Victims,* 11(4), 393-413.

Shepard, M. (1992). Predicting batterer recidivism five years after intervention. *Journal of Family Violence,* 7, 167-178.

Sinclair, H. (1989). *MANALIVE: Accountable programs for violent men.* (Available from MANALIVE Training Programs for Men, 345 Johnstone Drive, San Rafael, CA 94903)

Sykes Wylie, M. (1996, March/April). It's a community affair. *Family Therapy Networker,* pp. 58-66.

Williams, O. J. (1992, December). Ethnically sensitive practice to enhance treatment participation of African American men who batter. *Families in Society: The Journal of Contemporary Human Services,* pp. 588-595.

Williams, O. J. (1999). Healing and confronting the African American male who batters. In R. Carrillo & J. Tello (Eds.), *Family violence and men of color: Healing the wounded male spirit* (pp. 74-94). New York: Springer.

8

Undoing Harm to Children

The Duluth Family Visitation Center

Martha McMahon
with Jeremy Neville-Sorvilles
and Linda Schubert

Undoing the harm done to children by domestic violence is one of the eight key activities of a successful community intervention project. The Duluth Domestic Assault Intervention Project (DAIP) has been a national leader in most of these key activities but not in the area of undoing harm to children. Yet it has a special contribution to make. First, the DAIP organized the first visitation center in the United States to grow directly out of the battered women's movement. Second, from the beginning, those organizing the Duluth Family Visitation Center recognized that women's safety and children's safety are intimately connected. This connection between how domestic violence affects women and how it affects children is still not recognized by many agencies or institutions that work with children. Finally, the experience of the Duluth center shows that children cannot be protected from the consequences of violence if the dynamics of power and control in their families are not addressed. Indeed, ignoring the dynamics of power in their families exposes children to further harm (McMahon & Pence, 1995).

In this chapter, we describe the Duluth Family Visitation Center, explain its origins, look at some of its successes, and talk about the lessons to be learned from the difficulties it faces.

In the Beginning . . .

Duluth's visitation center began with a simple idea: providing a safe place for the exchange of or visitation with children. This would reduce the opportunities for violence, especially during the volatile period when a battered woman leaves her abuser.

Members of the DAIP assumed that they could organize a visitation center in the same way as they had done their other work. They expected to provide a needed service, and they also expected that organizing a visitation center would provide the springboard for doing the kind of institutional advocacy necessary to make broader social and policy change at the institutional level.

Institutional advocacy is a distinct approach to social change. It grows out of the recognition that social institutions such as the legal system are not autonomous systems separate from the everyday lives and private relationships of citizens. It sees that our institutions shape the dynamics of interpersonal relations in our families and not merely react to them, as is often assumed. We need to understand that social reality is constructed and that legal and other institutional discourses and practices play a role in how that social reality is produced and reproduced. For example, institutions provide sets of taken-for-granted meanings and cultural codes through which people understand and act on their worlds and relate to other people inside and outside those institutions. In the battered women's movement, institutional advocacy, therefore, shifts the focus of social change from individual victims themselves to institutionally organized practices that affect how, when, and why violence occurs.

Institutional advocates will maintain that there is no neutral method of intervention in domestic violence cases. For example, police officers who enter the home of a man who has just assaulted his wife for allegedly "flirting" with another man act in ways that either condone or confront the violence. We do not mean to imply that when an offender is arrested, the violence is therefore confronted or that separation means that the violence is condoned. That would be far too simplistic an understanding of how institutional responses mediate the relationship between an offender and his victim. Women in the battered women's movement have a saying: "Men batter because they can." That is, if you want to understand domestic violence as a social phenomenon, look at the institutional responses to battering rather than focus on the individuals who actually use violence.

In this chapter, we will explain that when a battered women's project intervenes to undo the harm done to children, as it did in Duluth, issues that are seldom addressed by other agencies that work with children become visible. The DAIP's work with children shows how certain institutional and cultural processes actually can undermine the goal of protecting children. We can learn of the ways in which the DAIP's efforts to protect children are affected by an adversarial civil divorce process, broader cultural assumptions about children and families, and the emerging rhetoric of "fathers' rights."

The DAIP and the Duluth Family Visitation Center find their work framed by the assumptions that social service agencies and professionals should be "neutral." Assumptions of neutrality shape how the DAIP works to protect children. Making such assumptions visible is helpful because it allows them to be put on the agenda for discussion by communities that want to address the harm violence does to children.

Before discussing the challenges the Duluth center faces, let us first look at the reasons for setting up the visitation center and how it works.

Why Organize a Visitation Center?

> We started the visitation center as a safe place for children to be exchanged for visitation. (DAIP staff member)

The Duluth Family Visitation Center opened in 1989. Like the DAIP, it is one of the five programs of Minnesota Program Development, Inc. (MPDI).

Women leaving violent relationships face the greatest risk of death or serious injury in the months following separation. A battered woman's chance of being killed by her partner rises more than 30-fold when she leaves him (Barnard, Vera, Vera, & Newman, 1982). As many as 75% of the visits to emergency rooms for treatment of injuries sustained as a consequence of domestic violence occur after separation (Stark & Flitcraft, 1988). Even when violence does not escalate after separation, the nonphysical forms of abuse typically do. The DAIP staff became involved in organizing a visitation center because they saw that children lock a battered woman into an ongoing relationship with a violent man (Regan, 1994; Sletner, 1992). Thus, not only are the highly charged issues of child custody and visitation being negotiated during the period of greatest risk for women, but the presence of children in a violent relationship means that the woman cannot free herself from involvement with her abuser.

For women who have been battered, separation from an abuser often shifts the site of the conflict from the privatized setting of the home to the public arena of the judicial system. Custody and access workers report that abusive men are more likely than nonabusive men to fight for physical custody of their children (Taylor, 1993); evidence suggests that they are also more likely to receive favorable rulings from the courts (Saunders, 1994). As Cain and Smart (1989) emphasize, children and child custody issues are now a significant part of the politics of gender. A man's relationship with his children, they argue, entails a power relationship with the children's mother, played out through the issues of custody and visitation. Children, who may once have been observers of violence in their homes, thus become central to the conflict between separating couples (Shepard, 1992).

One cannot work to undo the harm domestic violence does to children or make decisions about their future welfare without confronting the dynamics of power and control in their families. In the next section, we look at some of the ways in which children are drawn into those dynamics.

Children Are Not Just Bystanders

The violence needs to be named and addressed. How has the violence affected the children and his [the father's] relationship with them? We need to break through the denial that although he has done bad things to her, it hasn't hurt the kids. (Visitation center worker)

Undoing the harm that violence does to children means recognizing that children are both victims of and objects in struggles of power and control that do not end when their parents separate.

The DAIP staff had been aware of the intimate connection between women's safety and children's well-being before they became involved in the visitation center. They knew how witnessing violence hurts children. For example, 73% of the men who had been court mandated to the DAIP were either physically abused as children or had witnessed their mothers being abused (Minnesota Program Development, 1997). Their research indicated that children witnessed the abuse of their mothers in as many as 85% of cases (Minnesota Program Development, 1997). Children may see their father, stepfather, or their mother's boyfriend beat their mother; they may see her raped or even murdered (Hiberman & Munsen, 1978). Children can often accurately describe the violence they have witnessed (Jaffe, Wilson, & Wolfe, 1990). They often suffer psychological harm (Minnesota Program Development, 1997). Children themselves are often physically harmed in domestic violence (Jaffe, Wolfe, & Wilson, 1990).

The DAIP group facilitators had heard from battered women about children crying for hours before or after visitations with their fathers and of others who became very hostile or withdrawn for days following visitations. Duluth police records and battered women's accounts documented how, when kept away from their victims' homes by protection orders, violent men would use visitations with children as opportunities to harass or physically abuse their ex-partners. In 1985, more than 20% of the repeat offenses that were documented by the DAIP occurred during the exchange of children.

Men in court-ordered batterers groups expressed strong frustration at the difficulty of visiting with their children and forming good relationships with them. For many men, parenting had been limited to a disciplinarian role; others had a "second-hand" relationship, mediated through the children's mother. Men spoke of the pain of being kept apart from their children. Many felt that their partners stopped them from being with their children or used access to control them. Women in women's groups acknowledged that they sometimes used access to children to gain control over their ex-partners. As in Arendell's (1992) study of divorced men, some men were very angry at their partners for what "she had done to him." Because many of the men in the groups lived on low incomes, they lived with relatives or friends or in rented rooms and had no suitable place to bring their children to. They could not afford to take them to places that cost money. By 1985, a counselor who facilitated a men's group used the interagency meetings in Duluth to advocate for the need to provide a safe and nurturing place for such men to visit their children.

Finally, it is important to remember that children often want a relationship with both of their parents. Although some children are afraid of their fathers and are clear they want nothing to do with them, in very many cases, even children who have been abused by their fathers or who are afraid of them want to have a relationship with them. Thus, those who have to make decisions for children must (like the children themselves) deal with the tension between recognizing the harm done to the child, the potential for more harm, and the child's deep desire for a relationship with his or her father. Children must not be further disempowered or their agency denied in the gendered power struggles of custody and access.

The Duluth Family Visitation Center

> I see the visitation center as trying to prevent further harm. If there wasn't the center, they might see further assaults. Now they don't have to be afraid for Mom and Mom doesn't have to be afraid. (Visitation center worker)

The Duluth Family Visitation Center was designed with the safety of children and women as its first priority. It serves families with a history of domestic violence, and its goal is to minimize opportunities for violence associated with the visitation and custody of children. Upon formal request, the center provides information to the court or state agencies making custody and visitation decisions.

Families using the center are usually referred by the courts or by child protective services (CPS). Some parents use it as a drop-off and pickup site. Others must stay on-site because of concern that they might leave the city with the children or, in the case of an alleged history of physical or sexual abuse against the children, because the courts want all visitations or contact monitored.

Typically, those using the center include parents who have difficulty agreeing on visitation, show hostility or violence during pickup or return of children, have substance abuse problems so that the custodial parent does not feel comfortable with unsupervised visitation, have a no-contact order because of the risk to the victim of domestic abuse, or have children who are in care and the parent would rather visit them at the center than in the foster home.

The center is located at the YWCA, which is in a central location. There are two entrances, each with a separate waiting space, allowing the safe exchange of children. There are three spacious areas for visitation with age-appropriate books, games, and videotapes. There is a special place for babies and a relatively accident-free, toy-laden space for toddlers, a gym for older children to run in, and a space in which older children can read. A lot of effort has gone into making the center a pleasant, nonthreatening environment for children.

The formal goals and objectives of the visitation center are identified as follows in the manual that describes the center:

- To provide a safe and comfortable environment for children to visit with their noncustodial parent
- To provide a place where parents who have been abused by their partners can arrange for visitations and the exchange of children without being threatened or harmed
- To help parents develop good parenting relationships with their children by offering parenting classes and by modeling positive interactions with children
- To provide information and resources so that the courts and the criminal justice system can provide a coherent response to custody and visitation issues

The Center's Commitment to Advocacy

Duluth projects always started from women's experience, and we built our agenda for change and the focus of our institutional advocacy from that experience. We thought that when we created a visitation center, it would work the same. (DAIP staff member)

The center is currently staffed by four part-time workers and two coordinators. The visitation center offers its services to all victims of domestic abuse, and a small number of male victims do use it. However, relatively few male victims of domestic assault have custody of the children and find themselves in need of the kinds of services and protection from their abusers that the center offers. In practice, most of the victims of abuse who use the center are women and children.

As part of their role, staff provide victims of domestic violence with support and information about using shelters and about the legal, economic, medical, and counseling options available to them. They provide referral to education groups, including the DAIP women's and men's programs. They support women's efforts to reduce the impact of violence on themselves and their children by accompanying them to hearings and contacting police, probation officers, CPS, and guardians ad litem. They follow up on cases in which agencies fail to adequately protect women and children. They also gather data on the system's response to custody and visitation issues and to domestic violence to bring to interagency team meetings. In addition, they ensure that the Indian Child Welfare Act and the Heritage and Family Preservation Act are appropriately applied among the families they come in contact with.

The center's staff, however, are not women's advocates in the ways the DAIP staff or shelter workers are. Their advocacy role is far more limited because they need to adopt a more neutral position so that they can mediate the relationship between the woman and the man vis-à-vis the children. Thus, they cannot take the unequivocal position of advocating for the woman.

Having described the origins, goals, and workings of the center, we now look at some of its successes and difficulties.

Successes

> The Duluth center does a lot of positive work with social service agencies who deal with children in trying to come to some understanding on domestic violence and our philosophies. (Visitation center worker)

Although the Duluth Family Visitation Center meets its original goals of providing a safe place, it promotes safety in other ways too. Staff at the center prevent further harm to the children by trying to ensure that parents do not use the children as messengers to each other or get the children's help in negotiating the relationship, and by ensuring that neither parent degrades or insults the other in front of the children.

Staff at the center also find themselves having to address issues of appropriate parenting. Although there are parenting classes available through the center, staff often provide informal parenting education during visits.

The staff know that their visitation center must adjust to the dynamics of the violent relationship between the children's parents. They make it clear that the center will not be used by an offender to take hostile action against his or her former victim. This attention to the dynamics of violence distinguishes the Duluth center from visitation centers that are organized primarily through social service agencies.

The vast majority of offenders who come into contact with the center are men. Staff work with offenders to get them to focus on the needs of their children. This means staff must recognize the enormous psychological impact and sense of invasion a man might feel when what was once his intimate family relationship with his child is now mediated by the state. It means recognizing that his anger about this invasion is often projected onto his ex-partner (Arendell, 1992). Although not wanting to collude with an abuser who may be using custody and visitation as an opportunity to further manipulate his ex-partner, staff may work with him to help him to see how the sense of entitlement he feels in terms of his ex-partner ("Who is she to leave me?" "Who is she to take my children?") and his hostility toward her are spilling over and damaging his children. However, where the line falls between pragmatic working with an abuser to help him better understand his feelings and options and improve his relationship with his children and colluding with him is a constant source of tension among center staff. Differences of opinion on this issue often fall along gender lines.

Visitation center staff also promote better understanding of the power dynamics of domestic violence among other agencies in Duluth whose job it is to make decisions for families and children. Thus, members of coordinated community response from these agencies can get together and strategize about how to protect children with a better understanding of how power plays out in children's lives.

The center provides community police training so that officers are aware of the visitation center. Police officers can thus inform women who are at risk. This information could be made part of police protocol in which children are involved and in cases in which children are used as opportunities to violate protection orders or no-contact orders.

It Is More Difficult Than That . . .

> What battered women's activists intend when they start a project isn't
> necessarily what it becomes. The expectations of others have to be
> met too. (DAIP staff member)

Despite their success, Duluth organizers are not sure how to proceed. Their work is trapped within contradictory framings. A visitation center connects the work of many agencies. Whereas activists who
organize a shelter are clear in their commitment to advocate for
women who have been abused, others expect visitation center staff to
be neutral or to advocate primarily for children. They see children's
interests as one of competing sets of individual rights. But battered
women's activists do not see the interests of battered women and the
interests of their children as being in competition. On the contrary,
they see such a framing of women's and children's relationships as one
of competing individual rights and competing interests as legalistic,
patriarchal, and distortive of most mothers' actual relationships with
their children. Yet they are aware that the broader culture and legal
system often support such an oppositional framing of mothers' and
children's interests (Pollock & Sutton, 1985).

This framing of children's interests as being in competition with
their mothers' rights invites criticism of women who do not appropriately sacrifice themselves for their children or who seem unwilling to
agree with their ex-partners' demands for shared custody for the sake
of the children. The "sacrifice" demanded of an abused woman on
behalf of her children, however, is the denial of the dynamics of power
in the domestic violence that shapes her family's life. Such a sacrifice,
battered women's advocates caution, does not protect women or their
children but puts them at greater risk for new forms of harm.

One cannot try to undo the harm violence does in a child's life,
Duluth visitation center staff have learned, without addressing the
violence in the child's family. However, many of the institutions and
agencies with which they work do not see it that way.

Patriarchal Understandings of Protection

> I think that the key thing here is that we have a visitation center
> located out of a domestic violence agency rather than out of social

services. This increases the center's personnel's ability and propensity to connect their work with children into battered women's protection. . . . But we are a bit stuck about how to use the visitation center as a springboard for advocacy. We want to advocate for institutional change. For example, what is it about the [legal] institutions that make them poorly set up to act in the real best interests of children? One of the real problems is how the courts decontextualize the violence and miss the real nature of the harm done. (DAIP staff member)

When well-intentioned social service agencies or the judicial system take up the problem of domestic violence, they typically do it from the patriarchal role of protecting the victim rather than the goal of promoting social equality.

Women have been represented as victims in much public discourse on battering. People can understand the concept of *victim* without having to understand the social processes that produce victims. Battered women's advocates have strategically engaged such representations of battered women as victims and have had to balance the immediate needs for victim protection with the more radical and broader demand for equality. Some feminist critics have suggested that advocates have sometimes gotten that balance wrong by trading the political struggle for equality for the moral power of victimhood (Currie, 1993; Snider, 1994).

In a patriarchal society, it is often pragmatic for disadvantaged groups to speak as victims. First, it may be the only public voice allowed or available to those with little formal political power. Second, it allows groups or individuals to press for social change and social justice without appearing to challenge the underlying structural power arrangements. Those in power can feel sympathetic without feeling threatened.

But although the moral position of victim may be a politically strategic one for battered women, it is also a politically precarious one. Like recipients of charity, victims may be judged by their moral worth, their characters, or the emotional appeal of their case rather than the justice of their cause. And like recipients of charity, they remain dependent on the benevolence of their benefactors or protectors. They will also likely find themselves competing for their benefactors' good will. This century, the cultural moral worth of mothers gradually has been replaced with the historically increasing social worth of children (McMahon, 1995; Rothman, 1989). Fathers' rights groups, therefore, can use the image of children as the "real" victims of family conflict to undermine women's own moral claims as victims. Representations of children as embodying innocence and virtue and as redeemers of adult failures have slowly become powerful cultural themes throughout 19th- and 20th-century American society (Best, 1990). Idealized (White) womanhood has been removed from its moral pedestal in the sociocultural transformations of recent decades. Increasingly, mothers are portrayed as untrustworthy or potential enemies of their children rather than self-sacrificing and all-loving, as they were once ideologically portrayed.

It is important that debates about children in violent families and custody and access issues not be recast as a kind of competition among victims. In practice, rhetorical appeals to children's vulnerability, innocence, and need for protection do little to empower children or restore their agency (Kitzinger, 1988). The discourse of children's vulnerability, Kitzinger (1988) points out, is a patriarchal ideological barrier to children's liberation, and as a concept, it preempts discussion about the structural sources of children's oppression in our society. The rhetoric of child protection can reaffirm notions of ownership of children (Kitzinger, 1988), unless concern for children is conceived in a way that also respects their agency. Thus, talk of children's "best interests" may reinforce patriarchal notions of family relations as forms of ownership rather than promote the welfare and agency of children. Furthermore, by undermining the moral ground of women's challenge to male dominance in the name of children's best interests, patriarchal men acquire a new moral ground from which to fight political battles with feminists and reassert the male-dominated, often violent family form battered women's groups and others have been struggling to resist.[1]

Children are effectively reduced to property when child custody policies, often in the name of equality, embody the assumption that men and women are equally entitled to custody regardless of how much caregiving they did or the character of the relationships between children and their parents (Ehrensaft, 1990; Fineman, 1995). At the same time, if women are less than perfect mothers, they are judged more harshly than fathers for their "failure to protect" (Taylor, Barnsley, & Goldsmith, 1996), and patriarchal notions of their children's best interests may result in women losing custody of their children or having their mothering relationship with their children undermined and devalued.

Even women who have themselves been abused are blamed for their failure to protect the child victims who are increasingly seen as the real victims. Thus, battered women can lose their social claim to speak as mothers and their moral stature as deserving victims. When women's and children's interests are pitted against each other, public agencies and public opinion have to choose between victims rather than address the gendered power arrangements that oppress women and children.

Custody and Visitation

A lot of fathers who come in at intake deny that there is even a need for an order for protection. "She made it all up." "The courts always believe the woman." Or they say, "It's just me and their mother who can't get along, the relationship with me and the kids is just fine. She is trying to use this so I can't see my kids. I am going to go for custody." Most men are very angry about the restrictions on their relationship with their children. Very few see the visitation center in a positive way.

A dilemma of the visitation center is that of being drawn into giving assessment of who is the better parent or how custody is decided by the courts. (Visitation center worker)

The visitation center is directly and indirectly drawn into the power struggles between a violent man and his ex-partner. By being drawn into legal struggles over custody and access, the center is also drawn into the workings of an adversarial judicial system and of the state itself. Whether they recognize it or not, those who work to undo the harm violence does to children find they are part of the broader cultural and gender politics of society.

The workings of the legal system are blind to the dynamics of power in a violent relationship. The divorce and child custody system is slow, fragmented, and adversarial. Visitation center records may become court documents and thus part of the material of that adversarial legal system.

A visitation center worker logs a father's weekly visit. The visits are regular, and there is no evidence of inappropriate behavior, the log records. A year later, in court, the log is used by the father's lawyer to document the father's claim to the child and to challenge the mother's claim. If he wins, she must lose. In court, the log constructs the father as a good parent. He came regularly; he came on time. The log says nothing about the man's violence to the children's mother. The log says nothing about how he explained the violence to the children or if he did not. The log says nothing about what the violence has meant in the children's lives. The log says nothing about the mother's years of daily caring, which remains invisible in court documents, backgrounded, logged nowhere. "He came regularly; he came on time"—there was nothing inappropriate recorded about his parenting. The father's weekly visits stand in textual relief to the mother's invisible relationship with the children. The visitation center helps produce that text. His violence is reduced to one of 13 variables on a checklist to decide custody issues framed by assumptions about fathers' rights, mothers' responsibilities (McMahon & Pence, 1995), and decontextualized notions of a child's best interests.

"How can you talk about parenting without addressing his violence to the child's mother?" a visitation center worker asks. "How do I intervene in this family when everything I do is framed by a custody process that overshadows my work with children?"

Visitation center workers have learned that for children, like their abused mothers, there is no safe place to shelter them from the complex workings of power. The workers' challenge is no longer simply one of protection but of resisting those practices of power surrounding domestic assault. For them, this is the only way to undo the harm domestic violence does to children—to all the children in their community, the children they meet, and those they do not meet.

Protecting Parental Rights or Building Relationships?

> If there were not custody battles, the work of the visitation center would look totally different. But as long as the battle for custody looms, everything gets framed by that battle. Everything is tainted by it. . . . It's hard [to do this job] . . . when you know it [the records you keep] will be used to take her child from her. (DAIP staff member)

Some of the support for the visitation center comes from agencies and individuals who see in it an opportunity for men to repair disrupted relationships with their children or to build better ones. The desire to promote better fatherhood roles or to reconnect children and their fathers is widely seen as a social good and expresses a legitimate public interest in the workings of the center. But what does it mean when the child's need for a better relationship with his or her father or a father's desire to be a good parent is reduced to the issue of fathers' rights, as often happens in custody battles?

The notion of rights in custody battles expresses an ownership notion of family relationships. Custody lawyers will refer to a father's right to challenge a mother's claims to children. If cultural and legal meanings of fatherhood currently support a discourse of rights, motherhood, on the other hand, carries cultural implications of responsibility for children rather than rights to them. This cultural framing hurts women in custody battles waged within a legal system that is adversarial and individual rights based.

Court processes are designed to protect individual rights. They offer poor tools with which to try to build relationships. On one hand, the shadow of prospective custody battles looms over the work of the visitation center when it attempts to build healthy relationships between children and abusive parents. On the other hand, the shadow of court custody proceedings threatens to institutionally reduce the center's work to the role of helping to establish claims in legal custody battles that are framed in terms of rights to children.

From a visitation center worker's perspective, violence and custody are the backdrops that overshadow everything that happens at the visitation center, but at present there are few ways for them to directly address these issues and the harm that both do children.

Conclusion

The Duluth Family Visitation Center has been meeting its original goal. But the work of the center has exposed the urgent need to make the court system and the agencies that work with children in families in which there has been domestic violence better able to address the reality of violence in these children's families.

Interventions in these children's lives must respect the children's agency and also not reinforce the gendered power relationships that oppress women and children in families. Interventions to undo the harm that violence does to children cannot be built on simplistic assumptions about innocence and victims, good women, bad men, and bystander children, but must be based on careful understandings of the dynamics of power in violent families. In the long term, children's best interests are served by developing family forms based on equality and care rather than power and control in which children will have less need of protection from those who are supposed to love them.

Note

1. Not only do children make more compelling victims than women do in a patriarchal society, but they also make more politically attractive victims because they are nonthreatening to power. Children also allow men (individually and collectively) to claim the social identity of the father. In times such as ours, when traditional forms of male privilege have become harder to politically defend, the identity of father offers patriarchal men new grounds from which to resist claims for equality. It offers patriarchal men the moral grounds of fatherhood that reaffirm their ownership of children in custody and access cases.

References

Arendell, T. (1992). The social self as gendered: A masculinist discourse of divorce. *Symbolic Interaction, 15*(2), 151-181.

Barnard, W. W., Vera, H., Vera, M. I., & Newman, G. (1982). Till death do us part: A study of spouse murder. *Bulletin of the American Academy of Psychiatry and the Law, 10*, 271-280.

Best, J. (1990). *Rhetoric and concern about child victims.* Chicago: University of Chicago Press.

Cain, M., & Smart, C. (1989). Preface. In C. Smart & S. Sevenhuijsen (Eds.), *Child custody and the politics of gender* (pp. xi-xiii). New York: Routledge Kegan Paul.

Currie, D. H. (1993). Battered women and the state: From the failure of theory to a theory of failure. In K. Faith & D. Currie (Eds.), *A state of battered women* (pp. 37-60). Vancouver, Canada: Collective Press.

Ehrensaft, D. (1990). Feminists fight (for) fathers. *Socialist Review, 20*(4), 57-80.

Fineman, M. (1995). *The neutered mother and the sexual family and other twentieth century tragedies.* New York: Routledge Kegan Paul.

Hiberman, E., & Munsen, L. (1978). Sixty battered women. *Victimology: American International Journal, 2*, 460-471.

Jaffe, P., Wilson, K., & Wolfe, D. (1988). Specific assessment and intervention strategies for children exposed to wife battering: Preliminary empirical investigations. *Canadian Journal of Community Mental Health, 7*(2), 157-163.

Jaffe, P., Wolfe, D., & Wilson, K. (1990). *Children of battered women.* Newbury Park, CA: Sage.

Kitzinger, J. (1988). Defending innocence: Ideologies of childhood. *Feminist Review, 28*, 77-87.

McMahon, M. (1995). *Engendering motherhood: Identity and transformation in women's lives.* New York: Guilford.

McMahon, M., & Pence, E. (1995). Doing more harm than good: Some cautions on visitation centers. In E. Peled, P. Jaffe, & J. Edleson (Eds.), *Ending the cycle of violence: Community responses to children of battered women* (pp. 186-206). Thousand Oaks, CA: Sage.

Minnesota Program Development. (1997). *Duluth family visitation center operations manual.* Duluth, MN: Author.

Pollock, S., & Sutton, J. (1985). Fathers' rights, women's losses. *Women's Studies International Forum, 8*(6), 593-599.

Regan, K. (1994). *The Duluth Custody and Visitation Project.* Duluth: Minnesota Program Development.

Rothman, B. K. (1989). *Recreating motherhood: Ideology and technology in a patriarchal society.* New York: W. W. Norton.

Saunders, D. (1994). Custody decisions in families experiencing woman abuse. *Social Work, 39*(1), 51-59.

Shepard, M. (1992). Child-visiting and domestic abuse. *Child Welfare, 71*(4), 357-365.

Sletner, J. (1992). *Battered women's perspective on custody and visitation determinations.* Unpublished master's paper, University of Minnesota, Duluth.

Snider, L. (1994). Criminalization: Panacea for men who assault women, but anathema for corporate criminals. In D. Currie & B. MacLean (Eds.), *Social equality, social justice* (pp. 101-124). Vancouver, Canada: Collective Press.

Stark, E., & Flitcraft, A. (1988). Women and children at risk: A feminist perspective on child abuse. *International Journal of Health Services, 18*(1), 97-118.

Taylor, G. (1993). Child custody and access. *Vis à Vis: National Newsletter on Family Violence, 10*(3).

Taylor, G., Barnsley, J., & Goldsmith, P. (1996). *Women and children last: Custody disputes and the family "justice" system.* Vancouver, Canada: Vancouver Custody and Access Support Advocacy Association.

9

Evaluating a Coordinated Community Response

Melanie F. Shepard

Why Evaluate?

Developing and maintaining a coordinated community response to address domestic violence is a multifaceted undertaking that involves many different agencies and types of intervention and is influenced by complex political and social networks. The daunting task of evaluating the implementation of domestic violence interventions and their outcomes can seem overwhelming, if not impossible. Community practitioners struggling on a daily basis with the crises generated by domestic violence may view evaluation research as the concern only of academicians or administrators when funding sources demand it. During the past three decades of social program evaluations, it has become clear that evaluations frequently do not hold definitive answers about the success of programs. If this is the case, why bother with the expense and time to conduct an evaluation of project activities?

Evaluation research can be useful to community practitioners, administrators, and policymakers by providing information to guide decision making. According to Herman, Morris, and Fitz-Gibbon (1987), "Evaluation can help to set priorities, guide the allocation of resources, facilitate the modification and refinement of program structures and activities, and signal the need for redeployment of personnel and resources" (p. 11). Although program evaluation typically takes place in a context that places limitations on the reliability and validity of the findings, it does provide systematic information that is not otherwise available.

> Evaluation has meaning only if one believes that a rough idea of the relationship between program activities and outcomes is preferable to relying entirely upon hope and good intentions. Evaluation does not provide final answers, *but it can provide direction.* Thus evaluation does not lead to final statements about causal linkages, but can reduce uncertainty about such linkages. Therein lies its potential for utility. (Patton, 1986, p. 151)

The staff of community intervention projects can use evaluation data in a variety of ways. We already have seen in Chapter 5 how community intervention projects can develop monitoring systems to track the status of individual cases and to detect overall patterns of intervention within the system. Staff can use these data to determine if polices and procedures are being implemented as agreed on. Evaluation data also can be used to provide a detailed description of the project and what practitioners do. Projects such as the Domestic Abuse Intervention Project (DAIP) are not easily replicated unless there is an attempt to understand the different aspects of community intervention from the perspectives of those involved at different levels. Evaluations also can help to determine whether project goals and objectives are being met. Evaluators can assist in clarifying these goals with project staff and develop ways to measure outcomes that can be mutually agreed on. Scarce resources can be distributed so that interventions that have demonstrated intended outcomes can be funded over those that have not.

Finally, community intervention projects have an ethical responsibility to evaluate the impact of community intervention to address domestic violence. Advocates are well aware that many inappropriate interventions have taken place in the past that have led to further victimization. Although some intervention strategies may be presumed to be effective, we still do have not definitive answers about this. There is a tendency in the domestic violence field to jump on the bandwagon when a new approach emerges on the scene. However, without ongoing efforts to evaluate the efficacy of these approaches, battered women may be put at further risk. For example, researchers and practitioners are currently giving greater attention to risk factors and the determination of dangerousness (e.g., Campbell, 1995). The DAIP is also asking practitioners to do an assessment of dangerousness that can be used to make intervention decisions. However, the project recognizes that information on the efficacy of this approach is preliminary at this time and discourages practitioners from overrelying on this type of assessment to the exclusion of the woman's own perceptions of her safety and the practitioner's judgment. An evaluation project funded by the Centers for Disease Control and Prevention (CDC) includes an examination of danger assessment issues. Information from this study can be used later to make programmatic decisions about how to proceed in this area.

Initiating the Evaluation

Rossi and Freeman (1993) define *evaluation research* as "the systematic application of social research procedures for assessing the conceptualization, design, implementation, and utility of social intervention programs" (p. 5). Although this definition uses terminology that may be unfamiliar to many practitioners associated with community intervention projects, the evaluation should not be a mysterious process left to the "research experts." Evaluation research cannot be conducted without a collaborative effort between evaluators and project staff.

Developing a Collaborative Process

In the domestic violence field, project staff must carefully select an evaluator so that there will be a good match between staff expectations and those of the evaluator. This is not to say that evaluation activities always will be undertaken by external evaluators. Project staff may choose to conduct some evaluation activities on their own. Hiring a staff member solely for the purposes of evaluation, however, is probably beyond the means of most projects. When an external evaluator is selected, it is important that the evaluator understand the program philosophy and be comfortable working in a collaborative arrangement. Evaluators must understand that victim safety is paramount to any evaluation and must be carefully considered in the design of any evaluation project. A business mind-set will not serve an evaluator well, as community intervention projects are focused on victim safety, not efficiency and cost-effectiveness. Evaluators who come from a rigid scientific paradigm may find the constant permutations of community intervention projects frustrating and the type of research that they wish to undertake impossible to accomplish.

Activists in the domestic violence field are wary of researchers for good reasons. They have seen research data used to blame victims of domestic violence. They have encountered researchers who have discredited their experiences and used their knowledge of research methods to talk down to them. When I first approached the DAIP in 1983 about conducting my doctoral research at its agency, I knew that I had a lot to learn. I was an outsider and suspect because I was a "researcher." I also had recently come from the field as a practicing social worker where I had worked both as a child protection worker and a therapist. This was another strike against me because social workers, particularly in these roles, were considered to have widely engaged in practices that have been harmful to battered women. I was willing to be viewed as "suspect" and to have my intentions tested because I knew that the DAIP was engaged in groundbreaking work, and I was firmly committed to the feminist orientation of the program. Of course, I also needed some place to conduct my doctoral research, and the agency saw me as a cheap resource for conducting program evaluation activities. Developing a collaborative relationship was mutually beneficial.

I have observed that some researchers who do not have a collaborative relationship with activists resent having their research findings challenged. They do not think activists are qualified to question their research methods and seem to think that they are under attack because they refuse to adopt the "party line." I have never felt pressure at the DAIP to report findings that place the program in a favorable light. I know it has been important that I conduct research that has a feminist orientation and that focuses on victim safety. I sometimes have not liked being considered "one of them" or having my students at the university scrutinized before they can conduct research at the agency. However, I realize that this scrutiny is done for good reasons. True collaboration between researchers and advocates means opening ourselves up to each other's perspectives and examining the biases we have developed about a range of issues, including the causes of domestic violence, the role of professionals, and research methods.

Stecher and Davis (1987) point out that focusing the evaluation involves negotiations between people who do not always share the same beliefs, attitudes, or knowledge base. These negotiations are particularly important when evaluators and community intervention project staff meet to discuss developing an evaluation plan. Activists in the domestic violence field have often been at odds with researchers over how research questions have been developed, the types of methods used, and the interpretation of results (Yllö, 1988). Building a trusting relationship between the evaluator(s) and staff involves coming to a mutual understanding of each other's perspectives and accommodating these in developing the evaluation plan.

University-based evaluators may be viewed by domestic violence staff as being more concerned with pursuing their own research agendas than with the needs of battered women. Community intervention project staff may lack knowledge of research methodology that allows them to participate as fully as they would like to in discussions around the evaluation plan. Relationship building between myself as an evaluator and the DAIP staff has taken place over a number of years. They have been willing to address my interests as a university-based evaluator while learning more about the evaluation process through our exchange of ideas. At one point, a retreat was held with evaluators and program staff to discuss research concepts and how these relate to developing a long-term evaluation plan for a CDC-funded project. This retreat was helpful in developing a common understanding of what we were trying to accomplish together. Regular evaluation team meetings take place that include project staff and have contributed to our partnership.

The term *stakeholders* is used to describe the parties that have a stake in an evaluation, such as administrators, funders, staff, and clients. In a community intervention project, this could include a multitude of individuals representing the police, probation, women's advocates, men's program staff, and other community agencies. In addition to meeting with the DAIP staff, the evaluation team for the CDC-funded project has met with court advocates, probation officers, public health nurses, and employee assistance counselors. A questionnaire was pilot tested with women who had been battered. Feedback from these groups has allowed the project to focus evaluation ques-

tions and develop measurement strategies that reflect what stakeholders want to know and what can realistically be accomplished.

Types of Evaluation

As part of the collaborative process, evaluators and project staff
must reach agreement on the type of evaluation and research methodology to use. This involves exploring with staff what they want to find
out, how they hope to use this information, and what can be achieved
realistically given the resources available. Early in the process, a
decision should be made about whether it is feasible or acceptable to
use an experimental design.

The experimental approach emphasizes using controlled study
designs and quantitative methods of data collection and analysis. The
evaluator using this approach emphasizes objectivity and uses methods that will allow the findings to be generalized (or applicable) to
other programs. Recently, the Panel on Research on Violence Against
Women concluded that "there are few good evaluations of preventa-
tive or treatment interventions for either victims or perpetrators of
violence against women" (National Research Council, 1996, p. 136).
One of its recommendations is that "randomized, controlled outcome
studies are needed to identify the program and community features
that account for the effectiveness of legal and social service interventions with various groups of offenders" (p. 140).

The use of experimental designs has been difficult to implement
at the DAIP for a variety of reasons. Although it is desirable for
researchers to conduct this type of controlled study to lend validity to
the findings, project staff tend to view the program modifications
necessary to accomplish this as being detrimental. Domestic violence
staff are reluctant to make treatment and programmatic decisions
based on the demands of evaluation research. Randomly assigning
individuals to either no intervention or different types of intervention
raises ethical and logistical issues that are not easily resolved. For
example, providing no treatment to one group of batterers raises
concern that the denial of treatment might lead to future violence that
otherwise could have been prevented. In the case of court-mandated
treatment for offenders, the judicial system is unlikely to agree to
ordering different sentences to offenders of the same crimes in a
randomized fashion for the purposes of evaluation research. This is

not to say that controlled studies are not possible, only that they are difficult to accomplish. At the DAIP, we have conducted quasi-experimental studies that have used comparison groups without the use of randomization. This type of compromise has occurred frequently because an experimental design has been judged either to be impractical or to have a potentially harmful effect on the safety of battered women.

In Duluth, one aspect of our current evaluation does use a randomized comparison design. Male offenders are being randomly assigned to different educational models after they are referred to the DAIP. Evaluation staff have worked with project staff to resolve logistical issues, such as ensuring the programs were of equal length (a demand of the judicial system). In this case, only one portion of the models is different. Because there are so many components to a coordinated community response, it is unlikely that this one component alone will demonstrate a statistically significant difference unless it is a highly effective one.

Although experimental studies are held up as the model toward which evaluation researchers should aspire, they are fraught with difficulties when implemented in the real world. One of the best-known experimental studies in the field of domestic violence is that conducted by Sherman and Berk (1984), who compare the impact of arrest to other forms of police response. Arrest was found to reduce the chances of renewed violence at a 6-month follow-up when compared to separation or mediation. This study contributed to major changes in police policy throughout the United States. However, a series of studies funded to replicate these findings have not had clear-cut results and, in general, have been less supportive of arrest (National Research Council, 1996). Differences between communities, the types of individuals within these communities, and the range of structures in place to respond to domestic violence can make isolating the effects of single factors or components of the response an exceedingly difficult undertaking.

It is often more realistic to focus the evaluation on the program's goals and objectives. Instead of examining long-term outcomes that may be difficult to measure or evaluate, a goal-oriented approach focuses on identifying and measuring specific goals and objectives developed by the project to achieve these long-term outcomes (e.g., the prevention of violence toward women in the community). The evaluator must work closely with project staff to clarify the relationship between program goals, objectives, and activities. This can be a difficult undertaking as staff and evaluator(s) can become bogged down in formulating goals and objectives that adequately reflect the work they are trying to do. At the DAIP, we have spent many hours formulating goals and objectives for an ambitious project to enhance the coordinated response. Sometimes the goals seemed overly broad and overlapping; ultimately, they ended up narrow but more easily measured. Time might have been better spent on other activities than pursuing this laborious task. Patton (1986) describes similar struggles to develop goals and objectives that can result in conflict or "goals wars." When this goal-oriented approach begins to hamper the evaluation process, he suggests focusing the evaluation on what information is needed by decision makers.

Community intervention projects should develop clear goals and objectives that can be articulated to the community and funding sources. However, developing goals and objectives should not become an end in itself. Stecher and Davis (1987) identify the weaknesses of the goal-oriented approach as its "potential narrowness" and the "possibility of overlooking important issues" (p. 28). Exclusively focusing on this approach may lead community intervention project staff to miss important contextual factors. For example, the Duluth project has worked with probation officers to develop a sentencing recommendation matrix that requires probation officers to consider the offender's history of violent behavior and categorize the offender on a scale from 1 to 4, with a higher score indicating a more extensive history of violent behavior. The objective was met in that the new procedure was used in a majority of cases. An unanticipated outcome was that the probation officers identified many more of the offenders as a 1 than was expected by domestic violence practitioners and many more than identified by the DAIP men's program coordinator. Clearly, the new protocol has an unintended impact that must be studied further.

The type of evaluation selected should reflect the program's needs for information within the context of its current stage of development. When a community intervention project is initiated, different types of information are needed than when the project has been in place for some time. When a project is initiated, a needs assessment can be done to determine the problems and issues that are unique to that community. This might involve collecting descriptive information, such as the number of domestic violence calls to police, the rate of successful prosecutions, and the types of sentences imposed. Another option would be to survey battered women about their needs and experiences with services in the community. The DAIP always has emphasized drawing from battered women's experiences in developing programs and influencing policy.

During the program planning phase, community intervention projects can try out different strategies for addressing problems in the community and evaluate their effectiveness. Early in the history of the DAIP, the police were involved in a study that compared the use of officer discretion in determining arrests for domestic assault with using a mandatory arrest policy (Novak & Galaway, 1983). Although there were no statistically significant differences between the two groups based solely on arrest, the police department's positive experience with this new approach led to the adoption of a mandatory arrest policy. This is an example of how evaluation findings can be used as an impetus for policy changes by challenging misconceptions that a proposed change will have harmful effects (in this case, mandatory arrest). Agencies can be asked to try out a different approach and to withhold a final decision about its use until evaluation findings are available.

The program implementation stage requires that information be collected about how policies and procedures are actually operating. This involves collecting descriptive information about program activities and processes. The tracking and monitoring process described in Chapter 5 is an example of how the DAIP evaluates the implementation of policies and procedures. Other surveys have been conducted with both victims and offenders to determine what they have experienced in their interactions with the criminal justice system.

A recent study conducted by a student under my supervision illustrates how evaluation findings can be used to examine the routine handling of domestic violence cases. Staff at the DAIP initiated the idea for the study and provided extensive consultation, as well as necessary agency contacts to facilitate the data collection process. The study examined probation records to determine what information was being considered in presentence investigations, the types and frequencies of sentences imposed, and the extent to which judges accepted the recommendations of probation officers (Umlauf, 1996). The study found that the offender's prior criminal record and substance abuse were the factors most often recorded and reported in presentence investigations. The degree to which the offender had been violent and information from the victim were the factors least likely to be included in reports. Judges supported probation officer's recommendations 75% of the time. The DAIP had been encouraging probation officers to focus more of their efforts on determining the offender's history of violence and the risk to victims. These findings confirmed that these areas were not given priority. The study informs the DAIP that probation officers are heavily influential in determining the types of sentences given by judges.

Although evaluation efforts have informed decision making as Duluth's coordinated response has developed, this has not always occurred in a planful or systematic fashion. Project staff do not always think of consulting evaluation findings or conducting studies when they initiate changes. Community intervention projects may find it helpful to develop a strategy for information gathering that takes into consideration future plans and key decision-making points. However, because of frequent changes in public policy and in the policies of the community agencies involved in the project, it is not always possible to plan for future information needs.

A difficulty faced by evaluators at the DAIP is holding program components constant long enough to evaluate them. It can be frustrating to evaluators to find that program activities have been changed after the implementation of the study design. A strength of the DAIP is its openness to innovation and change. However, to an evaluator, it can be like trying to evaluate a "moving target." This is where a collaborative relationship can be helpful. If project staff understand the evaluation design, they will be more likely to involve evaluators in decisions around programmatic changes. Evaluators must clearly inform project staff of the impact of programmatic changes on the integrity of the evaluation. Ultimately, it is up to project staff to decide on the appropriate timing of changes. Evaluation needs should not supersede the community's ability to be responsive to the needs of domestic violence victims.

In choosing an evaluation strategy, it is important that project staff and evaluator(s) carefully consider the type of approach that will respond best to their information needs and fit with their style preferences. A range of methodological approaches should be employed to address the complex evaluation needs of community intervention projects. Methodological issues that arise in the evaluation process will be further discussed in the following sections.

Ethical Concerns

The privacy and confidentiality of research participants must be guarded carefully when conducting evaluation research. When contacts are made with battered women for research purposes, careful attention must be paid to their safety. Battered women may have partners who object to their participation in a research study. Procedures for contacting battered women should be reviewed carefully to ensure that adequate precautions are taken. Attention also must be paid to the informed consent of research participants so that they clearly understand the purpose of the study and the risks and benefits associated with it.

Currently, we are following up with battered women whose partners were arrested 18 months earlier. Contacting women for follow-up can place them in danger because their partners may see their mail or listen in on phone calls. Our procedure has involved sending them a letter informing them of the study and asking them to return a signed consent form, if they choose to participate. If they do not want to participate, they are asked to indicate this on the consent letter and return it in an enclosed envelope. Trained volunteers at the DAIP make phone calls to women who have not responded one way or another to determine whether they are willing to participate. Women are first asked if this is a good time to talk and if they are safe. Should they respond that they wish to participate in the study, they are asked to return the signed consent form before any further contact is made with them. These procedures result in a lower response rate because of the number of steps required to ensure safety and obtain informed consent. We have had to weigh the importance of having firsthand information from the women against the need to ensure that this information be obtained without negative consequences.

Changes in program implementation for evaluation purposes also should be considered carefully for any implications of potential harm or risk to battered women. For example, implementing dangerousness assessment procedures could lead practitioners or battered women to underestimate the risk in some situations, which could have harmful consequences. Victims, offenders, and practitioners must be informed that safety and treatment outcomes cannot be predicted with confidence.

Evaluating Project Implementation

Community intervention projects are engaged with many agencies in developing polices and procedures and in providing services to victims and offenders. The complexity of this process requires that procedures be in place to determine whether project components are being implemented as intended. This is a central issue for the management of community intervention projects, and the development of a monitoring process is discussed in Chapter 5. However, monitoring project implementation is also an important evaluation issue. In examining the project's effectiveness, the evaluator must have a clear understanding and description of what the project components are and whether they were implemented as intended. Information about project outcomes will not be useful if there is not adequate information about what the project activities actually were.

The evaluation should identify problems that prevent project activities or components from being implemented as intended. Rossi and Freeman (1993) identify three sources of implementation failure: incomplete treatment, delivery of the wrong treatment, and unstandardized treatment. Incomplete treatment is a critical issue for the men's program component of a coordinated community response. Most batterer programs experience dropout rates ranging from 40% to 60% (Gondolf, 1997). Although some dropouts do return to the DAIP men's program after intervention by probation, the completion of the program may take an extended period of time. The characteristics of dropouts also should be considered in examining program implementation and outcomes. For example, if dropouts are disproportionately men of color, this may be an indication that programmatic changes need to be made.

The many different practitioners and agencies involved in a coordinated response can lead to the wrong intervention being provided in some cases and to difficulties in maintaining standardized intervention. Some practitioners may be resistant to certain domestic violence policies and procedures and either not intervene at all or intervene incorrectly. For example, some probation officers may not follow through with initiating sanctions for failure to attend classes. Class facilitators differ in their styles and may use different activities and assignments, despite a standardized curriculum. Services to battered women are not uniformly provided to all women. For a variety of reasons, some battered women do not access services, but others do extensively. Furthermore, standardized intervention procedures may not be desirable in many situations. The lack of consistency in the implementation of project components makes community intervention projects difficult to evaluate. Failure to achieve a project goal may be due to poor implementation rather than the type of intervention provided. Evaluators must collect relevant implementation information during the evaluation process that should be considered when examining program outcomes.

The type of information collected in regard to program implementation should reflect the community intervention project's mission to enhance victim safety and hold offenders accountable for their behavior. Program polices, procedures, and activities should be considered in terms of whether they are implemented in a way that addresses this mission.

Methods of Data Collection

According to Rossi and Freeman (1993), four data sources should be considered in a monitoring evaluation: direct observation by the evaluator, service records, data from service providers, and information from program participants. Using a variety of methods can help the evaluator to develop a richer understanding of program processes. It is important that the evaluator select data collection methods that are unobtrusive and demand as little time and effort from practitioners as possible. Domestic violence practitioners are engaged in stressful and demanding work and will not be responsive to extensive demands on their time.

Direct observation by an evaluator can take place in a variety of settings: by riding along in police patrol cars, sitting in on men's groups, watching a 911 dispatcher in action, and attending court hearings. These kinds of activities have been undertaken at the DAIP to familiarize both project staff and evaluators with the work of these various agencies and practitioners. A systematic approach can be taken for evaluation purposes by developing a structure for recording observations. This could involve responding to structured questions about what occurred or be more loosely structured to capture the observers' impressions.

Service records are frequently used at the DAIP to monitor program processes. The DAIP has been working with public health nurses and employee assistance counselors to enhance their assessment and intervention efforts with battered women. On a quarterly basis, evaluation staff review records to determine the percentage of cases in which the enhanced procedures were used, as well as the types of intervention provided. This information is provided to practitioners in these settings and discussed with them. Ongoing feedback has increased the use of the enhanced assessment and intervention procedures in these settings. Data from the police and probation that are available through a computerized information network also are reviewed to determine the extent to which they are using enhanced procedures. For example, the police are asked to collect information for a dangerousness suspect assessment in each domestic violence–related incident. Data are routinely reviewed to determine the extent to which police officers are including this information in their reports.

Service providers may be asked to provide information beyond what is recorded in service records. Evaluators can conduct interviews with service providers or ask them to complete survey questionnaires. This could involve asking practitioners about their intervention with particular cases or about their experiences with certain project components. For example, public health nurses and employee assistance counselors were asked to complete a brief questionnaire about their use of enhanced assessment and intervention procedures. A recent study of child protection workers' responses to domestic violence cases asked them to provide information about their intervention with specific cases (Shepard & Raschick, 1999).

Program evaluators use information from program participants to determine their experiences with the intervention provided and their satisfaction with it. A recent study of participants in the DAIP men's program examined their experiences with a coordinated community response. The study focused on acquiring qualitative data during interviews with men to yield descriptive information about messages they received about their violence from different parts of the system. Men reported that they received the strongest messages about nonviolence from the men's classes (Heard & Winther, 1997). Currently, partners or former partners of men in the program are being interviewed about their experiences with different parts of the criminal

justice process. Preliminary results indicate that the majority of battered women interviewed found the civil, criminal justice, and shelter
interventions to be helpful but were split in terms of how helpful they
thought the men's program was (Shepard, 1997). Clearly, the different perspectives of victims and offenders are important to consider
when examining program implementation.

Evaluating Project Impact

Determining whether the coordinated community response en-
hances victim safety and increases offender accountability is central to
the impact evaluation of a community intervention project. Components of the coordinated response can be evaluated separately, or the
impact of the coordinated community response, as a whole, can be
studied. Research studies have tended to focus on certain aspects of
intervention rather than the entire community response. For example,
there have been many evaluations of batterer treatment programs
(Gondolf, 1997). Only a few studies have examined a coordinated
community response (National Research Council, 1996).

The evaluation of the enhanced coordinated response in Duluth
examines separate components, as well as the overall response. For
example, the public health component is being studied to determine
whether enhanced assessment procedures result in more battered
women being identified and referred to domestic violence services.
Although the desired long-term outcome is the elimination of domestic violence in the community, increased assessment and referral rates
by public health nurses are a short-term outcome that we hope will
lead to earlier identification and intervention. The overall community
response is being examined by comparing domestic violence rates
before and after the implementation of the enhanced intervention.
Designing an evaluation that can reasonably determine the differential impact of interventions that make up a coordinated community
response is extremely difficult.

Design Issues

Rossi and Freeman (1993) distinguish between full- and partial-
coverage programs when choosing an evaluation design. Community
intervention projects are designed to be full-coverage programs in that

they should extend to all community members involved with community agencies that address domestic violence. It is not possible to use randomized experiments to examine the entire coordinated response because control groups are not available in the community. Evaluation designs that can be used include studies that compare measurements before and after intervention, panel studies that use several repeated measurements, and time-series analyses that examine trends over time using many repeated measurements, case studies, and statistical controls. It may be possible to compare more than one community using a quasi-experimental design that uses matched control groups or statistical procedures to control for potential differences in these communities. The difficulty with this approach is that communities can differ from each other in many ways, making it impossible to control for all possible confounding variables.

Steinman (1990) used a before-and-after research design by comparing a preintervention period (prior to a coordinated response) to an intervention period (when a coordinated response was being used). Multiple regression analysis was used to examine the impact of police response on recidivism, controlling for several variables. He found that arrests by police prior to a coordinated response led to more abuse but served as a deterrent after a coordinated response was initiated. In some situations, a coordinated response was not found to be effective, such as when the offender had a criminal record.

Syers and Edelson (1992) used a panel study to collect information on woman abuse cases immediately after arrest and 6 and 12 months later. The least repeat violence was found among men who were arrested and ordered to treatment, followed by men who were arrested but not ordered to treatment, with the highest amount of violence among men who were not arrested. Gamache, Edelson, and Schock (1988) used a multiple baseline design to compare three community intervention projects and found significant increases in arrests, successful prosecutions, and the numbers of men court ordered to counseling after the projects were initiated in each of the three communities. These increases mirror what was found in the Duluth community after a community intervention project was initiated (Pence, 1985).

Tolman and Weiz (1995) used logistic regression analysis to examine the effect of arrest and prosecution on recidivism in a community that had adopted a coordinated community response. They found that arrest significantly deterred subsequent domestic violence incidents. The deterrent effect for arrest was maintained over a 18-month follow-up period. Offenders who had been arrested previously and who had previous police contact without arrest were more likely to be arrested again during the follow-up period. Recidivism rates for cases that were successfully prosecuted were lower than those that were not, but the differences were not statistically significant.

In a study conducted in Duluth, statistical procedures were used to determine which factors discriminated between those who recidivated and those who did not over a 5-year period (Shepard, 1992). The variables examined included demographic characteristics, length of the relationship with the victim, previous convictions for domestic assault, history of family violence, court-ordered chemical dependency evaluation, previous treatment for chemical dependency, duration of the abuse in the relationship, days served in jail for the domestic assault, completion of the DAIP program, type of court intervention (i.e., civil or criminal), and number of DAIP groups attended. Of the 100 men included in the sample, 40% were identified as recidivists because they were either convicted of domestic assault, the subject of an order for protection, or a police suspect for domestic assault. None of the variables that were related to the coordinated community response (e.g., jail time, type of court intervention, completion of the DAIP program, number of sessions attended) discriminated between recidivist and nonrecidivists. Men who had been abusive for a shorter duration prior to the program, court ordered to have a chemical dependency evaluation, treated for chemical dependency, abused as children, and previously convicted for nonassault crimes were more likely to be recidivists.

Although it was disappointing that aspects of the coordinated community response did not have more favorable outcomes, the study suggested the need to examine in more depth the characteristics of batterers. Current evaluation efforts are focusing on collecting assessment information about risk factors and determining if these are related to recidivism. The impact of providing enhanced intervention to those batterers who practitioners assess as needing higher levels of intervention also is being evaluated.

It is possible to assess the differential impact of variations in the type of intervention provided within a component of the coordinated community response using quasi-experimental or experimental methods. As mentioned earlier, the DAIP men's program is currently randomly assigning male offenders to different educational models for comparison purposes. Other project components could be evaluated using statistical controls to compare participants who received different interventions. For example, women who attended support groups could be compared to those who did not. My doctoral research at the DAIP compared men at different phases in the DAIP program. Lower rates of abuse were reported by offenders and their partners or former partners at later phases in the program. The greatest reductions occurred during the first 3 months of the program (Shepard, 1987).

It is important to determine whether a qualitative or quantitative approach best fits the needs of the program. The designs discussed here are primarily quantitative in origin and emphasize determining causality (linking project activities to project outcomes) and generalizability (being able to apply the findings to other settings). Qualitative inquiry operates out of a fundamentally different paradigm than the quantitative approach, which grew out of a scientific tradition. According to Chambers, Wedel, and Rodwell (1992), the paradigm for qualitative inquiry "assumes a world only partly understandable by rational investigation, a world in which the intrinsic nature of a thing [is] determined by their surroundings" (p. 18). The qualitative approach seeks to understand a phenomenon within the context in which it exists; it examines wholes and the relationship between parts. Community intervention projects that focus exclusively on quantitative methodologies may find them inadequate for understanding the processes that contribute to and maintain domestic violence in communities. Quantitative and qualitative methodologies can be used in an integrated fashion to yield richer information. Although advocates of this integration emphasize the use of quantitative approaches to examine program impacts and qualitative approaches to study program processes (Chambers et al., 1992), qualitative approaches also can yield important information about program impacts.

I have found that staff at the DAIP are, in general, more comfortable with qualitative methods that allow for examining contextual factors rather than discrete and narrowly defined outcomes. This approach also allows for the experiences and perspectives of battered women, offenders, and community practitioners to be heard. However, the process of collecting qualitative data can be time-consuming, and interviews can be difficult to arrange. The individuals who agree to share their perspectives may have very different experiences than those who do not.

Measurement Issues

How success is defined and measured should reflect the goals and philosophy of the community intervention project. What does it mean to increase victim safety? How can increased victim safety be measured? Is it enough to say that safety has been increased if no physical violence has occurred during the past year? Would safety be better defined in terms of women's perceptions of how safe they feel? What does offender accountability mean? How can it be measured? Is offender accountability increased if the system consistently enforces consequences for domestic violence, or does accountability include the kinds of messages the system gives the offenders about their violent behavior? These are the sorts of questions that evaluators and project staff must struggle with as they decide how to operationally define the outcomes they want to study.

Quantitative methodologies have been criticized in the field of domestic violence for measuring abuse in a reductionist fashion that overlooks critical contextual factors. This has led researchers to ignore the severity of violence or the use of violence by women as a means of self-defense in determining rates of abusive behaviors (Yllö, 1988). Qualitative methods do not emphasize the measurement of variables, relying more heavily on the observation of project processes and exploring the meaning of problematic issues with staff and program participants. On the other hand, quantitative methods focus on operationalizing outcome variables to measure whether project goals have been achieved.

Evaluators need the expertise of practitioners in the field to develop questionnaires, instruments, and measurement procedures that truly reflect the phenomenon being studied. If the information is to be useful to practitioners, evaluators must be willing to collect data that reflect what they need to know. This type of collaboration has resulted in many meetings at the DAIP to decide how to best word questionnaires, determine what criminal justice data should be collected, define desired outcomes, and many other related issues. For example, a questionnaire developed to interview women at follow-up about their experiences with the coordinated community response required that project staff clarify for evaluators the steps involved in civil and criminal justice processes and the types of questions that would be most helpful. Project staff emphasized the need to find out whether women perceived intervention as making them safer or whether intervention was provided in a way that was harmful. In addition to knowing whether abuse continued, project staff wanted to know about the women's well-being in different aspects of their lives. An interview format was developed that explored women's experiences in a qualitative format, which also used quantitative components.

Evaluators and project staff must carefully define the outcomes to be studied and choose more than one method of measuring them. For example, recidivism rates can be an indicator of the level of violence in the community. Reduced recidivism rates do not automatically translate to mean enhanced victim safety. Batterers may continue to offend without being identified by the criminal justice system. Battered women may not experience continued physical violence but have their safety continually threatened. Recidivism rates can be considered one source of data, which should be used in conjunction with multiple approaches. Collecting information directly from victims and offenders about abusive behavior through the use of standardized instruments to measure abuse or by interviewing them is another option. It should be kept in mind that research has shown that batterers report using much less violence than their victims report (Shepard, 1987).

Information collected qualitatively can be used to inform the development of quantitative instruments so that they more adequately reflect the phenomenon being studied. For example, the Abusive Behavior Inventory (Shepard & Campbell, 1992) was developed from the Power and Control Wheel (Pence & Paymar, 1993), which was based on the experiences of battered women. This instrument currently is being used to measure the physical and psychological abuse experienced by the partners of participants in the men's program. During follow-up interviews, women are asked to respond to the Abusive Behavior Inventory, as well as other questions.

Studies of batterer treatment programs frequently have focused on evaluating changes in psychological states or attitudes. At the DAIP, a recent study examined the extent to which participants in the men's program learned information from the curriculum, which indirectly reflected attitudinal change. The evaluator and men's program staff worked closely to develop questionnaire items that reflected the content of the men's curriculum. Men showed significant improvement when comparing pre- and posttest scores, although some men continued to disagree with certain aspects of the curriculum (Stringer, 1997). Although attitudes or emotional states may be an important part of the change process, programs ultimately must determine whether abuse has ended.

The methods of data collection selected are influenced by the availability of resources, feasibility of access, and issues of reliability and validity. Criminal justice or agency records, standardized or unstandardized instruments, interviews, and survey questionnaires have all been data collection methods used at the DAIP at one time or another. Each of these approaches has limitations, depending on the type of information that is desired. The use of criminal justice records to examine recidivism rates is a feasible data collection strategy if this information is easily accessible through local and state criminal justice agencies. One limitation is that local records do not reflect recidivism rates on the part of offenders who move elsewhere. In Minnesota, statewide data are only available for felony and gross misdemeanor offenses, requiring that data on misdemeanor offenses be collected on a county level.

Contacting victims and offenders at follow-up to administer questionnaires or conduct interviews has limitations as well. As noted earlier, locating and interviewing study participants can be a time-consuming process. We have found that battered women move frequently in the community and that it is difficult to find reliable addresses. Staff have begun asking battered women receiving advocacy services at the DAIP to list names and phone numbers of individuals who will know how to contact them in the future. Gondolf (1997) recommends the development of these sorts of tracking plans, as well as periodic follow-up every 2 to 3 months to "increase response rates and the validity of recall" (p. 87).

Finding reliable and valid instruments that measure outcomes of concern to community intervention projects, such as the safety and well-being of battered women, is difficult. Developing interview guides, instruments, or survey questionnaires is a time-consuming process and may not result in reliable and valid data. However, this is preferable to using standardized instruments that do not reflect project goals and desired outcomes.

Conclusion

Evaluation is an important part of developing, maintaining, and enhancing a coordinated community response to domestic violence.

Evaluation findings can be used to promote positive changes and to inform decision making. It is important that evaluators meet with project staff and carefully review evaluation findings and their implications. Too often, evaluation findings are simply ignored and placed in a dark closet waiting to be dusted off and used in a grant application. Project staff should consider what programmatic changes or adjustments are indicated by the findings, if any. Findings can be used to generate discussions with community agencies about the need for improvements in the coordinated community response. During the past 14 years, I have worked with the DAIP staff to evaluate different aspects of the coordinated community response. Although the relationship has been a productive one, there will always be some tension between me as the "researcher" and project staff. This tension can be a positive one as I can challenge staff to critically examine their interventions, avoid hasty conclusions about cause and effect, and be informed consumers of research findings. On the other hand, they can educate me about domestic violence and keep me grounded in the reality of this horror that so many women face on a daily basis. They can challenge me to consider the implications of various research designs and measurement strategies. Our long-term goal to make our community safe for women is the same, but our contributions to achieving this goal are different. We must work continually to respect our different perspectives and to learn from each other.

References

Campbell, J. (1995). *Assessing dangerousness.* Thousand Oaks, CA: Sage.

Chambers, D. E., Wedel, K. R., & Rodwell, M. K. (1992). *Evaluating social programs.* Boston: Allyn & Bacon.

Gamache, D. J., Edelson, J. L., & Schock, M. (1988). Coordinated police, judicial and social service response to woman battering: A multi-baseline evaluation across three communities. In G. T. Hotaling, D. Finkelhor, J. T. Kirkpatrick, & M. Straus (Eds.), *Coping with family violence: Research and policy perspectives* (pp. 193-209). Newbury Park, CA: Sage.

Gondolf, E. W. (1997). Batterer programs: What we know and need to know. *Journal of Interpersonal Violence, 12*(3), 83-98.

Heard, M., & Winther, M. (1997). *Study of Domestic Abuse Intervention Project men's group participant view of the coordinated community response.* Unpublished master's research paper, University of Minnesota, Duluth.

Herman, J. L., Morris, L. L., & Fitz-Gibbon, C. T. (1987). *Evaluator's handbook.* Newbury Park, CA: Sage.

National Research Council. (1996). *Understanding violence against women.* Washington, DC: Author.

Novak, S., & Galaway, B. (1983). *Domestic abuse intervention project final report.* Unpublished manuscript, University of Minnesota, Duluth.

Patton, M. Q. (1986). *Utilization-focused evaluation.* Newbury Park, CA: Sage.

Pence, E. (1985). *Criminal justice response to domestic assault cases: A guide for policy development.* Duluth, MN: Domestic Abuse Intervention Project.

Pence, E., & Paymar, M. (1993). *Education groups for men who batter: The Duluth model.* New York: Springer.

Rossi, P. H., & Freeman, H. E. (1993). *Evaluation: A systematic approach.* Newbury Park, CA: Sage.

Shepard, M. (1987, July). *Intervention with men who batter.* Paper presented at the Third National Conference for Family Violence Research, Durham, NH.

Shepard, M. (1992). Predicting batter recidivism five year after intervention. *Journal of Family Violence, 7*(3), 167-178.

Shepard, M. (1997, June). *Battered women's experiences with a coordinated community response.* Paper presented at the Fifth International Family Violence Research Conference, Durham, NH.

Shepard, M., & Campbell, J. (1992). The abusive inventory: A measure of psychological and physical abuse. *Journal of Interpersonal Violence, 7*(3), 291-305.

Shepard, M., & Raschick, M. (1999). How child welfare workers assess and intervene around issues of domestic violence. *Child Maltreatment, 4*(2), 148-156.

Sherman, L. W., & Berk, R. A. (1984). The specific deterrent effects of arrest for domestic assault. *American Sociological Review, 49*(2), 261-272.

Stecher, B. M., & Davis, W. A. (1987). *How to focus an evaluation.* Newbury Park, CA: Sage.

Steinman, M. (1990). Lowering recidivism among men who batter women. *Journal of Police Science and Administration, 7,* 124-132.

Stringer, D. (1997). *An assessment of educational components at Duluth's Domestic Abuse Intervention Project: Men's Non-Violence Program.* Unpublished master's research paper, University of Minnesota, Duluth.

Syers, M., & Edelson, J. L. (1992). The combined effects of coordinated criminal justice intervention in woman abuse. *Journal of Interpersonal Violence, 7,* 490-502.

Tolman, R. M., & Weiz, A. (1995). Coordinated community intervention for domestic violence: The effects of arrest and prosecution on recidivism of woman abuse perpetrators. *Crime & Delinquency, 41*(4), 481-495.

Umlauf, J. (1996). *Domestic assault: A comparison of pre-sentence recommendations and sentences imposed.* Unpublished master's research paper, University of Minnesota, Duluth.

Yllö, K. (1988). Political and methodological debates in wife abuse research. In K. Yllö & M. Bograde (Eds.), *Feminist perspectives in wife abuse* (pp. 28-50). Newbury Park, CA: Sage.

PART II

FUTURE DEVELOPMENTS
AND ADAPTATIONS OF
THE DULUTH MODEL

10

Just Like Men?

A Critical View of Violence by Women

Shamita Das Dasgupta

The Prologue: Specifying Aspects
of Domestic Violence

The fundamental concept of the Duluth model is simple. It is
centered on ensuring complete safety of battered women by establishing a complex network of comprehensive interagency coordination in a community. The critical component of this model is a legal
system that responds uniformly to cases of domestic abuse. Policies
are drafted recognizing the complex dynamics of domestic assault
cases.

AUTHOR'S NOTE: I would like to express my deepest gratitude to Anne Marshall, Ellen
Pence, and Sue Osthoff for their unwavering support and critical comments throughout
the development of this chapter. Thanks to Anne Bergman and Radhia Jaaber, who have
conducted many of the interviews. Various DAIP staff members have generously helped
me at different stages of this work. Thank you all. Anne Marshall continues to be the
driving force in this struggle for justice for women. Without her, this work would never
have been possible.

Despite Duluth's theoretical clarity and success, the program has encountered a major stumbling block in recent years. The problem is embedded in the significant increase of women who are charged and convicted of domestic violence and referred to rehabilitation groups. Are women who assault their partners "just like men?" Should they attend educational programs similar to those designed for male batterers? The Domestic Abuse Intervention Project (DAIP) has been working for several years at designing a program for women who use violence. Clearly, the answers to these questions and the design of their groups must be culled from women's experiences and grounded in theory. Claire Renzetti, editor of the journal *Violence Against Women*, articulates the concern that practitioners at the DAIP have felt about this issue:

> The topic [women's use of violence in intimate relationships] was being co-opted by supporters of the antifeminist backlash, who were arguing ever more loudly—and getting the attention of the media in the process—that women are as violent as men. Their claims are typically based on quantitative research that asks, using various scales, Who did what to whom how many times? These studies consistently show few, if any, gender differences in intimate violence. . . . What these studies miss—indeed, what they cannot measure given the nature of the methodology—is the context, motive, and meaning underlying each violent event. . . . A contextualized analysis of women's violence would show the gendered nature of the behavior; that is, when women use violence against an intimate partner, they are not acting "just like men." (Renzetti, 1997, p. 459)

This consciousness that a woman's use of violence against her intimate heterosexual partner is fundamentally different from a man's calls for a special concern in the coordinated community response system. That is, domestic violence must be contextualized to help practitioners find appropriate levels of responses to each perpetrator and victim. An example of such discriminatory practices already has been established in Duluth. Currently, the Duluth legal system offers a three-step pattern to respond to victims of battering who have been arrested on domestic violence charges:

1. City attorney trains police to distinguish cases in which suspects have used violence to defend themselves. If officers follow their training, only women who clearly have no claim to self-defense will be arrested.

2. Public defender interviews each woman arrested to determine circumstances of the case, even when she has admitted to using violence. A quick disposition by pleading "guilty," regardless of surrounding conditions of the incident, is thus avoided.

3. A woman (or male offender) who has not acted in self-defense but has a history of being battered by the partner against whom she has used violence can apply for entry into a diversionary program. The woman enters an admission to the prosecutor's record and is then diverted into the DAIP for a counseling/educational program with the stipulation that her case will be dropped upon the successful completion of the program, which includes a year of no further offenses.

An interagency focus group currently is looking into changing the current arrest policy to discourage the use of double arrests by requiring officers to arrest the primary aggressor when both parties have assaulted each other.

This chapter focuses on the controversial topic of women in heterosexual relationships who have perpetrated violence against their partners. Although a substantial body of knowledge exists about women who have killed their partners (Browne, 1987; Browne & Williams, 1989; Dutton, Hohnecker, Halle, & Burghardt, 1994; Jones, 1996; Jurik, 1989; Jurik & Gregware, 1989; Jurik & Winn, 1990; Kalichman, 1988; Mann, 1987; Roberts, 1996; Straus, 1993; Walker, 1989, 1992), little is know about women who have used nonlethal force in intimate relationships. In 1997, the DAIP sought to expand its understanding of women's use of violence by conducting interviews with 50 women ordered to attend groups for using violence. Interviews were conducted in four cities. This chapter is based on the transcripts of 32 of the 50 interviews conducted. The following discussion attempts to elaborate a theoretical groundwork for understanding the dynamics of women's violence against their male partners.

The Problem: Violence by Women

The arrest of women who have used violence against their partners has become a significant problem in recent years. Reports from around the country attest to the increasing number of women being routinely charged with domestic abuse. Some researchers and human service providers see no difference between men and women who assault their partners and believe that both groups should be treated similarly. In fact, many argue that in terms of perpetrating violence against their partners, women are hardly the victims. They promote that in intimate relationships, women initiate, retaliate, and use lethal force equal to men (Straus, 1993; Straus, Gelles, & Steinmetz, 1980). Based on their findings from the National Family Violence Survey conducted in 1975, Straus et al. (1980) contend gender neutrality of battering relationships. Despite evidence to the contrary, critics of the battered women's movement have used this study to claim mutuality of battering in heterosexual intimate relationships.[1] The following e-mail communication reflects the popularization of this sentiment:

> One of the most pervasive myths of our society is that domestic violence is something men do to women. Solid scientific research reveals that domestic violence is something women do to men more frequently than men do to women. While it is true that men account for most violence outside the home, women instigate most domestic violence and they injure men more frequently and more severely. (Sewel & Sewel, 1996)[2]

To support their claims, the detractors cite statistics from studies that have inquired into physical violence by heterosexual women toward their partners (Hamberger & Potente, 1994; Macchietto, 1992; Morse, 1995; Saunders, 1986; Steinmetz, 1977-1978; Steinmetz & Lucca, 1988; Straus & Gelles, 1986; Straus et al., 1980). They assert that because men and women mistreat each other in intimate relationships, such violence should be redefined as *mutual abuse* or *family violence* rather than wife or woman battering. Thus, although this concept of mutual violence or husband battering has brought legal and counseling focus on women, few programs have been constructed specifically for women. In general, these women have been referred to intervention programs that were primarily designed for male abusers. The following editorial is a testimony to this recent trend:

> Over the past several months, a public defender from New Hampshire has been telephoning me desperately in search of a batterers' treatment program for female batterers. . . . The problem is Massachusetts (like most other states) does not have a certified treatment program for non-lesbian female batterers. . . . All over the country, pressure is coming from judges, prosecutors and defenders for the development of female batterers' programs. (Klein, 1996, p. 1)

However, the crucial issue here is not the dearth of female batterers programs, but whether these women should be labeled batterers in the first place. The hasty attempt to equate men and women who have used physical force against intimate partners to batterers stems from the misinterpretation of the concept of battering itself. To comprehend battering only in terms of the incidence of violence is to misconstrue its full implication.

In most societies, moral and judicial systems are constructed to accommodate circumstances around transgressions. For instance, assaulting a potential robber is viewed differently from assaulting a person while robbing him. In the former situation, the act will legally be deemed self-defense with little moral repercussions, whereas in the latter, it will be considered criminal, as well as morally reprehensible. Again, circumstances surrounding a robbery (e.g., hunger, procuring medicine for a dying child, possessing a fashionable jacket, drug buy) may reduce or increase what we might think is an appropriate state response. In each case, societal reactions, as well the impact on the individual, will be dramatically distinct, and each will be judged by the full circumstances of the act committed. We must recognize that all violence is generally understood in its broad context that would include motivations, intentions, results, and consequences.

The Term: Defining and Understanding *Battering*

The first step to comprehend battering in its full import is to define the term itself. The DAIP's widely used Power and Control Wheel provides us with an inclusive framework for interpreting the behavior of men who batter. Generated by battered women themselves, this wheel explains a batterer's abusive conduct as a tool of intimidation and subjugation (see the Appendix).

Although each violent episode of battering may look like idiosyncratic outbursts of uncontrolled anger, stringed together, such incidents form a pattern of coercion in which abusers establish control over their partners. Furthermore, taken together as a historic and global phenomenon, battering looms as a systematic course of action rather than peculiar behaviors of a few demented individuals.

In fact, battering may or may not be established by actual acts of physical and/or sexual abuse. Coercing and terrorizing a victim are often accomplished by nonphysical manipulations. This ability to intimidate and dominate the female victim is authorized by the entitlement to master, historically attributed to the male gender role. Pence and Paymar (1993) write,

> A batterer's use of physical assaults or sexual abuse is often infrequent, but reinforces the power of the other tactics on the wheel (i.e., emotional abuse, isolation, threats of taking the children) that are used at random and eventually undermine his partner's ability to act autonomously. (p. 2)

Battering can thus be defined as acts that intimidate, isolate, and deny victims personal power and establish the abuser's control over them. Incidents and issues that apparently trigger conflict situations are therefore of little significance. Furthermore, intimate violence does not occur in a vacuum. It is nested within the sociocultural context of a nation and is maintained, as well as supported, by its structures. Religion, law, art, socialization patterns, education, economy, gender roles, and belief systems of a society legitimize men's violence toward women and simultaneously ensure that women assume responsibility for the abuse they suffer. It is the web of institutional, social, and cultural support for abuse that transforms male violence against women from incidental violence to battering and carries it from the realm of personal to the political.

> When discussing violence against women, it is important to understand that, even though each act of violence is perpetrated by an individual, violent behavior takes place in a sociocultural context. It is increasingly recognized that multiple levels of co-influences—from societal to individual—determine the expression of violence. Therefore, before one can begin to understand and address the phenomenon of violence against women—in all its various forms—one must understand the context in which that phenomenon is allowed to occur. (Koss et al., 1994, p. 3)

Unfortunately, most theories of battering fail to account for the sociohistorical aspects of this problem. As a result, understanding of battering continues to remain at a superficial level, promoted as a product of individual pathology and consequently to be treated by "therapy." However, such individualistic inquiries into battering are inadequate in explaining the following issues:

1. Historically, violence is a recognized strategy used to resolve conflicts. Whether in macro-, meso-, or microlevels (e.g., international wars, street gang fights, intrafamilial conflicts, etc.), aggressive behavior is a time-tested way of achieving goals. A theory, therefore, must examine battering, a patterned violence in intimate relationships, in terms of its objectives and goals.

2. Individuals engaged in a conflict do not necessarily possess equal negotiating power. Gender role, perceived authority, personal autonomy, ascribed status, social privileges, and cultural support determine power (im)balance between feuding parties. For example, the husband in a family is generally recognized by society to have more authority and higher status and be the greater contributor to family economy than his wife. He thereby enjoys more benefits associated with his role. These male advantages are supported by social institutions such as banks, employers, insurance companies, immigration authorities, churches, and sociocultural conventions. The ascribed power and privilege that a man brings to interpersonal conflicts with his partner therefore must be recognized in understanding battering.

3. Institutional interventions that are designed to support the individual with lesser power in domestic conflicts, such as law enforcement agencies, actually may increase the vulnerability of the victim. For example, statistics show that when women decide to seek help or leave abusive relationships, rather than ceasing, violence expands in lethality. Conversely, when male victims of assaults by their female partners leave the relationship, the violence typically ends. Women who assault their male batterers are made increasingly vulnerable to their abusers as they are subjected to growing incidents of arrest by police officers who may understand domestic violence as a simple "law and order" issue (Saunders, 1995). Studies have also shown that divorced women have significantly lower incomes following divorce, whereas divorced men have an increase in their incomes (Weitzman, 1985; Winner, 1996). This inability of women to just "walk away from violent relationships," the basis of various theories of female masochism, must be included in explanations of battering.

These issues underscore the social, historical, and political components involved in battering and domestic abuse. Thus, a valid perspective of intimate violence must endeavor to explicate battering in light of its sociocultural context, as well as various related issues.

The Confusion: (Mis)Understanding Violence by Women

Trying to understand women's violent behavior toward their male partners by focusing only on incidents of physical assault can be misleading. The dynamics behind women's use of violence in heterosexual relationships is distinct enough from men's to warrant a detailed analysis of the factors involved. A few researchers have asserted that the majority of women who use physical force against their partners are themselves battered women (Hamberger, 1997; Hamberger & Potente, 1994; Saunders, 1986). Although many women, like men, use physical force to make their male partners comply with their wishes or behave differently, a significant number of women use violence as a way to control or stop the abuse against their own selves (Barnett, Lee, & Thelen, 1997; Hamberger, 1997; Hamberger & Potente, 1994; Saunders, 1986; Vivian & Langhinrichsen-Rohling, 1994). Both legal acts of violence, such as self-defensive actions and acts of retaliation, are all directly linked to the fact that the woman offender is the ongoing victim of coercion, intimidation, and violence. Men, on the other hand, abuse their female partners without being victims themselves of ongoing abuse and intimidation. Most men who use repeated acts of violence against their partners generally do so to assert power and control in their intimate relationships (Barnett et al., 1997; Dutton & Strachan, 1987; Edelson, Eisikovits, Guttman, & Sela-Amit, 1991). Furthermore, Barnett et al. (1997) found that although a significant number of battered women use violence, few accomplish their goal successfully of controlling their partners' behaviors. It is, in fact, quite the opposite. Battered women's use of violence, according to Barnett and her colleagues, makes them even more vulnerable to their partners' aggression. In short, although women may have more varied motivations for assaulting their partners than self-defense and retaliation, few result in prolonged power, supremacy, and domination over their male partners.

In fact, if we examine the use of the various tactics of battering, it becomes clear that the effects of physical force by men and women are not the same at all (see Table 10.1).

Table 10.1 Gender Differences in the Tactics and Effects of Violence in Intimate Relationships

Tactic of Battering	Men's Use	Women's Use
Intimidation	Looks, action, and gestures can be used by men to strike fear in their partners, which may be followed up by threats of (or actual) physical and sexual abuse.	Rarely can women systematically engender fear in men by sheer acts of looking, gesturing, or behaving in a particular way. This may be due to the fact that very few women can consistently back up nonphysical threatening conduct with the potential of severe physical violence.
Isolation	Men may effectively isolate their partners by forbidding contact with friends, relatives, and neighbors. They may also prohibit women from working or joining schools, organizations, and so on.	A woman may try to limit her partner's contacts with relatives, friends, or acquaintances but seldom can achieve total control over his behavior.
Economic control	In general, men are the primary wage earners in families and thus may control all financial decision making. Even when women earn salaries, social norms dictate that their wages be controlled by their husbands.	Even though more and more women earn incomes, their financial contributions may be viewed as supplementary to their husbands' incomes. Few women can deprive their husbands of financial independence.
Personal power	Abusive men tend to deny their partners' decision-making skills or may demand authority over all family decisions, claiming their ascribed status in society.	Women's gender roles and socialization rarely allow them to deny their partners all decision-making power.
Sexual abuse	Men may use marital rape and sexual assault both as weapons of terror.	Although women may withhold sexual access and favors to manipulate their partners, this denial hardly has the same impact as a violent sexual assault.

The Reality: Interviews With 32 Women

> He was drunk and I was drunk. . . . He says you ain't going anywhere, and I said I am. I pushed him and he pushed me to the floor. I got up and I just tore into him. I scratched him right on the neck and he punched me in the mouth and cut inside of my lip. Next thing I know, I'm standing in the hallway, there's cops handcuffing me. (Christina, an interviewee, describing the incident that got her arrested)[3]

To develop an in-depth understanding of women's use of violence, 32 women who had either self-referred, had been arrested, or had been court ordered to treatment or educational programs for abusers were interviewed.[4] Of these 32 women, 18 were Euro-American (56.25%), 6 Native American (18.75%), 6 African American (18.75%), 1 Latino (3.13%), and 1 Asian American (3.13%). The women were mainly from the Midwest, the East Coast, and the West Coast and ranged in age between 19 and 50 years. Ten (31.25%) women were married at the time of the interview, and 22 (68.75%) were either single or divorced. The majority of women belonged to the working classes.

The interviews overwhelmingly revealed that nearly all women were either currently being or have been battered in intimate relationships. Many of the women's use of violence could clearly be identified as self-defense. For example, Jackie-Terri, a 28-year-old African American mother with two daughters, was arrested when she had sprayed mace on her husband and stabbed him with a knife. She had reacted when he had felled her to the floor and was beating her severely. Later, the charges against her were dismissed as the courts recognized her assault as self-defense at the testimony of her daughter. Dana, a White woman in her 30s, elaborated another such occurrence when both she and her husband were in a fight:

> I guess I just wanted him to leave me alone, you know, to keep away from me. So, I tried to use my hands to, like, fend him off. I went to do like this and he grabbed me and swung me around. I fell into my son's playpen and when I fell I just said, this is not working. So I grabbed a knife. It was the first thing I could think of just to keep him away from me, and so I came at him with it. He grabbed my arm and took the knife away from me. Then I grabbed another one and went at him.

Dana clearly recognized her male partner's physical superiority and the need to equalize the power differential with a weapon.

In fact, most women's use of a weapon in this sample was motivated by a desire to effectively ward off assaults or end an escalating pattern of aggression by their partners. Albeit their efforts, the majority of women were not only physically beaten but also emotionally controlled by their partners. Patricia, a 26-year-old African American woman, said, "He would not let me come out, sit on the porch, go out. When I'd go to the store, I had to return in 5 minutes or he would beat me up. He would not let me talk to anyone." In another interview, Patty's testimony to the escalating abuse in the relationship is typical of the group:

> At first it was just verbal, then it got into slapping me. I'd tell him it's not okay to slap me, that's abusive. He'd say, "Well, at least I didn't punch you." . . . Six months [later] he started getting more violent. He would throw me on the bed, try choking me. . . . [Once] he dragged me off the couch [by my legs] through the house when my son was there. . . . I was partly scared and partly angry and partly embarrassed because my son was watching this.

While discussing their current relationships, most women disclosed that they have been involved with multiple abusive partners. Marty, a 32-year-old African American woman, revealed that her abuse started at the hands of her foster father. After she started living on her own, two consecutive partners, including the current one, were extremely physically brutal to her. She asserted that her four sisters also were embroiled in highly abusive relationships with men. Most women were affected by these previous relationships to the point that they anticipated abuse and at times struck their partners preemptively. For example, before her marriage, Mei, an Asian woman brought up in a White American family, had been seriously involved with an Asian man whom she described as being "very physically abusive." "It is almost like I learned this [being physically abusive] from him. . . . I never used violence as a child or when I was growing up. . . . I saw him do it, [knew] how it felt, how it made me feel," stated Mei. She believed that this learning made her use violence toward her present husband to get her own way: "Violence [is] a tool or a way to get control or my way for attention."

Although all the women in this group admitted to having physically assaulted their partners, the motivation to terrorize or subjugate men did not clearly emerge from their narratives. Rather, the following set of intentions for their violent behavior could be identified from the interviews with women in the current study.

I wanted him to stop abusing me. Because the majority of women were experiencing violence in their relationships, a strong motivation for using violence was to halt further abuse. Rose, age 22, spoke about why she decided to respond aggressively toward her partner: "The first couple [of] times I would just let him hit me and I didn't do nothing. Then he would say, 'I'm sorry.' But then I just got sick of it and I thought if I fought him too he wouldn't do it anymore." Christina, a young woman who had taken boxing as a sport in high school, avowed that she was "more or less like a biblical woman" in the first year after meeting her future husband. "I was submissive. Anything my husband needed or wanted, I was there. I pampered him. He would take a shower, I would wash his feet; when he laid on the bed, I massaged him." However, after their marriage, he became sexually and physically abusive with her. Christina herself became violent: "I'm tired of putting up with this. I've been through other relationships that ended the same, abuse. I took it and the violence. [It was] too humiliating, too degrading. I'll go crazy if I don't stop this."

I wanted to stand up for myself. After they had endured prolonged abuse, many women decided that they could not bear it any more. They had to retaliate to salvage their self-worth as a human being. Christina, who had been in an extremely abusive relationship for 5 years, confessed that she felt better after she "jumped on him, hit him, and banged on his head" in a fight. "Yeah, I felt a lot better. Not better, but I felt that I could take care of myself when he was around. . . . My brothers were going to go after him and I said no. I said I can deal with him. I felt that I could take care of myself for once."

I wanted him to pay attention to me. Many of the women felt that their partners ignored them, and violence was the only way they could get some notice. Mary said that she generally became angry by her partner's indifference toward her: "He's very smug, very aloof about everything. I don't like that. I can't be like that. I want an answer; I want to figure it out." Consequently, she would "punch him or shove him or slap him." Terry also became resentful when her partner started neglecting her. She grew frustrated with his lack of communication and felt her aggressive behavior might elicit some reaction from him: "I'd have to say the more he ignored me the more upset I got. . . . I wanted him to give in and talk to me. . . . I was frustrated, hurt, angry."

I wanted to get some control over the situation. To gain control over potentially disruptive situations, many women used abusive behavior. Thus, when women sensed that their partners were spiraling toward physical violence, rather than waiting, they initiated it themselves. Christina said, "I wanted to be more in control. It becomes a head game relationship." Heather, a 40-year-old woman who had injured her partner with a knife, stated that she used violence to feel "a little bit more [in] control." In addition, she said, "I'd make him think a little bit or back off. Maybe I had a little bit of power. And that's the only way to have that kind of power."

I wanted him to take some responsibility. Women also reacted violently when men used their masculine privilege to shirk responsibilities of child rearing or household maintenance. Shannon, a 21-year-old woman who had been physically and sexually assaulted before by her partner, explained the circumstances of her single incidence of violence toward him:

> When my baby was 6 months old, [he was] really crying. I was feeding him all the time and thought he [her partner] needed some responsibility. . . . I kicked him so he would wake up. I tried to shake him at first, he wouldn't wake up. So then, I kicked him. . . . I felt very hostile, he should share responsibility too. The women shouldn't have to do the job the whole time even though I'm the mother. He should wake up once in a while and do it. I was just really angry that he wouldn't help.

I wanted him to respect me. Partners' breach of exclusivity often evoked physical aggression in women. Liz, a 20-year-old Native American, declared that she used violence for the first time when she caught her partner flirting with another woman. Adele, a 44-year-old woman, became enraged when she witnessed her husband flirting with another woman on their wedding night: "Our wedding night was terrible. He was flirting with another lady, more than flirting. He was kissing and hugging her. I just got physically ill and went to bed." Finally, when Adele started yelling at her husband, he became abusive toward her: "He just come up and boom, started getting physical, slapped me. I slapped him back. He would push me and I would push him back." Similarly, Rose, a Native American woman, confessed that she became physically abusive toward her husband when he was cheating with other women. "I [had] seen him at a party and he was sitting in the car. He had his window rolled down and didn't even know that I came up there. He was sitting there talking to somebody and I just reached in and punched him. I was so mad at him."

I wanted him to pay for his behavior. Revenge for misconduct and mistreatment was definitely on many women's minds while perpetrating abuse. Jenny, a 19-year-old Native American woman, had been secreting away money, which her partner stole: "He did steal $200 from me that I left at the house. I left it there so I could pay some of the bills and stuff. He ripped two of my books [also] when I was going to school." After she found out that he had stolen her money and books, she "punched him in the face." Heather articulated her motivation for being violent toward her partner quite clearly: "I wanted to hurt him just as he had hurt me. I was going to intentionally hurt him." Robin used physical force toward her extremely abusive partner to wrench a semblance of equity: "I guess I wanted him to feel fear. I wanted him to feel what it was like. What he would do to me."

I wanted to hurt him because he threatened my family. Often, women assault their partners when their children, relatives, or pets become targets of abuse. For a woman, children, other family members, and beloved pets may constitute an extended self. Thus, an assault on any of them may be taken as an attack on her. This group of 28 women also was no exception. Many of the women became physically aggressive with their partners when their children were being abused. Christina spoke of her decision to attack her partner when she suspected child abuse: "I found out he was molesting my daughter. She was 4 years old and in a lot of pain. He was sleeping on the bed. I woke up and my mind just snapped. I got up and took a rifle off the rack, pointed at him and I was going to blow him away. I, then, for an instant thought about my kids. They wouldn't have no mother." Misty, who had once injured her abusive husband, spoke of the abuse her son endured at his hands: "[He was] very abusive to me and my children. He got really bad with my older son. He would abuse him and hit him with a closed fist. It was like 'Oh! now I've got someone else to beat on.' He would hit him [her older son] with a closed fist and draw blood." The fear of her child being hurt made Jackie behave ferociously toward her boyfriend. She said, "I was 17. He punched me in the face while I was holding the baby. . . . When he did that, I put the baby down. I clubbed him back. He fell down a whole flight of stairs."

I am "tough." A few young women described their childhood socialization as learning never to be vulnerable. Patricia, a young African American woman, said, "I fought him. I fought him. I'd act you know like you're really scared but you'd act like you're really big and bad inside." They believed that being tough was the only way they could survive and achieve their hearts' desires in this world. Nonetheless, being tough did not prevent their victimization. Patricia voiced this issue clearly: "He is 6'3" and I'm only 5'6". So, he has the height over me. . . . He is the type that is scared of no one, he is scared of nothing." But when abused, they felt honor bound to respond in kind. This emulation of masculine-hardened behavior was mainly seen among the young interviewees. Jackie said, "I grew up fighting back because of my surroundings." Bobbie, a young Latina, became a gang affiliate by being the girlfriend of successive gang leaders and drug dealers. She declared, "I thought that [being physically violent] was the way I was supposed to get what I wanted and usually did." Although she was never physically abused by her lovers, Bobbie stated women in gangs were "just the pretty package on the side but we could have anything we wanted." She had participated in drive-by shootings and had fought other women with switchblades. When she decided to settle down with her husband, she missed the "spoiling" her gang leader boyfriends had provided for her. To get what she wanted, "I would try to hit him [her husband], beat him up. I mean, he was 6'4". . . . He'd leave because he wasn't used to violence in the home where he was raised."

Regardless of the degree of physical force women used, none of the interviewees believed that it made their partners fearful. Neither did it control their behaviors. This perception was not without its base in reality. A group of 10 men whose female partners had been arrested on domestic abuse charges and interviewed as a part of this study also denied that their partners' violence resulted in their experiencing prolonged or significant fear for their safety.[5] This finding is supported by studies that indicate that men in violent relationships, compared to their female counterparts, express little fear of their partners and wives (Barnett et al., 1997; Langhinrichsen-Rohling, Neidig, & Thorn, 1995; Morse, 1995; Russell, Lipov, Phillips, & White, 1989).

In the current sample, Jackie, a White woman in her 30s, thought she was tough, yet her conduct "didn't scare him at all; it didn't change any of his behavior." Similarly, when she attacked him, Adele stated that her partner "laughed at me, he thought it was funny. I tried to fight back and he just laughed." Even Bobbie, the ex-gang member, was not sure her physically larger husband had been afraid of her violence. Only when women picked up weapons, guns, knives, and household objects did their partners become temporarily afraid. Mei stated, "I don't think when I was attacking him with my hand he was afraid, only when I would start to use objects that could really hurt him with [such as] the salt and pepper shaker." Dana claimed that her partner became afraid when she picked up a knife because he was "caught off guard at that time." Quite often, aggression by women led to more abusive behavior on their male partners' part. Jenny was convinced that her use of violence had escalated his abuse: "He became more violent. Before he just pushed me, then he started hitting me, biting me." Christina declared that physical retaliation did not work with her partner: "Next time he uses more [violence] because he is more infuriated with me. [Once] he punched out all my windows." The main reason for the men's boldness seemed to be the size and strength differential with their partners. Shannon's statement summarizes the sentiments: "He is way bigger than me. It [violence] didn't change his behavior at all. It didn't really help."

When viewed in terms of motives, intentions, and consequences, these women's use of violence emerges as instrumental; that is, the incidents are directed toward the resolution of conflicts or control of immediate surroundings. For example, 20-year-old Mei confessed that she was the aggressor in their marriage. Although her husband did not generally initiate physical violence, he often exhorted her to be a "good little Asian girl" and not question his activities. Mei was left at home on a regular basis while he went out with his friends. It is easy to see what Mei was trying to accomplish with her physical attacks:

> After I had my baby [is when] the physical stuff started. If he wanted to leave, I would get real mad because he would leave me home with the baby and he would want to go out. . . . If he was walking out the door, I would step in front of him. If he tried to leave I would try to hit him, shove him. . . . I think most of that was just to get him to stay home. Even if that meant getting into a fight that was okay, as long as he would stay home. . . . I was only 16 years old. . . . He did a lot of shoving to restrain me. . . . I remember one time he hit me in the ear and it bruised black and blue. He was physically abusive too, but I started it all.

The dynamics of such violence do not accommodate the intent to systematically intimidate or consolidate power over the partner. In Mei's case, violence was used, probably as a last recourse, to achieve certain immediate goals. There is little indication that Mei's design was to create powerlessness in her partner. Rather, she herself felt powerless to change her husband's conduct.

Although during the interviews women elaborated various motivations for assaulting their partners, the overwhelming reason for their actions was protecting themselves. Patricia, an African American mother of three, said, "I'd actually fistfight him. I fought him when he came after me. I just wanted to get him off [of] me." Patty summarized the sentiments of many of the women: "I felt that I needed to protect myself. . . . I was like, get him away from me before I die. I needed to save myself and it [being violent] did work."

Despite feeling justified about assaulting their partners, most women suffered guilt over their behavior. Adele, who had picked up an instrument to attack her partner, said, "I got scared to think I could do something like that. That is what scared me." Heather articulated her feelings of wrongdoing as, "I knew how hurt I was when I was being abused and how bad I felt. For me to do that to somebody else, that hurts me more. To think that I could do that to somebody else!" Mei stated, "Just because for so long men have had the upper hand doesn't mean you go over to the other side. . . . Women shouldn't be able to hit men. If they do, maybe they don't create the same physical injuries, but its still breaking the boundaries. It is still abuse and can't be tolerated."

The Contrast: Distinguishing Violence
by and Against Women

The analysis of heterosexual women's use of violence in intimate relationships reveals the futility of equating violence by and against women. If we define battering as a pattern of intimidation and control that may or may not be established by physical abuse, then in most cases, women's use of violence cannot be termed as such. The motivations, intentions, results, and consequences underlying the acts must be analyzed to understand this violence. Similarly, not all partner-assaultive behaviors by men may be termed *battering* either. Only when a systematic pattern of conduct that provokes consistent fear and subjugation in the victim exists, do we recognize the condition of battering. The perpetrator who creates the situation is then the batterer.

Although both men and women may physically assault their intimate partners, in general, women have a lesser chance of systematically terrorizing their male partners. Men's and women's violence is distinct by what happens before, during, and after the abuse is perpetrated. A contrast of the two may be helpful in clarifying the argument.

Before

> In most societies, patriarchal ideologies imbue the male gender role with authority, dominance, and power. Individual men express this role in varying degrees and in different spheres of life such as occupations, social interactions, and leisure activities. The approval to master problems, situations, and people is integral to the male role. This permission to rule comes from institutions and the culture of a society. Customarily, the masculine role gets played out in intimate relationships by men establishing power and control over their female partners through belligerent emotional and physical assaults.

> In contrast, cultural ideals of femininity encourage subservience, passivity, and dependence on men. In short, men are taught to be aggressors, whereas women are taught to be willing recipients of masculine aggression.

> The cultural elements and institutions of a society provide moral and material support for male violence in intimate relationships. Men/husbands are expected to correct and control their wives/lovers physically, whereas women are considered to be the "beneficiaries" of these husbandly chastisements.

> No culture seems to provide room for women to engage in similar behavior.

During

Men's and women's motivations for engaging in abusive behavior are singularly disparate. The majority of women who use violence in intimate relationships either have been or are being battered. Thus, the primary motivation for women to become violent is self-protection. Women seem to be less interested in striking enduring fear in the hearts of their partners than in seeking respect and revenge, retaliating, stopping ongoing abuse, extracting attention and responsible conduct, or just expressing anger at and frustration with the situation.

Unfortunately, women's abusive behavior tends neither to significantly control their partners nor to produce desired outcomes. Most of the women interviewed for this study reported that their behavior actually resulted in swift retaliation from their partners and the escalation of the violence they were already experiencing.

The injuries inflicted by men and women on their partners also seem to be dramatically different. Because of the size and strength differential, women's violence in general causes less injury than men's assaults (Bachman & Saltzman, 1995; Saltzman et al., 1990; Steinman, 1991). The odds seem to even out only when women use weapons or objects that might cause serious damage.

After

Consequences of male abusive behavior tend to affect women by instilling long-term fear in them. This effect is deep enough to instigate changes in women's conduct on a more or less permanent basis. For example, abused women speak of walking on eggshells around their partners, suffering persistent anxiety, experiencing debilitating stress and paralyzing fear, modifying their habits and movements, and so on. They seem to focus much of their daily activities on avoiding their partners' next outbursts of violence. In fact, these consequences distinguish the violent behaviors of men and women.

Domestic violence and sexual assault crisis intervention agencies, mental health centers, and psychiatric wards of our country are teeming with women who are suffering from long-term effects of living in battering relationships (Koop, 1989). Even our jails have an overrepresentation of women who have been coerced to violent crimes by their partners (Richie, 1996). However, there are no comparable data on men who are experiencing trauma as a result of being subjected to ongoing violence by their women partners.

Women who have used violence against their partners seem not only to suffer from severe personal guilt but societal condemnation as well. By assaulting their husbands or male partners, these women are the

ultimate transgressors of prescribed gender roles. Thus, they are
genuinely self-critical. In addition, law enforcement officials may
treat them with more severity and contempt than their male counterparts. Sandy, an interviewee, stated that she believed the message
coming from officials is, "Please don't defend yourself." Regarding
police treatment of women, she declared, "It's almost a fun thing for
them cops now. [They think they] can arrest the women and the men
can do whatever they want." Monica repeated this perception: "[The
message from the system is] just lay there; take it; if he kills you, too
bad! But then they [the police] can do something about it." Furthermore, societies that believe in the stereotype of feminine passivity and
tolerance also may perceive a woman who uses violence against her
intimate partner as "unnatural," "freakish," and "criminal by nature"
and deal with her accordingly.

The judicial approach to violence against women generally has been incident focused. This method of addressing the problem actually may
be a disservice to women who use violence. Concentration on single
incidents generally has led to neglect of the situations surrounding
women's aggressive behavior. Thus, most women expressed complete
mistrust of the system. Patricia's disillusionment with the system is
quite typical:

> A woman [may] go out and kill a man, because she is tired
> of getting beat up [on] or she's tired of getting fouled and
> harassed, and she turn[s] around and do[es] something strong.
> [Then] they lock you up. They quickly lock you up. But when a
> man's trying to beat you and you call them [police], they'll come
> when you're dead, either laying on the floor or you're halfway
> dead. And if you're not dead, they're still going to do nothing
> else. So, what's the purpose of women going out and getting a
> restraining order anyway? There's no sense to it. I won't do it.

It is also important to note here that consistent abuse indubitably
will culminate in abusive behavior toward the perpetrator. Either due
to a drive for self-protection or the anger that abuse seems to generate,
the majority of victims of violence will ultimately retaliate in kind.
Thus, ignoring the context around violence by women leads to con-
fusion regarding its very nature. Dana, an interviewee, encapsulates
the problem precisely:

> I feel they are arresting more women [now]. I think that they are just
> trying to set, to make an example out of women to show that they
> are cracking down on domestic violence offenders and that nobody's
> going to get away with it. I think that they are trying to make an
> example out of women, but I think that the reason that more women

are committing domestic violence is because they are fighting back. I think if society is going to arrest a woman for assaulting her husband, they should also arrest the man for causing the woman to assault him. Because, you know, if these abusive husbands had been admonished back when they should have been, these women would not have to be fighting back now and you would not need to arrest all these women. So, I think they are going about it all wrong.

Dana's assertions are not so much a justification for women's use of violence but an explication of the circumstances that have led to such abuse. Like Dana, many of the interviewees believed strongly that because sociolegal systems erected to protect women have failed them so thoroughly, women's only recourse has been to retaliate in kind. Thus, despite unsuccessful results, many women have resorted to abusive behavior to gain immediate control over their partners' violence.

The Epilogue: Conclusions and Implications of Violence by Women

In recent years, many policymakers, academics, and community workers have been trying to present arguments that women are just as violent as men, if not more. Studies of women's use of violence have many theorists calling to nullify sociopolitical theories of domestic abuse that are based on the power differential between the genders. If women are as capable of battering as men, then how can we justify theories of domestic violence founded on masculine entitlement and the quest for power and control? Hence, studies on women's use of violence toward their intimate partners are considered to be disclaimers for the historical-structural theories of wife abuse.

Conversely, battered women's advocates, distrustful of the past record of societal and scholarly tendencies to blame women for their own abuse, minimize if not deny women's use of violence completely. For instance, many advocates tend to portray women as nonviolent by nature and thus incapable of mistreating others:

> The problem is that by creating batterers' programs for such women [who have used physical violence against their intimate partners], we are facilitating these gross miscarriages of justice. By responding to the demand for female batterers' treatment programs, we actually enable some police, prosecutors, and judges—all of whom should

know better—to take the easy way out: mutual restraining orders, mutual arrests, mutual programs, etc. Soon we will end up back where we started from, dismissing domestic violence as a mutual "family or relationship problem" that is inappropriate for criminal justice intervention. (Klein, 1996, p. 2)

However, both of these positions are extreme and present distorted realities. Historically, women in various societies actively have participated in political revolutions, terrorist groups, and numerous armed insurrections. Women have abused their powers as rulers in the public realm and also within the privacy of their homes. Women have committed violent crimes and joined gangs that are founded on brutality. Within the private domain and intimate relationships, women have abused their children and elderly relatives (Margolin, 1992; Wauchope & Straus, 1990). In the United States, battering in same-sex relationships also demonstrates women's capability of being vicious (Coleman, 1994; Renzetti, 1988, 1992). In fact, a woman's potential for violence is well supported in various psychological studies (Bandura, 1973; Frodi, Macaulay, & Thome, 1977; White & Kowalski, 1994). Thus, the question here is not whether women have the capacity to abuse but whether most women's violence expressed in the context of heterosexual relationships can be termed *battering*.

Little systematic research has been focused on women who use violence in intimate relationships. Yet women themselves have not been oblivious to their own abusive behavior toward their male partners. The following letter published in a popular magazine exemplifies this recognition:

> I am a married woman with a serious illness. I was raised by a mother who abused me until I was 15 years old, and now I abuse my husband physically and verbally. My self-esteem decreases every time I beat him. I hate myself for doing this to him, and he still cares for me. I can't afford a therapist. Please tell me what I can do. ("Husband Batterer," 1989, p. 12)

Often, such reports of women's violent behavior in heterosexual relationships have met with incredulity. Many advocates and theoreticians dismiss the notion of abusive women based on the reasoning that compared to women, cross-culturally men are significantly more aggressive (Eagly & Steffen, 1986; Fagot & Hagan, 1985; Hyde, 1984; Maccoby & Jacklin, 1974). The conviction has its own detrimental effects. For example, practitioners trained in this philosophy are shocked when they encounter a woman from another culture who has chased her partner with a cleaver or smashed a vase on his head. They may interpret such behavior as pathological and bizarre and distance themselves from the woman while demonizing her native culture. This belief in women's essential passivity is not necessarily shared by all cultures but has Judeo-Christian roots. Hindu and Islamic cultures, for instance, perceive femininity as dynamic and powerful (Mernissi, 1975; Mookerjee, 1988; Wadley, 1988). Consequently, women from these societies may be less inhibited in using physical force across situations than their counterparts from Western nations.

This study addresses the complex theoretical issues that surround the realities of women who assault their partners. The 32 in-depth interviews in this sample have yielded findings to indicate that the most pervasive and persistent motivation for women's use of violence is ending abuse in their own lives. The majority of participants in this study were battered as well as routinely assaulted by their male partners and reciprocated the violence to affect immediate change. It should be noted that we did not seek women who had been battered but women who were currently in a program because they had been court ordered or referred to for counseling because they had used violence. Most of these women were focused on wrenching a semblance of control in their own lives and surroundings by the use of physical force. Unfortunately, many practitioners in the field have confused all violence by women, regardless of their antecedents, motivations, and consequences, as battering. This chapter tries to untangle some of the issues in this very complex and difficult problem.

Even though women's use of violence in intimate relationships is unequivocal, the earlier discussion suggests that the inclusion of partner-assaultive women in intervention programs designed for (male) batterers would be neither appropriate nor efficacious. Gender sensitivity cannot be sacrificed to achieve uniformity of responses in domestic violence intervention work. Differential treatment of groups does not necessarily indicate injustice, nor is this strategy without precedence.

Unfortunately, the infrastructures that have developed to deal with battered women generally fail to provide appropriate services to women who have used violence against their intimate partners. The predominant services around the country focus on assisting the victims, thereby leaving no room for the inclusion of abusive women. However, violent behavior by women cannot be connived at either.

As mentioned before, curricula for women who engage in violence for reasons other than self-defense tend to emulate those designed for the batterers. Consequently, these programs cannot offer adequate solutions to the problem.

Educational programs for women must take into account the fact that men and women do not enjoy the same cultural and institutional validations for using violence in intimate relationships. Neither do they engage in abusive behavior for the same reasons. Sociohistoric factors that endow male violence against women with approval and authority also infuse it with cultural power that is absent from women's equivalent behavior. Thus, in formulating an intervention program for women in heterosexual relationships who have assaulted their partners, the following issues must be considered:

1. Since the majority of women have been and are being battered, it is important to address the issue of battering and power and control.
2. Since the justice system tends to focus on incidents of violence, it is likely that women's behavior will be viewed in segments rather than in their contextual entirety. Therefore, it is important to train appropriate personnel to understand women's use of violence holistically and contextually.
3. Frequently, alcohol or drug abuse plays a significant role in violence of any kind. The issue of substance abuse needs to be addressed in women's intervention programs.
4. Exploring behavioral alternatives to violence in any given situation must be included in any intervention program.
5. Issues related to race, class, ethnicity, nationality, and residency status in the United States must be incorporated in the curriculum.

Awareness of the gender dynamic in domestic conflicts is leading community intervention projects such as the DAIP to incorporate greater sensitivity toward perpetrators by contextualizing their actions. A step toward this is to replace the mandatory "flat" arrest policy by inclusion of the "primary aggressor" language. By definition, a primary aggressor is the person who is most in control of the violence being perpetrated and is most likely to cause physical harm to the other partner. By the same token, the most vulnerable person in a domestic conflict situation also has to be distinguished and protected. Obviously, such policy changes go beyond the immediate incidence and foreground the couples' relationship on its history and context of abuse. It remains to be seen whether such determinations in conducting domestic violence arrests ameliorate some of its problems and render justice more sensitive, as well as appropriate.

Notes

1. For a discussion on the validity of this study, see Ritmeester and Pence (1992) and Kurz (1993).

2. Both authors identify themselves as "one of the original incorporators of our local abuse shelter."

3. All names of interviewees have been changed to protect their privacy.

4. The Duluth program is the only one that does not refer to women who have been arrested as "abusers" and the group as an "abusers' group." Instead, Duluth refers to them as "groups for women who use violence." This chapter was written after 32 of more than 50 interviews were transcribed. It is based on these interviews.

5. The Duluth project interviewed 10 men whose female partners had been court ordered to educational groups for women who use violence. Although some of the men declared that they might have been scared of their partners at the time of the assault, no one claimed that the violence made them generally afraid of their partners or believed that their safety was threatened.

References

Bachman, R., & Saltzman, L. E. (1995). *Violence against women: Estimates from the redesigned survey* (Report No. NCJ-15438). Rockville, MD: U.S. Department of Justice.

Bandura, A. (1973). *Aggression: A social learning analysis.* Englewood Cliffs, NJ: Prentice Hall.

Barnett, O. W., Lee, C. Y., & Thelen, R. E. (1997). Gender differences in attributions of self-defense and control in interpartner aggression. *Violence Against Women, 3*(5), 462-481.

Browne, A. (1987). *When battered women kill.* New York: Free Press.

Browne, A., & Williams, K. R. (1989). Exploring the effect of resource availability and the likelihood of female-perpetrated homicides. *Law and Society Review, 23*(1), 75-94.

Coleman, V. E. (1994). Lesbian battering: The relationship between personality and the perpetration of violence. *Violence and Victims, 9*(2), 139-152.

Dutton, D. G., & Strachan, C. E. (1987). Motivational needs for power and spouse-specific assertiveness in assaultive and nonassaultive men. *Violence and Victims, 2,* 145-156.

Dutton, M. A., Hohnecker, L. C., Halle, P. M., & Burghardt, K. J. (1994). Traumatic responses among battered women who kill. *Journal of Traumatic Stress, 7*(4), 549-564.

Eagly, A. H., & Steffen, V. J. (1986). Gender and aggressive behavior: A meta-analytic review of the social psychological literature. *Psychological Bulletin, 100,* 309-330.

Edelson, J. L., Eisikovits, Z. C., Guttman, E., & Sela-Amit, M. (1991). Cognitive and interpersonal factors in woman abuse. *Journal of Family Violence, 6,* 167-182.

Fagot, B. I., & Hagan, R. (1985). Aggression in toddlers: Responses to the assertive acts of boys and girls. *Sex Roles, 12*(3/4), 341-351.

Frodi, A., Macaulay, J., & Thome, P. R. (1977). Are women always less aggressive than men? A review of the experimental literature. *Psychological Bulletin, 84,* 634-660.

Hamberger, L. K. (1997). Female offenders in domestic violence: A look at actions in their contexts. *Journal of Aggression, Maltreatment, and Trauma, 1*(1), 117-129.

Hamberger, L. K., & Potente, T. (1994). Counseling heterosexual womenn arrested for domestic violence: Implications for theory and practice. *Violence and Victims, 9*(2), 125-137.

Husband batterer. (1989, July). *Essence, 20,* 12.

Hyde, J. S. (1984). How large are gender differences in aggression? A developmental meta-analysis. *Developmental Psychology, 20,* 722-736.

Jones, A. (1996). *Women who kill.* Boston: Beacon.

Jurik, N. C. (1989, November). *Women who kill and the reasonable men: The legal issues surrounding female-perpetrated homicide.* Paper presented at the 41st annual meeting of the American Society of Criminology, Reno, NV.

Jurik, N. C., & Gregware, P. (1989). *A method for murder: An interactionist analysis of homicides by women.* Tempe: Arizona State University, School of Justice Studies.

Jurik, N. C., & Winn, R. (1990). Gender and homicide: A comparison of men and women who kill. *Violence and Victims, 5*(4), 227-241.

Kalichman, S. C. (1988). MMPI profiles of women and men convicted of domestic homicide. *Journal of Clinical Psychology, 44*(6), 847-853.

Klein, A. (1996). Editorial. *National Bulletin on Domestic Violence Prevention, 2*(11), 1-3.

Koop, C. E. (1989, May 22). *Violence against women: A global problem.* Address by the surgeon general of the United States, Public Health Service, at a seminar of the Pan American Health Organization, Washington, DC.

Koss, M. P., Goodman, L. A., Browne, A., Fitzgerald, L. F., Keita, G. P., & Russo, N. F. (1994). *No safe haven: Male violence against women at home, at work, and in the community.* Washington, DC: American Psychological Association.

Kurz, D. (1993). Physical assaults by husbands: A major social problem. In R. J. Gelles & D. R. Loseke (Eds.), *Current controversies on family violence* (pp. 88-103). Newbury Park, CA: Sage.

Langhinrichsen-Rohling, J., Neidig, P., & Thorn, G. (1995). Violent marriages: Gender differences in levels of current violence and past abuse. *Journal of Family Violence, 10,* 159-176.

Macchietto, J. G. (1992). Aspects of male victimization and female aggression: Implications for counseling men. *Journal of Mental Health Counseling, 14*(3), 375-392.

Maccoby, E. E., & Jacklin, C. N. (1974). *The psychology of sex differences.* Stanford, CA: Stanford University Press.

Mann, C. R. (1987). Black women who kill. In R. L. Hampton (Ed.), *Violence in the black family: Correlates and consequences* (pp. 157-186). Lexington, MA: Lexington Books.

Margolin, L. (1992). Beyond maternal blame: Physical child abuse as a phenomenon of gender. *Journal of Family Issues, 13*(3), 410-423.

Mernissi, F. (1975). *Beyond the veil: Male-female dynamics in modern Muslim society.* Cambridge, MA: Schenkman.

Mookerjee, A. (1988). *Kali the feminine force.* New York: Destiny Books.

Morse, B. J. (1995). Beyond the conflict tactics scale: Assessing gender differences in partner violence. *Violence and Victims, 10*(4), 251-272.

Pence, E., & Paymar, M. (1993). *Education groups for men who batter: The Duluth model*. New York: Springer.

Renzetti, C. M. (1988). Violence in lesbian relationships: A preliminary analysis of causal factors. *Journal of Interpersonal Violence, 3*, 381-399.

Renzetti, C. M. (1992). *Violent betrayal: Partner abuse in lesbian relationships*. Newbury Park, CA: Sage.

Renzetti, C. M. (1997). Editor's introduction. *Violence Against Women, 3*(5), 459-461.

Richie, B. E. (1996). *Compelled to crime: The gender entrapment of battered black women*. New York: Routledge Kegan Paul.

Ritmeester, T., & Pence, E. (1992). Cynical twist of fate: How processes of ruling in the criminal justice system and the social sciences impede justice for battered women. *Southern California Review of Law and Women's Studies, 2*(1), 255-292.

Roberts, A. R. (1996). Battered women who kill: A comparative study of incarcerated participants with a community sample of battered women. *Journal of Family Violence, 11*(3), 291-304.

Russell, M. N., Lipov, E., Phillips, N., & White, B. (1989). Psychological profiles of violent and nonviolent maritally distressed couples. *Psychotherapy, 26*, 81-87.

Saltzman, L. E., Mercy, J. A., Rosenberg, M. L., Elsea, W. R., Napper, G., Sikes, R. K., & Waxweiler, R. J. (1990). Magnitude and patterns of family and intimate assault in Atlanta, Georgia, 1984. *Violence and Victims, 5*, 3-17.

Saunders, D. G. (1986). When battered women use violence: Husband-abuse or self-defense? *Victims and Violence, 1*(1), 47-58.

Saunders, D. G. (1995). The tendency to arrest victims of domestic violence: A preliminary analysis of officer characteristics. *Journal of Interpersonal Violence, 10*(2), 147-158.

Sewel, S., & Sewel, B. (1996). *Facts about domestic violence you will not see in the media* [On-line]. Retrieved November 27, 1996 from 72752.76@compuserve.com.

Steinman, M. (1991). The public policy process and woman battering: Problems and potentials. In M. Steinman (Ed.), *Woman battering: Policy responses* (pp. 1-18), Cincinnati, OH: Anderson.

Steinmetz, S. K. (1977-1978). The battered husband syndrome. *Victimology: An International Journal, 2*, 499-509.

Steinmetz, S. K., & Lucca, J. S. (1988). Husband battering. In V. B. Van Hasselt, R. L. Morrison, A. S. Bellack, & M. Hersen (Eds.), *Handbook of family violence* (pp. 233-246). New York: Plenum.

Straus, M. A. (1993). Physical assaults by wives: A major social problem. In R. J. Gelles & D. R. Loseke (Eds.), *Current controversies on family violence* (pp. 67-87). Newbury Park, CA: Sage.

Straus, M. A., & Gelles, R. J. (1986). Societal change and change in family violence from 1975 to 1985 as revealed by two national surveys. *Journal of Marriage and the Family, 48*, 465-479.

Straus, M. A., Gelles, R. J., & Steinmetz, S. K. (1980). *Behind closed doors: Violence in the American family*. New York: Anchor.

Vivian, D., & Langhinrichsen-Rohling, J. (1994). Are bi-directionally violent couples mutually victimized? A gender-sensitive comparison. *Violence and Victims, 9*, 107-124.

Wadley, S. (1988). Women and the Hindu tradition. In R. Ghadially (Ed.), *Women in Indian society: A reader* (pp. 23-23). Newbury Park, CA: Sage.

Walker, L. E. A. (1989). *Terrifying love: Why battered women kill and how society responds*. New York: HarperCollins.

Walker, L. E. A. (1992). Battered woman syndrome and self-defense. *Notre Dame Journal of Law, Ethics, and Public Policy, 6*, 321-334.

Wauchope, B., & Straus, M. (1990). Age, gender and class differences in physical abuse of American children. In M. Straus & R. J. Gelles (Eds.), *Physical violence in American families: Risk factors and adaptations in 8,145 families* (pp. 133-148). New Brunswick, NJ: Transaction.

Weitzman, L. J. (1985). *The divorce revolution: The unexpected social and economic consequences for women and children in America.* New York: Free Press.

White, J. W., & Kowalski, R. M. (1994). Deconstructing the myth of the nonaggressive woman: A feminist analysis. *Psychology of Women Quarterly, 18*, 487-508.

Winner, K. (1996). *Divorced from justice: The abuse of women and children by divorce lawyers and judges.* New York: HarperCollins.

11

The Silence Surrounding Sexual Violence

The Issue of Marital Rape and the Challenges It Poses for the Duluth Model

Kersti Yllö

During the past two decades, domestic violence has emerged as a significant social problem, not because it is a new problem but because feminist activists brought the issue to public attention. There is no doubt that the Duluth Domestic Abuse Intervention Project (DAIP) has been a leading force in this movement. Duluth's Power and Control Wheel, depicting the primary abusive behaviors experienced by women living with men who batter, was developed by battered women involved in the project and has been translated into more than a dozen languages and dialects (Pence & Paymar, 1993, p. 2). The Power and Control Wheel is not only at the core of the Duluth model but also

AUTHOR'S NOTE: Thanks to Frances McIntyre, chief of the criminal division, Office of the Attorney General of the Commonwealth of Massachusetts, for her insights on the issue of prosecuting marital rape.

223

has become the icon and essential tool of the wider battered women's movement because it speaks to so many women's experiences across cultures.

The wheel depicts the issues of power and control at its center and violence—physical and sexual—around the circumference. The question that I would like to raise in this chapter is why, despite its equal billing on the wheel, sexual violence is essentially ignored within the Duluth model and in broader efforts to deal with woman abuse. Although there has been a tremendous outcry against physical violence in marriage, there has been relative silence regarding marital rape. In comparison to the tremendous research and tireless advocacy focused on battering, academics and activists alike have said little and done less about wife rape. A recent national survey of 621 battered women's shelters and rape crisis centers, for example, found that only 4% included marital rape as an issue of concern in their mission statements (Bergen, 1996, p. 96). Scholars have written only three books in 15 years on the topic (Bergen, 1996; Finkelhor & Yllö, 1985; Russell, 1982/1992). So, it is clear that the Duluth DAIP is not alone in overlooking marital rape.

Ellen Pence and Michael Paymar describe the mission of the Duluth model as follows:

> As a monitor of the justice system, we pressure that system to impose consequences for continued acts of violence. As an organization committed to social change, we challenge local institutions to think about their own complicity through their actions or inactions. As an organization that works directly with offenders, we confront batterers' behavior and question their beliefs in the most compassionate way that we can. (Pence & Paymar, 1993, p. xiv)

The DAIP recognizes that the issue of marital rape poses a difficult challenge to the Duluth model (otherwise, this chapter would not have come into being). The DAIP is concerned that it has not adequately pressured the criminal justice system to impose consequences for acts of marital rape. Although the Duluth model is known internationally for its attention to police training around domestic violence, those trainings are silent on the issue of wife rape. Although the DAIP has worked with thousands of abusive men over the years, not one of them was court ordered into the program because raping his wife was his primary offense, despite the fact that more than half of the battered women in the Duluth program indicate that they have experienced sexual abuse (E. Pence, personal communication, 1997).

The Duluth model has had extraordinary success in helping local institutions, such as the courts, social services, and hospitals, reflect on their own complicity in domestic violence and change. Yet the entire coordinated community response to battering is complicit in its failure to recognize the problem of forced sex, hold marital rapists criminally accountable, and protect the safety and integrity of marital rape victims. On the community level, as well as in the culture at large, efforts to challenge the taken-for-granted "right" of husbands to coerce their wives sexually lag at least two decades behind our work on physical violence.

The one area where the Duluth model does address sexual violence is in its education groups for men who batter. It is one of the eight themes addressed in the curriculum. The thematic unit (Sexual Respect) clearly articulates the issue of marital rape and challenges it (Pence & Paymar, 1993, pp. 132-145). This 3-week curriculum piece is well designed and represents one of the few models for intervention with wife rapists. The problem is that the Duluth model fully subsumes marital rape under the broader rubric of battering and in so doing excludes perpetrators who rape but do not physically batter their victims. Furthermore, the model fails to hold rapists fully accountable because their sexual violence is not challenged until three quarters of the way through the curriculum. Although the men have had their physically abusive behavior challenged at every step of the way (beginning with a restraining order or arrest or voluntary intake), their sexually abusive behavior does not come up as an issue until quite late in group. Although the group leaders may hold them accountable, sexually abusive men must sense that this is an isolated confrontation rather than a part of a coordinated community response.

What Is Marital Rape?

Before I begin to discuss the definition of *marital rape* and its various forms, I want to address the loaded term *rape* and our reluctance to use it in this context. Rape is an ugly word, and we tend to preserve it only for heinous acts. To be a rapist is to be a monster in our culture. The power of these words is based on our cultural belief that rape is a very rare crime committed by a very small number of evil men. The myth that rape is perpetrated by crazed strangers in dark alleys persists, despite considerable evidence to the contrary. The reality is that rape is a rather common occurrence, and rapists are rather ordinary men (Russell, 1982/1992). Unfortunately, until this reality becomes widely understood, efforts to label sexual assault in marriage as rape are regarded with suspicion. Naming a husband who forces his wife to have sex without her consent a rapist is seen as an overreaction. Language is powerful, and I urge all to use loaded terms such as *rape* and *rapist* carefully. At the same time, I feel that they must be used where they properly apply. To back away from a term such as *wife rape* is to retreat from the whole issue. The depth of our resistance to using the word *rape* in cases of marital sexual assault is a measure of the entitlement husbands enjoy.

At the core of marital rape, like all rape, are the issues of force and consent. However, the nature of the marriage makes these issues all the more complex. Marriage is assumed to be a sexually intimate relationship; it is not even legal until it is "consummated." Consequently, the popular view is that if you have had sex with someone hundreds of times, what is the harm of one more time? The basic misconception reflected here is the idea that the harm of rape comes from the sex rather than from the violation of the victim's autonomy, bodily integrity, and trust. For wives, this violation is compounded by the sense of entrapment. When you are raped by a stranger, you live with a frightening memory; when you are raped by your husband, you live with your rapist.

Forms of Coercion

Unquestionably, most marital sex is consensual. Nevertheless, many women feel impelled by their husbands to have sex. As one respondent to Hite's (1976) early sex survey reported,

> In my relationship I am forced to give sex because of the marriage vows. My husband has on occasion threatened to withhold money or favors—that is, permission of some sort or another—if I do not have sex with him. So I fake it. What the hell. When the kids are older I just might lay my cards on the table. (Quoted in Finkelhor & Yllö, 1985, p. 85)

It can be argued that doing one's "wifely duty" in the context of an unequal power relationship should be regarded as rape, especially when that relationship is supported by the force of law. Sex as wifely duty has been the legal and normative situation historically and still is the case in most cultures. Oppressive as such coercion may be, I would argue that calling it rape means substantially expanding—and, at the same time, diluting—the meaning of the word *rape*.

In our study of marital rape, David Finkelhor and I (1985) found it useful to distinguish between different forms of coercion. *Social coercion* is the pressure women feel as a result of cultural expectations or social conventions. As one woman in our study put it,

> I know I was feeling coerced and not doing it willingly most of the time. But in a way I'm not sure it was done by him. It was really my own upbringing and the things that I'd been taught. . . . My allowing it is what makes it not rape. (Finkelhor & Yllö, 1985, p. 86)

This kind of social coercion regarding marital sex is institutionalized in our culture and internalized in individuals. Although such coercion can be degrading and detrimental, especially when accompanied by other forms of male entitlement and control, it does not fall within a useful definition of rape.

Interpersonal coercion occurs when a woman has sex with her husband in the face of threats that are not violent in nature. Husbands who threaten to withhold money or have an affair or who become nasty toward the children are guilty of interpersonal coercion. The coercive nature of such threats is especially salient in a marriage in which a woman's dependency and powerlessness undercut her bargaining position. Nevertheless, when such threats are not associated with any physical coercion, the sex that follows cannot be regarded as rape.

Threatened or actual physical coercion, in contrast, is at the core of rape. Physical threats can range from explicit threats to kill a woman if she does not comply to the implied threat that she will get hurt if she does not cooperate. The implied threats are especially potent in relationships in which a husband has battered his partner in the past. The actual use of physical force also has a wide range, from the use of greater size and strength to hold a woman down to the infliction of extensive injuries.

There is no question that social and interpersonal forms of coercion can be oppressive and harmful. Some may chose to label these forms of coercion as rape for the political purpose of drawing attention to the violation inherent within them. Nevertheless, for the purpose of intervening on behalf of marital rape victims in a wide range of institutional settings, it is most useful to limit the definition of marital rape to the legal standard of the use or threatened use of physical force, without the consent of the woman.

It is also important for practitioners, activists, and researchers to note that many women whose husbands have physically forced them to have sex, despite their active resistance, and who feel deeply violated by the assaults do not define their experience as rape. As I noted earlier, rape is a culturally loaded term. The stereotype that rapes are perpetrated by strangers in dark alleys, combined with notions of "wifely duty," make it very difficult for many wives to identify marital rape as "real rape." The continuing silence around the issue of marital rape in the media as well as in the criminal justice, medical, and social service systems contributes to many victims' sense that their violation is unspeakable. Significant changes in these institutions will have to be made before women can fully name their own experience.

Physical and Sexual Violence

A further important distinction must be made between physical and sexual violence in marriage and other intimate relationships. Diana Russell, pioneer researcher on the issue of sexual violence, points out that

> the tendency to see wife rape as the exclusive problem of battered women has led to an important segment of wife rape victims being overlooked—those who are never beaten, or those for whom wife beating is a much less significant problem than sexual abuse. (Russell, 1982/1992, p. 101)

Russell's groundbreaking book, *Rape in Marriage,* published in 1982, remains the most rigorous and thorough study of the subject to date. In her study of a representative sample of 644 wives, she was able to examine the overlap between battering and rape. She found that in 54% of marriages in which wives were abused, physical violence was the major or only problem. In 23%, marital rape was the major or only problem, and in 22%, the two were of approximately equal significance from the women's point of view (Russell, 1982/1992, p. 91). She concludes that "wife rape cannot and must not be subsumed under the battered woman rubric" (p. 101).

It is precisely Russell's (1982/1992) challenge that posed such difficulties for the Duluth model. The entire program is focused on the problem of physical battering. It is true that this approach is valuable for the majority of abused wives. Nevertheless, Russell's data indicate that a large number of victims are not adequately addressed. Nearly a quarter of abused wives who are "only" raped have no voice in the current system. More than one in five abused wives who are both raped and battered have to contend with a program that validates and responds to only a part of their experience.

Legal Issues

Beyond making the distinction between wife beating and wife rape, it is necessary to examine the legal definition of marital rape and to recognize how it has been regarded differently from other forms of rape. Rape traditionally has been defined legally as forced intercourse without the consent of the woman, other than one's wife. This last phrase is known as the "spousal exemption," and for centuries, it made the marriage license a license to rape. This exemption derives from British common law and particularly from the writing of an early British jurist by the name of Lord Matthew Hale. He proclaimed in 1680 that

> the husband cannot be guilty of rape committed by himself upon his lawful wife, for by their mutual matrimonial consent and contract, the wife has given up herself in this kind unto her husband, which she cannot retract. (Quoted in Finkelhor and Yllö, 1985, p. 2)

In other words, the marital vow "I do" was taken to legally imply consent any time, any place, and under any circumstances. The Hale doctrine became part of the U.S. criminal code, and marital rape was legal until the 1980s, when most states eliminated, or at least limited, the spousal exemption. When North Carolina became the final state to criminalize marital rape in 1993, feminist activists claimed an important victory. Through concerted testimony and lobbying, feminists managed to fundamentally redefine rape, and in that process, they redefined marriage.

The victory is not as sweet as it might be, however. Although marital rape has been criminalized, it is still regarded as distinct—and suspect—in many states. Half of the states still impose special restrictions or conditions with regard to rape by husbands. In many jurisdictions, a woman must be separated from her husband or have a court order active against him at the time of the assault to file rape charges. Such restrictions rest on the continuing assumption that, whether forced or not, sex is a husband's right and a wife's duty. These restrictions continue to allow cohabiting husbands in many states to rape with impunity.

Also, many states have enacted statutes of limitation for marital rape that are far more restrictive than for rape in general. The restricted time frames for reporting marital rape rest on the premise that wives will fabricate rape charges to advantage themselves in divorce proceedings if not legally prevented from doing so. The old idea that a rape charge is easy to make and hard to defend against certainly influenced the state legislators who limited the criminalization of rape in marriage. This notion has hampered efforts to prosecute all forms of rape, but it has been particularly insidious in the case of marital rape. The concerns of legislators (as well as police, prosecutors, and public) about "vengeful wives" are quite palpable in their dealings with marital rape.

The fears that the courts would be flooded with unfounded cases in the wake of criminalization have proven to be unfounded. Marital rapes continue to be the most underreported of sexual assaults. In those cases in which charges have been brought, the conviction rate has been high. However, this high rate is attributable to the fact that marital rape cases that go to trial are usually brought in conjunction with other charges such as assault and battery, kidnapping, and attempted murder. The evidence for use of force in these cases tends to be overwhelming.

Leaving aside for the moment the difficult issue of whether one can legally prove that a rape has occurred, marital rape can be fairly simply defined as forced sex without the consent of the woman in cases in which the perpetrator and victim are legally married. This definition appears clear and succinct, yet there are ambiguities embedded within it. First, the phenomenon of "marital" rape is not limited to legally married couples. Cohabiting couples have relationships quite comparable to husbands and wives, and there is evidence that cohabiting women experience even higher rates of violence than wives (Yllö & Straus, 1983). Recognizing the similarity between cohabitors and spouses, many states have, unfortunately, extended aspects of the spousal exemption to men who are not even legally married to their partners. Because the dynamics of forced sex are quite similar for cohabitors and marrieds (Finkelhor & Yllö, 1985) and the criminal justice system often fails to draw a distinction between the two, it makes sense to include cohabitors in our definition of marital rape and in our interventions.

Prevalence of Marital Rape

Given the explosion of research on many forms of family violence, it is surprising how limited the research on marital rape has been. The two representative sample surveys that provide estimates of the rates of marital rape are more than a decade old. However, there is little reason to believe that there has been a decline in forced sex in marriage, so they remain our best estimates. Russell's (1982/1992) representative survey of women in the San Francisco area revealed that 14% of the women who had ever been married had experienced a rape or attempted rape by their husbands or ex-husbands. Russell argues that this figure is probably an underestimate for a number of reasons: (a) It is likely that some respondents were unwilling to admit to experiences of forced marital sex; (b) the prevalence of forced oral, anal, and digital sex, as well as penetration by objects, was seriously underestimated because data regarding these acts were not directly solicited; and (c) the sample excluded women with no fixed abode or who resided in institutions such as prisons, hospitals, shelters, or halfway houses. It is likely that women who have experienced the trauma of marital rape are overrepresented among such residents. Russell concludes that her calculation that one in seven women are sexually assaulted by their husbands is a conservative estimate.

David Finkelhor and I surveyed a representative sample of 323 Boston-area women with children and discovered that 10% of the married or previously married women indicated that their husbands have "used physical force or threat to try to have sex with them" (Finkelhor & Yllö, 1985, p. 6). Furthermore, the study found that fully 25% of the separated or divorced women in the sample had experienced such assaults. These estimates are likely to be low due to the same factors identified by Russell (1982/1992). Still, their relative consistency with the rates found by Russell provide rather strong evidence that rape in marriage is a widespread problem.

The Marital Rape Experience

Perhaps one of the reasons that marital rape is ignored is that its trauma is not readily apparent. The violation of self-determination and the breach of trust are at the core of wife rape. Consent is the issue, and women's autonomy and bodily integrity are at stake. Such violation is not as publicly apparent as a black eye or a broken nose. Yet, unless one grants women the right to autonomy over their own bodies and understands the serious trauma that results from the violation of that autonomy, then one cannot understand rape.

At a Senate Judiciary Committee hearing, Alabama Senator Jeremiah Denton commented on rape in marriage:

> The issue is whether the . . . drastic punishments for rape should apply. The answer depends on whether the anguish caused by intercourse forced by a husband is equivalent to that inflicted by intercourse forced by someone else. . . . The character of the voluntary association of a husband and wife . . . could be thought to mitigate the nature of the harm resulting from the unwanted intercourse. (Quoted in Finkelhor & Yllö, 1985, p. 137)

Senator Denton's idea that being married alleviates the harm of rape suggests that he is not sufficiently focused on the issue of women's autonomy. The shock, terror, and betrayal of wife rape are often exacerbated rather than mitigated by the marital relationship. Among Russell's (1982/1992) survey respondents, the women who had been raped by their husbands reported greater negative long-term effects (including inability to trust men and form intimate relationships and sexual dysfunction) than victims of any other kind of rape. As one of the women I interviewed (whose husband had been physically and sexually violent) described the rape,

> My whole body was being abused. I feel if I'd been raped by a stranger, I could have dealt with it a whole lot better. . . . When a stranger does it, he doesn't know me, I don't know him. He's not doing it to me as

a person, personally. With your husband it becomes personal. You say, this man knows me. He knows my feelings. He knows me intimately, and then to do this to me—it's such a personal abuse. (Finkelhor & Yllö, 1985, p. 118)

Types of Marital Rape

If marital rape cannot be subsumed under the wife-beating rubric, then how is it different? In *License to Rape* (1985), David Finkelhor and I developed a typology of marital rape based on the experiences of our 50 interviewees. The first type, *battering rape,* describes the experience of the women who are the victims of physical beatings and forced sex. The sexual violence, often combined with verbal degradation, is an additional means by which husbands inflict pain and humiliation. Batterers who also rape appear to be at the more brutal end of the physical violence continuum. They often inflict serious physical injury and then force their terrorized and sometimes semi-conscious wives to have sex with them. The sexual violation appears to be the final debasement.

Nicholas Groth (1979) studied men who were convicted of rape (none of whom had been convicted of marital rape) and developed a typology based on the men's motivations. Our category of battering rapes seems to be consistent with his category of "anger rapes." These men are enraged and hateful and want to inflict serious harm. They use far more force than necessary to overcome their victims, and the forced sex appears to be just one part of this broader dynamic of hostility.

Another type of marital rape, *obsessive rape,* seems to be the least prevalent but most cruel. Some obsessive rapists batter their wives apart from the forced sex, and others do not. What sets them apart is their fusion of violence and sexual arousal. They are hypersexual and perverse, and they are willing and even prefer to use force to carry out their sexual obsessions. Also, these men tend to be deeply involved with pornography. In our in-depth interviews, women reported that their husbands were aroused by hitting and harming them during sex, used objects to rape them, planned sexual assaults, simulated stranger rapes, took degrading pictures, and kept written records and descriptions of the rapes. One woman described her husband's efforts to pull out her vagina with a pair of pliers. When she went to the hospital hemorrhaging, no one inquired about the cause of her injury.

These obsessive rapes are consistent with what Groth (1979) identifies as "sadistic rapes," in which aggression becomes eroticized and the victim's suffering is a source of pleasure for the perpetrator. It is important to note that the presence of sadism in these rapes should not be taken to imply a corresponding masochism on the part of the victim. Although sadomasochistic sexual relationships do exist, they are characterized by the masochist's consent to certain scenarios. The victims of the obsessive rapes described above were unwilling participants who were forced into sex without their consent and despite their resistance.

A final type of marital rape is *force-only rape,* which occurs in relationships that are generally free of other physical violence. The husband uses only as much force as is necessary to coerce his wife into sex. This coercion often involves just using his greater weight, size, and strength to hold her down. It sometimes includes twisting an arm behind her back and holding a pillow over her face. As terrifying as such bodily force can be, the husband's purpose does not appear to be the infliction of physical injury but rather the overpowering of resistance. These relationships tend to be characterized by power struggles over issues such as money, children, and especially sex. Force-only rapes are consistent with the dynamics Groth (1979) identifies in "power rapes," which are motivated by the need for dominance and control. The goal is not so much to harm the victim as to possess her sexually. This type of forced sex, especially in marriage, is the sort that was fully legal until recently. It has been defined as an entitlement of marriage. When husbands perpetrate these force-only rapes, they are taking that to which they believe they are entitled as husbands. And their beliefs are firmly grounded in our legal tradition and prevailing cultural norms.

Force-only rapes are very difficult to prosecute due to a lack of injury and corroborating evidence and because the perpetrators are men who do not, for the most part, otherwise violate the law. It is ironic that the marital rapists who are least likely to be convicted are probably the ones who would be most restrained by laws, institutional responses, and social norms that clearly condemn forced marital sex. The victims of these force-only rapes (who, in our nonrepresentative sample, made up 40% of the total) are completely excluded from Duluth model interventions at present. The men who perpetrate this type of rape are not held accountable by anyone at any point.

The Impact of Marital Rape

Because marital rape remains largely concealed by the more public issues of battering and stranger and acquaintance rape, its impact on victims also remains in the shadows. The assumption articulated earlier by Senator Denton that rape by a husband is just not particularly harmful remains widespread. A 1996 study confirms earlier research indicating that wife rape is not taken seriously (Monson, Byrd, & Langhinrichsen-Rohling, 1996). The study found that most women tend to regard forced sex by husbands as rape and as a violation of the victim's rights. In contrast, the men in the study were significantly less likely to regard forced marital sex as rape and also less likely to see it as a violation of the victim's rights.

Our findings contradict the assumption that wife rape is not a serious assault. The women in our study reported that the forced sex they experienced had wide-ranging and sometimes debilitating consequences. In the immediate aftermath of rape, women reported four primary feelings: betrayal, anger, humiliation, and guilt. These feelings tended to change over time, yet most of the women reported long-term emotional effects, particularly an inability to trust men, an aversion to sex and intimacy, and a lingering, sometimes acute fear of being assaulted again (Finkelhor & Yllö, 1985, pp. 117-118).

The data from Russell's (1982/1992) survey indicate that the long-term effects of wife rape are more serious than for stranger rape. Of the women raped by husbands or ex-husbands, 52% said that the long-term effects had been great in comparison to 39% of stranger rape victims. Moreover, the victims of wife rape in our study revealed that almost all of them felt that the sexual violence was more devastating than the physical abuse they had experienced. As one woman described it,

> The physical abuse was horrible, but that was something I could get over. It was like a sore that heals. When he forced me to have sex with him, that was more than just physical. It went all the way down to my soul. He abused every part of me—my soul, my feelings, my mind . . . and I don't think there is anything worse than that. (Finkelhor & Yllö, 1985, p. 135)

Although it is beyond the scope of this chapter to discuss the impact of marital rape in any detail, the points made earlier are very important. Limited though it is, the available research suggests that marital rape can be more devastating to victims than either stranger rape or physical abuse. This should serve to strengthen our resolve to respond more adequately to this problem.

Creating a Coordinated Community Response to Marital Rape

When it comes to marital rape, the Duluth model does not now uphold its basic principles of protecting victims, holding assailants fully accountable, and changing the way the community thinks. Surely, the first steps in creating a coordinated community response to rape in marriage are to take the problem seriously; recognize its nature, scope, and impact; and create appropriate interventions. It would be easy to assert that the Duluth model should just intervene in sexual violence using the same means it has successfully applied to physical violence. However, it does not follow that intervention in sexual violence should simply be equivalent to intervention in physical violence. This is particularly salient because the Duluth model is primarily a criminal justice intervention in which legal definitions, evidence, and conviction rates are at issue.

Any individual, agency, or institution trying to intervene in marital rape must face a significant tension. On one hand, there are the demands of holding the perpetrator fully accountable for raping his wife. We would like to post notice that "violators will be prosecuted to the fullest extent of the law." On the other hand is the reality that the majority of marital rape cases are impossible to prove in a court of law.

From the point of view of prosecutors, marital rape cases present the same difficulties as other rape cases, only more so. Inevitably, the credibility of the victim becomes an issue. Rape shield laws were designed to protect victims from inappropriate inquiry into their sexual histories. However, they do make allowances if there was a prior sexual relationship between the defendant and "alleged" victim to address the issue of consent. For married or cohabiting couples, this creates a very large hole for admissible evidence. In addition, the "bias" of the witness comes into question. The defense makes the argument that the alleged victim/witness has a vested interest, holds a grudge, or has something to gain in terms of divorce, custody, or finance by making the rape charge. Given the likelihood that reasonable doubt can be created in the minds of jurors when there is little other evidence than the victim's testimony, it is not surprising that prosecutors are not anxious to take on marital rape cases. It is also no wonder that victims are not eager to put themselves through the anguish of a trial. Consequently, the ultimate sanction that hangs over the heads of batterers—jail time—is rarely a real threat to wife rapists.

So what is an intervention program to do? Victim safety can be addressed most expediently (at least for those women who are both battered and raped) by focusing on the physical violence. Restraining orders, arrests, indictments, and convictions are much more likely outcomes if this path (the path of least resistance) is taken. Victims are also spared the humiliation of public discussions of this very private violence. But the safety and privacy of these victims come at a price—the continued silence surrounding sexual violence. If police are trained according to Duluth model guidelines, they will learn little about the crime of marital rape, and they will not be held accountable for holding the perpetrators accountable. When police respond to a domestic abuse call and focus on physical abuse without investigating for possible rape, the message that marital rape is unspeakable is reinforced. If a husband is charged with sexual assault, the failure to prosecute further reinforces the message that wife rape is acceptable or at least beyond the ability of system to intervene. When marital rape is not explicitly challenged, then it is condoned, and husbands walk away secure in their sense of entitlement to their wives' bodies.

What seems ironic about making these points about marital rape is that they are the same points we used to make about physical violence. The Duluth model has been at the forefront of challenging the notion that men are entitled to violate their wives and that family privacy and shame should prevent vigorous intervention. But the DAIP did not invent its intervention strategies overnight. They evolved from thousands of conversations with hundreds of battered women who talked about their experiences and how various systems and interventions had helped or failed to help them. Similarly, survivors of marital rape must be included in revisions and expansions of the model if we are to create genuinely useful change. We need to learn more from them about how the criminal justice system—as well as social services, medical and mental health services, shelters, and rape crisis centers—could better respond to their needs. We need to learn how to integrate concerns for safety and privacy with validating the experience of rape and holding perpetrators accountable. All of this begins with open discussion of the issue.

In raising the issue of marital rape (and other critiques) in this volume, the editors make clear that the Duluth model is not a finished product simply to be replicated. It is a model of intervention and social change that is evolving, and it requires all of us to address difficult and pressing issues. It is an approach committed not only to institutional change but to social transformation. One of the most fundamental feminist transformations we can create in society is the redefinition of marriage. The criminalization of marital rape has been an important step. But we now need to go further to end institutional complicity and to create a meaningful community response to this form of domestic violence. The issues I have raised in this chapter are difficult ones, and there are no easy answers. The answers will come only out of extended open discussion, further research, and new strategies of intervention.

References

Bergen, R. K. (1996). *Wife rape: Understanding the response of survivors and service providers.* Thousand Oaks, CA: Sage.

Finkelhor, D., & Yllö, K. (1985). *License to rape: Sexual abuse of wives.* New York: Free Press.

Groth, N. (1979). *Men who rape.* New York: Plenum.

Hite, S. (1979). *The Hite report on female sexuality.* New York: Knopf.

Monson, C., Byrd, G., & Langhinrichsen-Rohling, J. (1996). To have and to hold: Perceptions of marital rape. *Journal of Interpersonal Violence, 11,* 410-424.

Pence, E., & Paymar, M. (1993). *Education groups for men who batter: The Duluth model.* New York: Springer.

Russell, D. (1992). *Rape in marriage.* Newbury Park, CA: Sage. (Original publication 1982)

Yllö, K., & Straus, M. (1983). Interpersonal violence among married and cohabiting couples. In D. Olson & B. Miller (Eds.), *Family studies review yearbook* (Vol. 1, pp. 308-315). Beverly Hills, CA: Sage.

12

Hamilton Abuse Intervention Project
The Aotearoa Experience

Roma Balzer

In July 1991, the Hamilton Abuse Intervention Project (HAIP) in the north island of Aotearoa (New Zealand) was officially launched. Using the Duluth model, the New Zealand project provided an integrated criminal justice and community response to domestic violence. The pilot was 2 years in preparation and operative for 3 years. In 1996, the project dropped its pilot status and now continues to provide advocacy for battered women, education programs for batterers, and monitoring of government agencies. The story of this effort is filled with twists and turns, good decisions and (in hindsight) poor decisions, successes and failures, and an endless supply of political lessons for its organizers. In this chapter, I focus my discussion on the decision of Maori activists in the refuge movement like myself to support the pilot project in Aotearoa.

Early in 1989, the National Collective of Women's Refuge (NCWR) received a copy of a report written by Ellen Pence of the Domestic Abuse Intervention Project (DAIP) in Duluth, Minnesota

(Pence, 1989). What the refuge found attractive about this report was that it directly challenged popular and often victim-blaming psychological theories that mask the social causes of violence toward women. For Maori activists, it was not just the fact that the model encompassed a social analysis but that it also allowed an analysis that accounted for the impact of colonization on Maori life and violence against Maori women by Maori men. Implicit in the DAIP analysis that contextualized violence within a cultural framework of power, domination, and control based on gender entitlements was a parallel analysis that explained tactics used against Aotearoa's first nation people (Maori) by a more dominant and powerful force, British colonizers and neocolonizers. The Duluth report had widespread appeal to both Maori and non-Maori women within the refuge movement as it provided a framework that explained the current status of women and Maori within New Zealand, a status that evolved through the culturally supported subjugation of both groups. The Maori liberation struggle, the struggle of battered women to be free of domination by their abusers, and the broader women's liberation struggle are fundamentally quite different movements, but similarities in their struggles exist. Refuge workers promoted the establishment of a Duluth-type approach because they could see the potential within the DAIP report for creating significant systemic change for the benefit of battered women, many of whom were Maori.

The DAIP report, "Batterer Programs: Shifting From Community Collusion to Community Confrontation" (Pence, 1989), laid out a framework for collaborative action by government and community agencies working in the field of stopping family violence that was to become the blueprint for a national pilot in Aotearoa. It prescribed that criminal justice agencies and frontline battered women's advocacy groups work collaboratively to do the following:

a. Intervene consistently whenever there was an act of violence.
b. Provide support and advocacy for battered women throughout the criminal process and to ensure that the needs and wishes of battered women were represented within the criminal system.
c. Hold offenders accountable by imposing sanctions that were incrementally more severe for repeat acts of violence.
d. Develop agency protocols for the handling of family violence offenses that directed the actions of individual practitioners and required sharing information among agencies.

e. Systematically monitor and assess practitioners' compliance with the protocols.

f. Evaluate intervention practices on an ongoing basis from the standpoint of victim safety.

Women's safety was the theme that became the underpinning course of action in these cases. The role of advocates became paramount in the interagency effort. The roles of battered women's advocates as critics of an ineffective system were to change as they became key players in the coordination of the reform effort. The refuge submitted the report to the Family Violence Prevention Coordinating Committee (FVPCC), a government ministerial committee that had been established 3 years earlier specifically to coordinate the activities of government and community groups working in the field of family violence. Representation on the committee was made up of senior officials of head office government agencies and national coordinators of victims' advocacy groups and men's programs.

After the first reading of the report, FVPCC members agreed that there was potential for initiating a similar project within Aotearoa, and a steering committee was formed. The task of the steering committee was to investigate the suitability of a Duluth-type model to local conditions and to report back with recommendations to the larger committee. The steering committee looked at the project from a number of aspects, including its adaptability to the local environment, its suitability to our political reality, its feasibility of being adopted by the necessary groups or agencies in Aotearoa, its usefulness in making battered women safer, and its advantages for women. The bottom-line question for many of us was how the suggested processes necessary for keeping women safe would benefit or disadvantage the Maori. To even understand this question, one needs to have some knowledge of the history of Aotearoa and the impact colonization had on the Maori.

Historical Perspective

Aotearoa (New Zealand) consists of two large and a number of smaller islands. It is situated southeast of Australia in the Pacific Ocean, the last large landfall before reaching the Antarctic. This series of islands was first settled by Pacific voyagers, generically known as the Maori, more than 1,000 years ago. Small tribes settled mainly around the shoreline, with some tribes moving inland to establish their permanent bases. Each tribe is named after the sea vessel that transported the ancestor or leader from which they originated. Within each tribe are a series of smaller subtribes made up of extended family groupings. The subtribe assumed the name of their leader at the time of establishing the subtribe and comprised three to four generations of a family, including great grandparents, grandparents, parents, aunts, uncles, and children.

The continuance of the community meant that the welfare of the individual was the responsibility of the collective community. A union between a couple was often arranged with the well-being of the whole tribe being considered. "Marriages" bound two tribes together by blood, settled old grievances, cemented kindred ties, secured land or treaty ties, and/or were based on mutual attraction. The basis for the marriage often dictated which tribe the couple was to eventually reside with. Partners were not involved in an exclusive or nuclear relationship; in fact, more importance was often placed on the relationship of an individual with peers of the same gender.

Roles for men and women were prescribed by the tribe and related directly to the need for continued survival. The elderly, because of their previous years of work, experience, and accumulated knowledge, were afforded an elevated status that usually included the responsibility of raising children belonging to the tribe. As such, elders had the vitally important task of securing traditional knowledge and protocols into the minds and behaviors of future generations. Child rearing was a valued role in the tribe. Young fit men and women had their own roles as protectors (including warfare), food gathers and cultivators, shelter providers, arts and crafts workers, teachers, and healers.

From the early 1800s, Aotearoa frequently was visited by English and European whaling and trading boats. In 1840, a treaty between the Maori and the English Crown entitled the British to establish a government to minister over their own people. The treaty assured Maori sovereignty while entitling the British to establish a government to administer over their own people. At the time of signing the treaty, there were an estimated 300,000 Maori and 3,000 English or European settlers. Within 60 years of signing the treaty, Maori numbers were reduced to less than 30,000, whereas European and English numbers swelled to around one quarter million. Land wars, disease, influenza, and alienation from tribal lands and cultural practices decimated Maori society. In this climate of Maori genocide, the existence of an indigenous culture and the right to self-determination were subsumed under British imperialism.

In the past 100 years, 97% of the land mass has been wrested from Maori hands. Control of the waterways and natural forests is currently held by the New Zealand government. The British institutions that were allowed under the treaty to govern British subjects became the government of all Aotearoa's inhabitants. Today, Aotearoa has a population of 3.8 million: 350,000 Maori, 300,000 from the Pacific basin and Asia, and the balance from Europe, the Middle East, and the Americas.

The Decision to Use the Duluth Model

Members of the domestic violence steering committee made a commitment to acknowledge the history of Maori colonization and to honor the spirit of the Treaty of Waitangi. In practical terms, this meant that any proposed intervention project would seek a remedy that was inclusive of Maori and that would meet the needs of Maori as defined by Maori.

Because of this commitment, a two-part research project was undertaken. First, a research team from the dominant culture (Pakeha-European) was commissioned to examine the DAIP model and its applicability to Pakeha society. A second team of first nation people (Maori) was commissioned to examine whether the principles and practices held in the DAIP model could adequately accommodate the needs of indigenous people and concomitant developments within their own communities.

The Pakeha team's report stated,

> Historically, culturally and structurally there are many similarities between North American and Pakeha society. The two share a common cultural basis in European society. Both have a basis in colonization and in their domination of the indigenous people. Both have variants on the democratic, pluralist political model and have a market lead economy. The criminal justice systems of both societies derive from the same model but have since partly diverged. (Family Violence Prevention Coordinating Committee, 1989)

The report held that although the cultural mix of each country is different, the dominant culture of each country is derived from Europe and England, from which they share significant basic ethos and cultural constructs.

The Pakeha team discussed in their report the extent to which the Eurocentric culture had defined the shape of society within Aotearoa. New Zealand's parliament and legislation were modeled on a Westminister-style government, major institutions have been rooted in English structures and modes of practice, and religious observance is Christian based. The idolization of the power and supremacy of the individual as prescribed by patriarchy has, until recently, gone largely unquestioned. Western religion both influenced and reflected the culture of European people. It provided the framework within which standards of moral and ethical behavior were formed and often determined penance or penalties for breaches of those codes. In the area of non-Maori (Pakeha) women, the Pakeha team concluded that

the concept of natural order [discussed in the DAIP report] in which men have power over women as a right is an integral part of the western belief system, and as such, is fundamental to Pakeha society. . . . The culture brought by the British settlers included a clear sense of the division between the public and private world as part of natural order [discussed in the DAIP report]. . . . This division has usefully served the control needs of western society for over 2,000 years. The public/private division as part of the natural order has facilitated violence within the family and has acted to preserve a power hierarchy within the home. It has reinforced women's dependency, lack of economic choices and relative powerlessness. . . . The patriarchal family system allied to the economic system is one of the basic structures of Pakeha society having been transported here during colonization. This system has provided Pakeha males with a range of historical and cultural mechanisms to support them in their role as head of the household, with all that position implies. Patriarchal traditions include powerful facilitators of violence within them because of the nature of the power relationships between men and women. Where a society includes significant power inequalities, there is likely to be a legitimization of violence. Violence towards women and children and between males can be seen as an expression of a society out of balance. . . . The experience of community groups active in the family violence field, and research which is based on the reality of women's lives, lead us to conclude that the analysis presented in the Duluth

Domestic Abuse Intervention Project is valid. The cultural facilitators identified in the Duluth analysis are equally present in Pakeha culture despite differences in the colonial experience. The analysis of these cultural facilitators of violence is both consistent with feminist theory and with a significant body of research emerging in this field. (Family Violence Prevention Coordinating Committee, 1989)

The Maori team also found that the analysis in the Duluth report accounted for the historical development of violence in Maori families. The team identified four factors of colonization that had a direct and a causal impact on family violence: the denigration of Mana-Maori (Maori identity), the contravention of the Treaty of Waitangi, the breakdown of the tribal structures and subsequent fragmentation of the *whanau* (family), and the infiltration of an ideology of male supremacy on Maori consciousness. The Maori report states, "It is therefore no surprise that in a society which is maintained by forcing relationships based on inequality and subjugation, as has been experienced by Maori through colonization, violence against more vulnerable members of a community is endemic" (p. 2). In probing the effect of colonization on Maori women in particular, we found that "seemingly to the detriment of Maori women, religious morality has become integrated into the Maori subconscious and so too has western thought and attitude in areas affecting the status and role of women" (p. 3). Probably most pervasive for Maori women is the Christian view of women as the original sinner, which frequently has become the rationalization for the subjugation of all women by men.

The Maori report talked about how records of Pakeha (European) historians were inaccurate descriptions of the social relationships that existed in Maori society. Maori women were portrayed and perhaps largely understood to be like European women, subservient to men. Missing from Pakeha understanding of Maori social structures was the place and value of Maori women in decision-making positions as educators, as holders of specialized knowledge, as military strategists, and as warriors. Unlike English women's social-political and economic condition in 1835, Maori women had control over their own assets; kept the products of their labor; were esteemed for their importance in the arts; had formal and central roles in ceremonies and their role as "carriers of the people" (childbearing), without which the continuation of the tribe would be impossible; and were treasured rather than debased.

He tapu te tinana o te wahine no te mea he whare tangata (Sacred is
the body of women as it bears the house of mankind). (Family Violence Prevention Coordinating Committee, 1989)

The far more egalitarian and balanced relationships shared between Maori men and women were ultimately appropriated and then
replaced with Eurocultural, economic, and religious restrictions and
interpretations of women as dependent, weak, the original sinner, un-
clean (during menstruation and childbirth), subservient (made from
the rib of Adam), and with the spiritual and moral ability to "bring
down" or harm man. Cultural and economic structures that debased
women were coupled with a consciousness that privileged the individual as opposed to the collective. The imposition of this new reality
and these new values began to alter the collective consciousness of
Maori. The importance of self superseded the individual's responsibility to the group, and as the consciousness of self changed, so did
the values of the collective. The overall effect was that as Western
patriarchal beliefs became absorbed into the Maori psyche, women
and children began to be seen in terms of their economic value as
opposed to their value as vital members of the extended family. The
life, health, and continuation of the people as women's work were
devalued, and children's role in the tribe was altered, making both
women and children vulnerable to abuse.

Rather than being advantaged by the shift into what colonists
claimed to be an advanced civilization, Maori women doubly suffered—first from the overall affect of foreign invasion and again
through the reduced stature in the eyes and actions of Maori men.
This reduced status has been compounded by the masking of abuses
and silencing of Maori women through society's general acceptance
of men's dominion over their family. It became difficult to distinguish
whether the hostility that battered Maori women encounter is because
of their age, gender, or ethnic origin; thus, their struggle for identity,
status, and autonomy is today as much with their partners as it is with
Pakeha (European) culture. Through all the changes Maori have
experienced over the past two centuries, European cultural values
toward women possibly have been the most destructive to Maori
people as a whole. They have formed immeasurable and potentially
irreversible divisions based on gender that require the subordination
of women to the will and desire of men.

The breakdown of structures and mechanisms of social control within Maoridom meant that there were often no internal mechanisms to control or even contain the violence. Increasing physical and economic isolation of families from their tribes or extended families made it impossible to maintain Maori lore or governorship over their own people, and Maori communities' ability to impose and enforce sanctions against their own people diminished as Pakeha institutions resourced, legislated, and asserted their right to define social norms and standards. For many Maori, their way of dealing with the emerging violence between couples was to not deal with it at all or to actively shield incidences of violence toward women and children by protecting the offender from possible state intervention. There developed an unspoken understanding that the enemy from outside (the state-Pakeha) was much worse than any possible enemy within.

Over the past century, Maori men's reaction to violence has grown to become one of justification and rationalizations, whereas Maori women's reaction has become one of acceptance. Similar to the situation with European society, turning a blind eye or blaming the victim is the standard as opposed to direct action, and as a consequence, individual women and children are sacrificed to violent men and remain vulnerable to society's contempt and disdain.

As Maori activists in the refuge movement, we found the Duluth model to be the first practical programmatic approach to domestic violence that did not obscure or mask these historical realities. Alternative approaches were based in Eurocentric psychological explanations of the abuse, which isolated abusive men from their community, describing them as somehow defective and suffering from anger problems, fears of abandonment, or poor self-esteem. Their violence toward women was not seen as a logical outcome of how social relations were institutionally, economically, and culturally constructed but as somehow deviant.

Ironically, the New Zealand government that institutionalized the denigration of things Maori and the devaluing of women is the same entity that Maori and Pakeha women must now turn to for protection from their batterers. This is particularly true for urban Maori women, whose access to police and courts is relatively easy and immediate. However, the state's responses to battered women have been haphazard and inappropriate, often failing battered women on fundamental safety and protection issues. Not only are state intervention mechanisms poorly designed to intervene, but they are imbued with a belief that there are "good victims" and "bad victims," and protection is weakened for bad victims. Few Maori women fit the criteria for the good victim. Safety for battered Maori women becomes a major issue when state responses are inappropriate or inadequate and have resulted in women not seeking further help from intervening agencies or remaining in unhappy relationships, sometimes endangering their own lives and those of their children. It was the position of the Maori team that although the physical act of violence in Maori and in non-Maori families appeared the same with seemingly similar consequences to the victim, it was important to develop responses that accounted for the way that Maori women sought and used help. Equally important was the need to hold Maori offenders accountable, but only to their own community.

However, that position is compromised when the legal institutions women turn to for help treat cases as if the violence is primarily a relationship issue. In Aotearoa, the government, supported by emerging batterers programs, set an intervention agenda that prioritized rehabilitating offenders through counseling, education programs, or community-based sentences rather than focusing on the needs or autonomy of battered women. As a consequence, addressing the greater issue of societal acceptance and endorsement of men's violence goes unchallenged and unchanged. The Duluth model offered a striking alternative. Its combined used of the civil court process (offering women autonomy) and the criminal process (holding abusers accountable), as well as its philosophical commitment to accounting for historical relationships of dominance and the insistence on building a partnership between advocacy groups and the system that prioritized victim safety, drew us to the model.

Both teams eventually wrote reports that reached similar conclusions. The first was that any effective intervention strategy had to account for the culturally supported belief that people, primarily men, have the right to control their partners within a marriage, and even though violence was officially made illegal, it was still tolerated in all but the most blatant cases of going too far. Although the practice of wife beating had very different historical roots in Maori and non-Maori cultures, it was now present in both. The two teams also had concurred on a number of other points, including an agreement that (a) intervention priority must be given to the safety and protection of women and their children, (b) consistent consequences needed to be imposed on batterers for each and successive acts of violence, (c) intervention agencies needed to be monitored in the performance of their duties, and (d) collaborative relationships between government agencies and the community needed to exist to provide strong and direct intervention when necessary.

How this intervention might occur was left to the steering committee to decide, although there was an expectation of both groups that indigenous involvement at every level and throughout every stage of implementation would be essential to ensure that the needs of Maori were being met. They also raised the concern that programs for Maori batterers or battered women should be developed for and provided by Maori. After serious consideration, the steering committee accepted that a criminal justice response designed along the same lines as the DAIP was appropriate for Aotearoa, and a recommendation for the establishment of a pilot project was made to the full FVPCC committee.

Reaction to the Report

The idea of establishing a DAIP-type pilot met with resistance almost immediately and from some unexpected quarters. The National Rape Crisis movement—along with its sister organization, Te Kakano O Te Whanau (Maori Women's Rape Crisis)—held the belief that by focusing on and resourcing services for male offenders, the pilot would take essential funding away from women's groups working with the victims of abuse. At this time, these groups, along with women's refuges, were struggling to survive on woefully inadequate funding, received limited recognition for their work, and experienced widespread community anathema toward any issues associated with women and violence. Because the program included a rehabilitation component for abusers, the project was seen as demanding access to scarce funds that would be further stretched to accommodate services for abusers. None of the existing models was seen as effective from the perspective of women's safety or autonomy. It was feared that the pilot would require more work from already overworked women's advocates while ultimately only making superficial changes for battered women. The two women's rape crisis groups withdrew from the steering committee. The NCWR was the only women's advocacy organization that stayed with the proposed pilot project.

The next wave of resistance came from Maori government department workers. A series of meetings with Maori officials clarified their concerns that a project such as the one we were proposing would be counterproductive for Maori overall. Their opposition centered on two major themes. First, Maori already featured highly on all (negative) statistics (school dropout rate, unemployment levels, crime statistics, beneficiary recipients, medical ill health), and this project could expose Maori to further community condemnation. Anxious that racist practices within government agencies would be legitimized by using the state as the primary means of intervention in family violence cases, they articulated their concerns to the FVPCC committee. In addition, this group believed that the project flew in the face of Maori initiatives to reclaim control over their own resources and reestablish customary practices, including the development of an independent Maori legal system. In essence, opposition to the project built up around what appeared to be an expectation that the state would interfere more in Maori lives rather than less. Maori representatives on the steering committee met with dissenters to the project on a number of occasions without any real resolutions being reached at that time. Although the Maori government workers' desire to stop the project were not realized, their opposition gave further strength to the argument that if the model were to be used in Aotearoa, it would be required that a Maori-controlled, Maori-centered program be offered as part of the overall project.

Ownership of the project became hotly debated within the steering committee itself. The Duluth model's success was largely linked to the role of the DAIP as an independent, community-based group that played a key role in policy development, networking, and tracking cases. Government officials began to step away from the project as funding implications surfaced. None of the government officials on the steering committee wanted to financially commit their department to a project they did not completely control, even when a collaborative approach to stopping violence was being touted. The role of an independent group in monitoring government agencies was seen as potentially explosive. However, prior to and even during the struggle over funding, consensus on how the pilot project might progress went relatively smoothly.

The Pilot Project

With the full (FVPCC) committee's approval, the steering committee began the search for a community that would be agreeable to implementing the pilot. This was not a problem, and after a series of meetings with local groups and agencies, the city of Hamilton was selected. There were numerous reasons for deciding on Hamilton as the ideal city to pilot the project, including its ethnic breakdown, the support of local refuge and several agencies in the community, and its size. Maori representation in Hamilton was equivalent to national figures—approximately 10% Maori inhabitants. Located in the upper center of the north island, Hamilton is a university town with a static population of 110,000 people. In 1986, Hamilton had piloted a police arrest policy for domestic assaults.

Although the project was to be a locally based, it would be overseen by the FVPCC, which selected and hired its coordinator. Having DAIP literature and eventually close contact with the DAIP's staff was useful, but we still had to, in essence, reinvent the model. We began our work by forming a support and supervisory team of workers who were attached to the two local women's refuges—one Maori, one Pakeha. Three staff members were hired to carry out the first phase of the HAIP. Over the following months, the three staff members spent hundreds of hours struggling with the issues associated with implementing the project in a way that would be most beneficial to battered women. These were months of talking, negotiating, and congealing senior-ranking individuals into accepting that improvements in practitioners' performance was not only necessary but imperative. Theories on spouse abuse that individualized the violence and measured it by degree of dysfunction within the family unit were widely accepted by community leaders and deeply entrenched in the thinking of practitioners in the system. Therefore, the notion that we should shift our focus from changing how individuals relate to being abused to how as a community we intervene was neither appreciated nor accepted by many. The logistics of getting full participation from agencies and practitioners were greatly helped by enlisting and eventually securing the aid of senior representatives from government departments as the main contact people.

Six months prior to the start date, police training on the newly negotiated protocols began. Community corrections training followed, and the establishment of office facilities for the intervention project were under way. The last group to be approached were the local judges. At this meeting, all the other intervention agencies were represented by their most senior personnel, including the district commander of police, the regional and local manager of community corrections, coordinators of each refuge, the chief court registrar, and the HAIP coordinator and research consultant. With support for the aims and intentions of the project gained from the judges, the project was officially launched 2 months later.

The HAIP trust or governing body comprised six Maori and six non-Maori men and women who had been nominated by the two refuges as people they worked with and trusted within the local community. All policy documents acknowledged the unique status of Maori within Aotearoa and the commitment by HAIP to challenge all facilitators of violence and abuse, including those of racism and cultural imperialism.[1] The initial team of three who established the HAIP rapidly expanded to nine, including two battered women's court advocates, men's program coordinators, administrators, women's program coordinators, and national and local trainers. A team of 30 volunteers also helped manage the workload, and within the first 2 years, 800 violent men eventually entered programs offered by the HAIP. Refuge workload increased by 300% in the first 12 months. Since the end of the pilot period and subsequent withdrawal of FVPCC involvement, the project has become firmly based in the local community and continues to advocate for improvement in services for battered women and their children.

The research conducted by the government involved interviews with 132 battered women who had some form of contact with the police or the HAIP due to an incident of violence. They were asked whether they felt the Hamilton community was more responsive to their needs (now as opposed to 5 years prior). Did they believe their children were exposed to or were living with more or less violence? Were they themselves living with less violence? More than 90% of those interviewed felt they and their children were safer or living with less violence since the implementation of the pilot project. From our point of view, active intervention in all instances of family violence was beneficial to battered women, Maori and non-Maori.

Conclusion

At the end of the pilot period, the political climate within New Zealand had changed dramatically. Government officials who had worked alongside the establishment of the project and taken a personal interest in its success were being directed to make substantive cuts to their budgets, and the restructuring of all major institutions was under way. Home office government officials who took over from the original people looked at the project more specifically from the point of view of whether there were cost savings for their departments or for government. Whether women were safer as a result of intervention was not necessarily a priority of these officials. Monitoring of agencies' performance was the one area of expenditure in which these officials could see funding cuts being made, and they offered the alternative of government agencies monitoring their own performance, thereby eliminating the need to fund an outside agency to carry out this task. The most important element of the project was gutted. An assessment of HAIP funding identified that approximately 65% of funds received were for different forms of monitoring government performance, and this level of funding was withdrawn from the project. All other funding was targeted at service delivery only. The immediate effect of the government's action was to almost cripple the HAIP, which has not occurred, much to the surprise of some. However, it has had much wider and longer-lasting ramifications.

In taking the action that it has, the government has decided against making the HAIP experiment standard national practice. It has once again left it to local groups to argue for a collaborative government and community-based program effort to confront this violence. It has retreated from a commitment to its own obligation to be accountable to a broader vision of intervention. No funding is available through any of the conventional funding sources for the independent monitoring of agencies and practitioner performance. In many parts of the country, government agencies give mere lip service to interagency collaboration, and victim's advocacy groups are accorded the status of service providers with little or no allowance for them to critique how agencies' performance affect battered women.

The project has still made an impact that cannot easily be rolled back through funding cutbacks. The work of government agencies in

Hamilton and the HAIP has set a standard for domestic violence work that influences every major effort in this area nationally. Much of what the HAIP built into its program is now considered standard practice for effective and accountable intervention, including (a) offering advocacy and educational services to Maori women and men by Maori staff, based on the historical and cultural experience of Maori people; (b) having men and women cofacilitate abuser groups; and (c) designing all legal advocacy programs to have an individual and systems advocacy component. The HAIP has paved the road for collaborative government advocacy partnerships previously unknown in this field. During the course of the project, researchers from the University Waikato worked closely with the project to create a system of feedback from victims of abuse to project staff. This work led to a broader research project that was a catalyst for the passage of legislation, which many consider to be the most progressive domestic violence legislation in any country with a European-based legal system. Hamilton agencies continue to be strong advocates for this form of intervention. Even though they are no longer obligated to work cooperatively with the project, they continue to do so because they helped to create it and have found this new style of intervention to be more beneficial to them as practitioners, to abusers, and, most important, to victims of battering.

Note

1. For a detailed description of the project, write to the HAIP at P.O. Box 19051, Hamilton, New Zealand.

References

Family Violence Prevention Coordinating Committee. (1989). *The cultural facilitators of family violence: A Pakeha perspective.* Research published by the Family Violence Prevention Coordinating Committee.

Pence, E. (1989). Batterer programs: Shifting from community collusion to community confrontation. In L. Caesar & L. K. Hamberger (Eds.), *Treatment models for spouse abusers* (pp. 24-50). New York: Springer.

13

Pick 'n Mix or Replication

The Politics and Process of Adaptation

Robyn Holder

This chapter explores the influence of the Domestic Abuse Intervention Project (DAIP) and the Duluth model on developments in two locations and the adaptation issues involved. The first location is the London Borough of Hammersmith and Fulham (Britain), an inner-city area comprising 175,000 people. The second is the Australian Capital Territory (ACT), a small, landlocked city-state of 300,000 people in the federated system of Australia. In neither location has a Duluth-style system actually been implemented in full. Both are still evolving.

Influence of the DAIP and the Duluth Model

During an after-dinner speech in a sheep shearing shed deep in rural New South Wales for a police conference on domestic violence late in 1997, nearly every single person there revealed that they had seen or used the Power and Control Wheel graphic (see the Appendix; Pence & Paymar, 1993). One officer present wryly pointed out that there must not be a corner of the world in which this wheel had not turned.

At its simplest, then, the DAIP has created deceptively simple tools that, at a glance, provide clarity to a wide range of audiences on an often confusing phenomenon. The various materials generated by the DAIP that are now in circulation in Britain and Australia use a language that feminists are comfortable with, are based on concepts that we applaud, are easy to use, and are flexible to adapt.

What also appeared to be revolutionary was the systemic nature of the model. Traditionally, feminists in Britain and Australia have focused the bulk of their attention on inadequate police responses to domestic violence (Easteal, 1993; Edwards, 1989; Hatty, 1986; Seddon, 1993). After all, it was claimed, police were the uniformed agents of patriarchal capitalism who most obviously (inevitably?) let women down. They were also the most accessible as targets of our criticism. In the Duluth model, we could see an approach that attended to police, the prosecutors, the courts, and probation both singly and as a whole. The fact also that the Duluth model encompassed a whole city and a whole city's institutions in its set of interlocking protocols gave us a clear and concrete example to show those in positions of influence and power in our own communities what actually could be done.

Therein lies another feature of the Duluth model that has been influential. It spoke of itself not only as seeking social change but of institutional change as well. The people at the DAIP buried themselves in the minutiae of practice, of the day-to-day realities of police and probation officers. They sought to place themselves in the shoes of prosecutors and judges to better understand the internal ideological references and culture of these critical players. What became apparent was how much the agencies were directed by their paper-routine and procedural mechanisms when confronted by domestic violence as much as by the populist victim-blaming beliefs also located in broader society.

The notion of intervention à la Duluth has come to be understood in two ways. First and foremost is the notion of it as an assertive, public, and focused use of the combined and collaborative power of some of society's most powerful institutions into a hitherto private battleground. Second is the idea of the outsider's intervention into the day-to-day workings of those same traditionally closed and conservative institutions to critically refocus the attention of their operations.

Rather than stand at a distance from these agencies and loudly point out their deficiencies, it became apparent to us in Britain and Australia that the feminists in Duluth were not only prepared to get inside but were actually there already. The results were extraordinarily practical and almost breathtakingly simple. The approach that had been developed appeared to rest on a clear understanding of the power dynamics located in the personal, institutional, and social spheres. The political analysis was sophisticated, but the adoption of change management methodologies frequently used in private corporations made it all effective. It appeared also that the DAIP had been able to do all this without diluting its political language. In fact, liberation theology, community development theory, and antiracist practice appear to have been grafted seemlessly to its feminist heart.

Although the above factors have been critical to the influence the Duluth model has come to have in Britain and Australia, the fact is that it can also easily be spoken of as 'a model'. One can now say in either country that one is "implementing the Duluth model," and listeners will generally nod sagely and with approval. The fact that the model is made up of a number of different components in reality also means that the model can mean any number of things, depending on where you locate yourself and what information you have. In the early 1990s, rather too many simply took the Duluth model to mean the power and control curriculum for violent men (Pence & Paymar, 1993). Although this still does happen, there are more who now articulate their work as an adaptation of "the coordinated community response."

Adaptation of the Duluth model in either Britain or Australia necessarily means operating in cultural, social, economic, structural, and political contexts that are as vastly different from each other as they are from the United States. It also means taking into account the different orientations and histories of the respective women's and refuge movements. A critical similarity between the two jurisdictions is, however, their shared criminal justice heritage. This likeness, as well as the difference between that and North American jurisprudence, generates just one of the adaptation issues it has been necessary to confront.

Using the Duluth Model in Britain

It is deliberate to choose the words *using* the Duluth model in Britain rather than *adapting* it. It has been very advantageous to use the example provided by the DAIP around which to strategize and negotiate with key players. But it is and never was the whole game.

Interagency working on the issue is more common (Hague, Malos, & Dear, 1996; Harwin, Hague, & Malos, in press). The Domestic Violence Forum in the London Borough of Hammersmith and Fulham is one such example (Harwin et al., in press). As a developmental and coordinating tool, interagency forums have introduced stakeholders other than women's refuges into the central arena of domestic violence policy and program development, thereby extending not only the number of perspectives calling to be heard but also potential competition over whose perspective and priority on the issue will predominate.

Research conducted in Hammersmith and Fulham in 1989 revealed that women experiencing abuse make between 5 to 12 separate contacts before finding a sympathetic and helpful response (McGibbon, Cooper, & Kelly, 1989). Moreover, they overwhelmingly seek help first from female family and friends, second from slightly more remote providers such as general practitioners, a more distant third from police, and still fewer from a range of other sources such as refuges, law centers, and advice bureaus. These revelations of women's help-seeking behavior helped focus attention on a wider range of providers than perhaps the Duluth model uses.

The central problem of attrition on women in their help seeking also ensured that issues such as the availability and accessibility of information, documentaton of good practice, consistency in response messages, publicity for providers, and effective interagency communication were paramount in Hammersmith and Fulham in the forum's early years. The objectives were to reduce the number of unproductive contacts women were forced to make and increase the number and quality of empathetic and responsive access points she may find.

It could be asserted that these aspects of service delivery and coordination had to be addressed before use of the Duluth model could be seriously considered in Hammersmith and Fulham, particularly given the core functions of housing, social services, and child protection and the related responsibilities of community development that fell within local government remit. There were also tactical decisions involved in addressing the accessible targets first, building trust among key opinion formers, using available opportunities and openings, and nurturing the allies found in the more hostile cultures of the police and probation.

The forum also sought to reveal gaps in service provision that affected more than one existing stakeholder. Therefore, the Duluth model was crucial in Hammersmith and Fulham in encouraging the two local refuge groups to allow the development of a new project to provide an education program for abusive men and support groups for partners. Without doubt, refuges have heard countless women express ambivalence about responses that criminalize the behavior of violent men and a wish that there be "help" for them (Edelson & Eisikovits, 1996; Mooney, 1994). In the past, at least at an express policy level, most refuge workers tended to ignore these awkward positions. The power and control curriculum developed by Pence and Paymar (1993) was cautiously sanctioned, its focus being on getting violent men to accept responsibility for their actions and on teaching nonviolent alternatives within a feminist analysis of domestic violence as a functional method of subjugating women. Refuges and others in the forum accepted the establishment of a local Domestic Violence Intervention Project (DVIP) with the provisos that it offer parallel support services to women, whether or not their partners were participants in the men's program, and that it not seek funds from sources traditionally accessed by the refuges.

The education curriculum and the DVIP were also influential in both stimulating further the interest of police and probation in domestic violence work and in providing them with something they could relate to. The police officers used the existence of the project to encourage women to continue with criminal proceedings so that their men could actually be helped by referral to the program. They also used the same argument to encourage fellow officers to follow the Met's proarrest policy. Probation officers viewed the program as a nonpunative and rehabilitative response to offenders and an intriguing development that piqued their professional curiosity (Burton, Regan, & Kelly, 1998).

The survival of the DVIP in Hammersmith and Fulham owes much to the commitment of its workers and management committee and to some creative fund-raising efforts. But it could not be said that a Duluth model existed in the borough. The first years (1990-1995) of the Domestic Violence Forum were crucial to later activity that sought more deliberately to install the other components of the model. In fostering open and effective dialogue across a wide range of agencies, a sense of common purpose, and mutual trust, as well as in gaining acceptance for basic feminist principles of good practice in responses to women and children experiencing violence at home, interagency work in Hammersmith and Fulham cultivated the seed bed for a program of collaborative criminal justice/community intervention.

Following a weeklong workshop facilitated by Ellen Pence in 1995, the forum established a Criminal Justice System Working Group. This group began more purposefully to seek the establishment of the Duluth model in full. An increased level of dialogue and negotiation was pursued with the local magistrates court and with the Crown Prosecution Service. A consultant was commissioned to examine the British legal framework and found no legal impediments to the full establishment of the model (Edwards, 1998). A party of the key stakeholders visited Duluth in 1997, and a collaborative bid for just over one million funds sterling over 3 years was submitted to the National Government's Single Regeneration Budget Challenge Fund. Although the bid was unsuccessful, the partnership framework created in this collaboration continues to seek implementation of further core components of the model. The work of the Domestic Violence Forum in improving responses from the health, social service, and housing authorities also continues but is also largely unfunded.

Adapting the Duluth Model in Australia

Six sites are known at this time that claim, in part, to be adapting the Duluth model in Australia: Melbourne (Victoria), Perth and Armadale (Western Australia), Brisbane (Queensland), Adelaide (South Australia), and the Australia Capital Territory (ACT). Australia has a very active domestic violence sector, and there is much interagency activity. In every state and territory, there are also a number of services for violent men. Some are located in corrections departments, and others are within social/family service contexts (National Crime Prevention, 1999).

This chapter will focus on the adaption of the Duluth model in the ACT.

The ACT is unique in Australia in a number of ways, not least for having a 24-hour community-based Domestic Violence Crisis Service (DVCS). The DVCS was established in 1988 with a feminist philosophy written into its constitution (Hopkins & McGregor, 1991). Its relationship to the Australian Federal Police (AFP) is as set out in legislation and in an agreed memorandum of understanding. When police are called to a domestic violence incident, the communications operator is required to notify the DVCS, which then dispatches one of its own workers. Police at the scene are then required to offer the services of the DVCS to the victim and seek her consent for the worker to enter the premises. If consent is not given, the DVCS worker returns to the central office location. If consent is given, the DVCS worker will assist the victim in a number of ways. She may be accompanied to a hospital or alternative accommodation, her options will be discussed in terms of legal protection and other services, and she will be offered assistance at court. The intention is to respond to the crisis and not to offer an ongoing service.

The ACT, like all other jurisdictions in Australia, has paid considerable attention to legislation both as a method of enhancing women's protection but more particularly as an instrument to direct practice change, especially in police departments. It is noticeable that, when talking about legal protection for domestic violence victims in the ACT, almost every police officer, crisis advocate, or support worker will discuss accessing personal protection orders first before turning to the possibility of criminal proceedings. This is a big difference to the approaches taken in Britain (Barron, 1990; Bonney & Trimboli, 1997; Stubbs & Eggar, 1993). The combined affect of this emphasis, the role of the DVCS, and the way in which police appear to simply remove the alleged perpetrator from the scene have all resulted in a very low arrest rate and even lower (to the point of nonexistence) charge rate (Mugford, Easteal, & Edwards, 1993).

The policy separation between the civil and criminal areas of domestic violence responses was consolidated in the ACT in two publications of its Community Law Reform Committee (ACT CLRC, 1995a, 1995b). The CLRC reviewed the operation of civil and criminal proceedings in relation to domestic violence not as interlocking and complementary processes within one system but as entirely separate systems. The CLRC report on domestic violence and the criminal law recommended the setting up of a "Duluth style system" (ACT CLRC, 1995a, p. 108).

The report recommended that a domestic violence project coordinator be responsible for this, and a domestic violence advisory council should be charged with overall responsibility for policy and strategic direction. In the ACT, the ready recourse to politicians, the legislature, and legislation as a principal (if not the primary) strategy of effecting change is a significant difference between it and change strategies in Hammersmith and Fulham. It appears that there is far less trust or experience of interagency problem-solving negotiations as there was in Britain.

The actual process followed in developing the ACT's Interagency Family Violence Intervention Program (FVIP) sought first to have the key agencies articulate and agree to the guiding principles and objectives of their combined intervention and then to slowly work through, step by step, how these objectives may be achieved in the local context. Participants involved in this evolution were influenced not only by Duluth and the Hamilton Abuse Intervention Project in New Zealand but also by the program surrounding the family violence court in Manitoba, Canada; other criminal justice initiatives in the United States (notably in Quincy and in San Diego); and developments in Britain.

In debating what might or might not work in the ACT, stakeholder agencies understood that the actual core components of all these exemplary projects were essentially very similar. It appeared as though the differences between them were related to local factors, such as which component was to be prioritized, the range of services available, the lead agency to the initiative, the resource constraints of the area, the relationship and history between the key players, and the positions adopted by the women's sector and by prosecution authorities. Of prime importance here are the eight key components of community intervention projects described in Part I of this book. Jurisdictions considering adapting the Duluth model need to recognize these as activities or functions and that adaptation is, in large part, about finding the means of implementing them and the places for locating them that are appropriate and meaningful for that area.

The principles that were most strongly articulated in the interagency committee charged with devising and implementing the FVIP were those relating to achieving a greater degree of responsibility for perpetrators' actions and to increasing the accountability of the criminal justice system to domestic violence victims. These and other policy positions were drafted piece by piece into a new and detailed interagency protocol document. Essentially, however, the ACT's adaptation of the Duluth model revolves around the more active case management of domestic violence criminal matters by those agencies charged with the statutory responsibility of processing them—that is, the police, the prosecution, the court and corrections—but with specific victim input. The core components of the program are the following:

> Police will encourage and reinforce that where prima facie evidence of an offense exists, best practices require that action be taken in the collection of evidence and the active pursuit of charges.
>
> The office of the Director of Public Prosecutions (DPP) will implement an approach that, consistent with the independence of the DPP, incorporates the provision of advice to the AFP on questions of evidence, ensures appropriate charges are prosecuted, and enables the wishes of victims to be given appropriate weight in the prosecution process.
>
> The magistrates court will create a separate list into which all domestic violence criminal matters are processed and around which court support is provided to victims.
>
> Corrective services will provide magistrates with a new sentencing option in an education program for violent perpetrators.
>
> The DVCS will reorient its service to enable it to provide more ongoing support to victims following police referral (ACT Attorney- General's Department, 1998).

Interestingly, the most intensive negotiations were those with the DPP. In the ACT, unlike in Hamilton and most other Australian jurisdictions, summary prosecutions in the magistrates court as well as proceedings on indictment in the Supreme Court are handled by the independent statutory office of the DPP. However, like all DPPs in Australia and their counterparts in Britain, the ACT DPP jealously guards the independence of its decision making. The jurisprudence and culture of these bodies are vastly different to their more politicized counterparts in the United States. In the United States, it is possible, if not desirable, for a district attorney to talk publicly about "winning" a case. The language is alive with metaphors of combat and competition with the defense. In the British and Australian contexts, prosecutors are supposed to act and consider all matters with the balance required of an attorney-general.

The debates about mandatory arrest, the role of the victim/witness in decisions to proceed, and prosecution strategies were lively. In the end, it was felt that the terms *mandatory arrest* and *proprosecution* actually disguised the retention of a considerable degree of discretion.

A number of other graceful and cogent arguments put by eminent criminologists were also persuasive on the committee philosophy. In a discussion on the operation of Manitoba's family violence court and its specialist prosecution unit, Professor Jane Ursel has argued that if the feminist intervention forced a victim to give evidence against her wishes or if a matter proceeded despite her reasonable protestations, then somewhere we had lost the plot. The Crown attorney in Manitoba will pursue "rigorous prosecution" but "not at the expense of the victim." She argues that "this dual and frequently contradictory mandate was a much closer reflection of the complex nature of these cases than the old simplistic definition of conviction as success" (Ursel, 1997, p. 272). Furthermore, Eve and Carl Buzawa, in their excellent review of research and policy in the United States, are "concerned that the primary goal, the cessation of battering and victim satisfaction with the process, can easily be subverted to serve an organizational goal—for example, increasing the rate of convictions regardless of victim needs or desires" (Buzawa & Buzawa, 1996, p. 176).

In finding a policy position that sought to acknowledge the victim's ambivalence (often, though not always) in proceeding against her abuser, the ACT DPP committed itself to take steps that ensure the witness is properly protected from intimidation and harassment and is adequately supported. A newly created witness assistant position is to be instrumental in this. In essence, as Professor Betsy Stanko has commented, "The criminal justice system cannot be considered a solution. It is a resource."[1]

The ACT Interagency Family Violence Intervention Program is being implemented as a 12-month fully evaluated pilot. The evaluation is not using measures that could determine "success" or "failure." Rather, the evaluators participate as active observers to the process, offering critical feedback that is used to continuously refine and focus the interventions of the agencies. The efficacy of this coordinated intervention in the Australian criminal justice context has never been fully explored or tested in practice. The evaluation will provide signposts for the agencies and victim advocates on future directions based on measures of victim satisfaction, recidivism, outcome and process satisfaction for justice personnel, and resource management.

Reflections on Adaptation

Given that the Duluth model has not been fully transplanted in either the British or Australian location, one hesitates to discuss "lessons." It may be more appropriate instead to offer comment on implementing the model. In fact, talking about the model actually disguises and may even skew the process of continual reform of criminal justice responses to domestic violence. Although it may serve as a good motivator and guide, too often people speak of the model as though it were a complete, one-size-fits-all package. It raises also an assumption that once the collaborative structure is sorted, then the work is done. Furthermore, discussion of innovations in domestic violence responses as models can degenerate into catwalk competition—this model is better than that model—when, in reality, an eclectic approach may suit a broader range of jurisdictions.

Even if one does seek to adopt the core functional components of the Duluth model, the notion of adaptation may be more concretely understood in terms of implementation. Implementing these core components may then be more easily articulated in terms of strategic development, institutional change, and, crucially, of systemwide reform. Then, various corporate change methodologies can be employed usefully across agencies, large or small. This language and method of working can feel alien to community activists. The skills necessary for developing the implementation strategy may be different from those required for the equally hard task of maintaining the momentum and direction of the collaboration over time.

It is important to read about the development, philosophy, and components of the Duluth system but not be limited to that. Duluth is only one jurisdiction that has generated reform in domestic violence responses. It is a fundamental tenet of community development that change needs to be "owned," be responsive to local circumstance, and be cognizant of local resources. It follows that every adaptation of the Duluth model will be different in some aspect.

Acknowledging adaptation as both a process and a strategy of implementation also reveals that the debate about whether interagency work or intervention programs are "better" than the other is in fact spurious. Each is part of the same continuum and of the same multilayered dynamic. The implementation of a collaborative intervention on domestic violence will never end.

In placing oneself, one's organization, or one's community in the middle of a change process, it makes it easier (on so many levels) to adopt a working assumption that everyone else comes with their best intentions, that they desire the most effective response possible to the victim (or perpetrator) from their organization, and that it is an accepted part of a service's operation (whether government or nongovernment) to seek continual improvements in delivery. Moreover, it is in the capacity of human beings and human society to be transformed. These assumptions do not mean suspending one's critical faculties nor one's preparation for the very real possibility of resistance to change.

Also, vital to the implementation process is the practice of dialogue, discussion, consultation, and debate—in fact, communication on every level. The process outcomes are the creation of trust, common purpose, and direction; the creation of a common pool of information and shared history; and mutual comprehension. A collaborative intervention requires the construction of a new relationship between agencies and between activists and professionals that is neither confrontational nor adversarial.

The bedrock of this is the creation of individual working relationships. Perhaps the single most effective strategy of institutional change is to find and nurture potential allies. Posing questions (e.g., "How can I help you assist your agency in this process of change?") facilitates a problem-solving approach that does not push people too hard. It is vital to avoid duplicity and maneuvering—you need to be trusted as well. Do not, however, rely on individual allies to carry the whole change process for their organization.

Scan the structure, roles, and practices of all the relevant agencies in a critical and constructive analysis. Ask what they do, what victims say they do, what they could do better, and what else could be done. Consider also the nature of the relationships between agencies and the perceptual issues and expectations that are stated or unstated.

Deal with the principles and objectives of intervention first. Through this, create a vision of what an alternative practice and an alternative system may actually look like in reality. Then go back and work it through step by step. Acknowledge that implementation is a negotiating, problem-solving process through differing interests, and detail is all important. Persistence pays, but always keep in mind the end goals of improving victim safety and victim satisfaction.

Let this process reveal where new resources need to go or where existing resources need to be reallocated. Ownership of the end result of the collaboration will be subverted if the structure of the DAIP in Duluth is transplanted before the local needs reveal what is relevant and required. A little bit of money can be a dangerous thing. Having money at the beginning can too often degenerate into "how much can I grab for my agency/interest group."

Nothing focuses the legal mind quite like the possibility of a written protocol. Information and agreements will not be lost, the process will continue beyond personnel (and political) changes, and transparency is facilitated. The written protocol, as a living document, is a critical means of achieving accountability.

Inevitability, the changes of practice and procedure sought for domestic violence in any given agency will disclose a systemic problem that has nothing to do with that issue. In the ACT, for example, discussion on how corrective services could monitor compliance of offenders with court orders revealed that they had no systematic procedures for monitoring compliance in any offender category.

Immersion in the day-to-day practicalities and overall constraints of each agency's operations will generate information on what they do and provide an understanding about why they do it. If individuals within a system are to accept and implement change, they need to see the value of it to themselves, to the overall role of their agency, and to their perception of their clients' needs. The touchstone should always be, however, how this or that will be experienced by the victims of domestic violence.

Perhaps above all else, it is vital to keep a focus on the lived experience of victims of domestic violence in all its diversity and complexity. Understandings of the dynamic and purposes of women's coping skills, their survival strategies, and their help seeking should guide developments. The lives of women, men, and children are not simple. We should avoid putting too simple solutions in place for them.

Can One Critique the Duluth Model?

The people and programs that comprise the Duluth model have been tremendously influential in Britain and Australia. The DAIP represents many different things to many different people. For activists against domestic violence in particular, it is an exemplar in feminist practice, feminist strategizing, and feminist aspiration. At this distance, it represents feminists keeping hold of an increasingly complex and sophisticated agenda in a way that is continually creative, dynamic, and adaptive. However, the impetus for reform and the drive for adaptation will not always come from feminists. Disquiet has been voiced about the different language of change that domestic violence initiatives are adopting, language that perhaps suggests adjustments in objective away from root-and-branch social change to the more limited institutional change. Co-option is always a concern for the wary feminist activist, and the question of just who is changing whom is a live one. Change is definitely not a one-way street.

The advent of new and possibly more powerful stakeholders in the domestic violence policy-making field has created concerns that refuges will lose their control over the agenda. As Dobash and Dobash (1992) have pointed out in their thought-provoking work *Women, Violence and Social Change,* the women's refuges that consider themselves by definition revolutionary may be in danger of being placed in a position of conservatives resisting the inevitability of the changes they previously sought by questioning the legitimacy of the change agents. In a number of jurisdictions, the motivation and innovation for the adaptation of the model have not come from an obvious feminist source. It must surely be an inevitable consequence of a multisystems approach that the lead may come from unexpected quarters and may change over time. This should not be problematized. It is a dynamic movement on a complex issue that has begat related dynamic and complex responses.

The portrayal of the Duluth model as a coordinated community response to domestic violence could also be viewed as too broad a sweep. Is it, in fact, a total community response? Is it a community response at all? Isn't it more accurately a coordinated criminal justice response? That surely is the locus, the nexus, of what DAIP does. The influence that the model has had is perhaps distorting the potential for a wider range of responses that could be articulated from the diverse bases of community concern.

It is from this position that perhaps the most serious questions about the Duluth model arise. Is this sort of collaborative criminal justice intervention really what we should be focusing our energies and resources on? The various pieces of research into women's help-seeking behavior reveal an enormous array of strategies and of contacts made (Australian Bureau of Statistics, 1996; Cavanagh, 1978; Gondolf & Fisher, 1988; McGibbon et al., 1989; Mooney, 1994). Accessing the police, the courts, and even refuges comes way down the list. And yet that is what we have built our policy and program responses around. Have we got it only partially right or quite, quite wrong?

In Australia, the recent national women's safety survey identified that very low numbers of women respondents who had experienced physical or sexual violence actually sought help from police or crisis services (Australian Bureau of Statistics, 1996). This finding generated a flurry of anxious research contracts to try and find out why. The real line of enquiry should have been to find out more about what women actually do, when, at what point of the relationship, with whom, for what purpose, and with what expectations and results.

The question of resources cannot be avoided with these questions still largely unanswered. Although maybe, from my British experience, I have learned to keep working on domestic violence issues with little or no resources for far too long! Women disclose to friends and family first, but which resources do we apply to informing, supporting, and empowering these informal networks that are so crucial to women of all backgrounds but especially those from marginalized communities? More women victims of domestic violence access the health and medical services than any other profession. Has any jurisdiction placed as much strategic emphasis and dedicated as much policy attention and money to this area as has been applied to the criminal justice system? Research suggests that child abuse is likely to be found in two of three cases of domestic violence (Holder, Kelly, & Singh, 1994). Where are the resources devoted to creating an effective collaboration between the domestic violence sector and child protection authorities?

Perhaps the resource question is wider even than this. Can communities of 8 million people such as London (or even 300,000, such as in Canberra) with complex and overlapping administrative boundaries afford a model developed for a unitary city of 90,000? Multiply this by the number of large metropolitan cities and by the number of largish rural towns in Britain, and multiply it by the number and geographical reach of some of Australia's remoter regions—what is actually affordable and possible? It is a central thrust of the ACT's pilot program to create the collaboration with minimal new resources attracting to the central tasks of policy development, coordination, and monitoring. The resource emphasis is on direct services. It remains to be seen whether the model can be adapted in the ACT or in Hammersmith and Fulham without the level of resources that the DAIP has drawn to itself or that which the Hamilton project required.

For other people considering adapting the Duluth model in their jurisdiction, the conclusion can only be, to paraphrase Hannah Arendt, to think and think hard about what you are doing (Women's Research Centre, 1988).

Note

1. Professor Elizabeth A. Stanko (Director, Centre for Crime and Justice Studies, Brunel University, UK), at a seminar in Camberra, ACT. August, 1997.

References

ACT Attorney-General's Department. (1998). *Responding to domestic violence: The ACT inter-agency intervention program protocols and resources*. Canberra, Australia: Author.

ACT Community Law Reform Committee (CLRC). (1995a). *Domestic violence and the criminal law report* (No. 9). Canberra, Australia: ACT Attorney-General's Department.

ACT Community Law Reform Committee (CLRC). (1995b). *Domestic violence and the criminal law report (No. 11)*. Canberra, Australia: ACT Attorney-General's Department.

Australian Bureau of Statistics. (1996). *Women's safety Australia*. Canberra: Australian Government Publishing Service.

Barron, J. (1990). *Not worth the paper: The effectiveness of legal protection for women and children experiencing domestic violence*. Bristol, UK: Women's Aid Federation.

Bonney, R., & Trimboli, L. (1997). *An evaluation of the New South Wales apprehended violence order scheme*. Sydney, Australia: New South Wales Bureau of Crime Statistics and Research.

Burton, S., Regan, L., & Kelly, L. (1998). *Supporting women and challenging men: Lessons from the Domestic Violence Intervention Project*. Bristol, UK: Policy Press.

Buzawa, E., & Buzawa, C. (1996). *Domestic violence: The criminal justice response* (2nd ed.). London: Sage.

Cavanagh, C. (1978). *Battered women and social control*. Unpublished master's thesis, University of Stirling, Stirling, Scotland.

Dobash, R. E., & Dobash, R. P. (1992). *Women, violence and social change*. New York: Routledge Kegan Paul.

Easteal, P. (1993). *Killing the beloved: Homicide between adult sexual intimates*. Canberra: Australian Institute of Criminology.

Edelson, J. L., & Eisikovits, Z. C. (Eds.). (1996). *Future interventions with battered women and their families*. Newbury Park, CA: Sage.

Edwards, S. (1989). *Policing domestic violence.* London: Sage.

Edwards, S. (1998). *Is change possible? An exploration of the applicability of Duluth principles of inter-agency coordination to the crime of domestic violence.* Hammersmith and Fulham, UK: Community Safety Unit/Domestic Violence Forum.

Gondolf, E., & Fisher, E. (1988). *Battered women as survivors.* Lexington, MA: Lexington Books.

Hague, G., Malos, E., & Dear, W. (1996). *Multi-agency work and domestic violence: A national study of inter-agency initiatives.* Bristol, UK: Policy Press.

Harwin, N., Hague, G., & Malos, E. (in press). *Domestic violence and multi-agency working: New opportunities, old challenges?* London: Whiting & Birch.

Hatty, S. E. (Ed.). (1986). *Domestic violence: Proceedings of a national conference.* Canberra: Australian Institute of Criminology.

Holder, R., Kelly, L., & Singh, T. (1994). *Suffering in silence? Children and young people who witness domestic violence.* London: Hammersmith & Fulham Domestic Violence Forum.

Hopkins, A., & McGregor, H. (1991). *Working for change: The movement against domestic violence.* Sydney, Australia: Allen & Unwin.

McGibbon, A., Cooper, L., & Kelly, L. (1989). *What support?* London: London Borough of Hammersmith & Fulham/Polytechnic of North London.

Mooney, J. (1994). *The hidden figure: Domestic violence in north London.* London: Police & Crime Prevention Unit, London Borough of Islington.

Mugford, J., Easteal, P., & Edwards, A. (1993). *Domestic violence* (Research Paper No. 1). Canberra, Australia: ACT Community Law Reform Committee.

National Crime Prevention. (1999). *Ending domestic violence? Programs for perpetrators.* Canberra: Commonwealth of Australia.

Pence, E., & Paymar, M. (1993). *Education groups for men who batter: The Duluth model.* New York: Springer.

Seddon, N. (1993). *Domestic violence in Australia: The legal response.* Sydney, Australia: Federation Press.

Stubbs, J., & Eggar, S. (1993). *Effectiveness of protection orders in Australian jurisdictions.* Canberra: Australian Government Publishing Service.

Ursel, E. J. (1997). The possibilities of criminal justice intervention in domestic violence: A Canadian case study. *Current Issues in Criminal Justice, 8*(3), 272.

Women's Research Centre. (1988). *In women's interest: Feminist activism and institutional change.* Vancouver, Canada: Author.

Epilogue

We have heard critiques of and praise for our work at the Domestic Abuse Intervention Project (DAIP) from all over the globe—it is sexist or antimale, it is too focused on changing men, it is not feminist, it is too focused on convictions, it does not address lesbian battering, it is Eurocentric, it is an organizer's miracle, it has the best analysis of violence, it is the best program in the country, its groups are the only way to work with offenders. For us, it is none of these things. The DAIP is a 20-year experiment in reshaping the way a community thinks about and reacts to the use of violence and coercion and threats within intimate relationships. It is more about how we develop that response than it is about the response itself.

In this book, we did not want to ask people to write about the specifics of our dispatch or police policy. We did not want a debate about the pros and cons of a no-drop prosecution policy, nor did we want to describe in detail our sentencing matrix. Those policies will change. We were more interested in the evolving process of trying to use existing institutions and agencies of social control to act on behalf of victims of battering. That has meant that we did not get to start from scratch. We started this work with practices and ways of thinking that have been produced and reproduced over centuries. This is not a social phenomenon created in our community, but it is continually re-created here. The lessons from Duluth are mostly about dialogue, patience, learning from our mistakes, persistence, basing our frame of reference on the experience of those who are battered, losing slogans, and taking up the complexities and not covering up the relationship of the violence to the social realities of a society steeped in class, gender, and race inequities.

This book is an incomplete description of the DAIP. It says nothing of how we have managed ourselves as an agency. It does not tell the story of going from a hierarchy to a collective; it does not talk about how the visitors from New Zealand took all of our materials, films, forms, and policies and left us with the understanding and practical ability to operate an agency with equal decision making between Native American staff and nonnative staff. It does not adequately address all of the unintended consequences of our reform efforts. It gives a glimpse of the process and ends with an invitation to visit. Remember: It is never hot in Duluth.

—Ellen Pence

Appendix

Figure Appendix.1. Power and Control Wheel.
SOURCE: Domestic Abuse Intervention Project. Reprinted with permission.

Index

About the Editors

Melanie F. Shepard is Associate Professor and Director of the Department of Social Work at the University of Minnesota, Duluth. She has been involved in evaluation activities at the Domestic Abuse Intervention Project (DAIP) since 1984. She has published articles and chapters on domestic violence topics, as well as other issues related to social work education. She developed an instrument—the Abusive Behavior Inventory—based on the DAIP's Power and Control Wheel. Currently, she is the lead evaluator for the Enhanced Domestic Abuse Intervention Project, which is funded by the Centers for Disease Control and Prevention. Dr. Shepard has facilitated groups for abusive men using the Duluth curriculum. She also has been a group facilitator for battered women support groups and for women who have been arrested for domestic abuse. In addition to teaching social work students, she has practiced social work in the fields of child welfare and mental health.

Ellen L. Pence is one of the founders of the Domestic Abuse Intervention Project (DAIP) in Duluth, Minnesota. She has been active in institutional change work for battered women since 1975. She has worked on legislative efforts, legal reform projects, and shelter development in Minnesota and has trained practitioners, advocates, and educators throughout North America, New Zealand, Australia,

Europe, and Central America. Dr. Pence is the author of several educational manuals and curricula for classes for battered women, men who batter, and law enforcement trainers. She is also coauthor of *Education Groups for Men Who Batter: The Duluth Model,* as well as many articles, particularly on the legal response to domestic assault, and she is the producer of several educational videos. Currently, Dr. Pence coordinates the development of coordinated community response projects on U.S. Marine installations. The USMC model is based on the Duluth DAIP model of intervention in domestic assault cases. She also provides keynotes, trainings, and technical assistance to other communities. She has conducted specialized trainings on domestic violence issues for law enforcement officers, prosecutors, legal advocates, social activists, human service providers, health care workers, chemical dependency counselors, educators, judges, probation officers, politicians, religious leaders, and policymakers. She also has conducted on-site consultations with policymakers and community activists on policy development in the area of confronting domestic violence.

About the Contributors

Mary Asmus graduated from the University of Minnesota, where she received B.A., summa cum laude, and J.D. degrees. She is chief prosecutor for the Duluth City Attorney's Office, where she has been instrumental in developing the office's policies and procedures for the prosecution of domestic violence cases. She has conducted many police and prosecutor trainings regarding effective investigation and prosecution techniques for domestic abuse cases. She has contributed to *Domestic Violence: The Law Enforcer Response*, a training manual for police officers. She also has spoken about the criminal justice system's response to domestic violence at numerous conferences across the United States and Canada. In addition, she coauthored "Prosecuting Domestic Abuse Cases in Duluth: Developing Effective Prosecution Strategies From Understanding the Dynamics of Abusive Relationships."

Roma Balzer is Coordinator of the Hamilton Abuse Intervention Pilot Project (HAIPP) in New Zealand (Aotearoa). She has been an active organizer in the Maori women's domestic violence movement and has been an organizer in the Refuge movement for 20 years. She worked for a local Refuge for 6 years and was on the national executive board of Refuge for 3 years before she became the first national coordinator (Maori) in 1986. She was raised in Rotorua among the Arawa people.

Her mother's tribes are Ngai te Rangi, Ngati Ranginui, and her father's tribe is Te Arawa. She is the mother of 3 children.

Shamita Das Dasgupta is an immigrant from India and currently Assistant Professor with the Psychology Department at Rutgers University–Newark. She is a cofounder of Manavi, the pioneering organization for South Asian women in the United States. She is a community worker, and her research interests lie in the area of violence against women in South Asian contexts. She has authored a book of folklore with her daughter, *The Demon Slayers and Other Stories: Bengali Folktales* (1995), and has recently edited another, *A Patchwork Shawl: Chronicles of South Asian Women in America* (1998).

Dennis R. Falk is Professor and Director of Graduate Studies in the Department of Social Work at the University of Minnesota, Duluth. He has taught at the college and university level for 25 years, focusing his recent teaching on social research and human behavior. He has conducted or supervised more than 60 research projects and written two dozen articles and papers and one book on group dynamics, evaluations of human service programs, domestic violence, and educational technology. He is currently participating in the evaluation of the Enhanced Domestic Abuse Intervention Project in Duluth.

Denise Gamache, M.S.W., is an associate director of the Battered Women's Justice Project, a national resource center on the civil and criminal justice system's response to domestic violence. In 1975, she helped establish the Harriet Tubman Women's Shelter in Minneapolis and worked as a women's advocate there for several years. As the community intervention coordinator of the Domestic Abuse Project, she was responsible for initiating and supervising an advocacy project within the county attorney's office, working in collaboration with local women's shelters, the courts, and law enforcement agencies. She then served as the prevention coordinator for the Minnesota Coalition for Battered Women, trained secondary teachers in the use of domestic violence prevention materials, consulted on the development of a video-based curriculum on dating violence, and coauthored a prevention curriculum for elementary students. Later, she served as a director of WHISPER, Inc., a program fighting the sexual exploitation of women and youth. She has published several papers related to her work in the field. In 1994, she received a Gloria Steinem Award from the Ms. Foundation for Women.

Nancy Helgeson has been the Domestic Abuse Information Network (DAIN) coordinator for the Domestic Abuse Intervention Project (DAIP) since 1994 and has seen the DAIN through all phases of its development. For 2 years prior to this, she was the DAIP men's program co-coordinator and facilitated education groups for men who batter their partners. She has been involved in the development and production of two DAIP manuals: *Power & Control: Education Groups for Men Who Batter* and *What About the Kids? Community Intervention in Domestic Assault Cases.* In addition to her responsibilities at the DAIP, she works part-time with people who are actively chemically dependent.

Robyn Holder currently works in the Australian Capital Territory as the Victims of Crime Coordinator. She is also Chair of the Domestic Violence Prevention Council and of the Interagency Intervention Program. Previously, she worked in the London Borough of Hammersmith and Fulham's Community Safety Unit, where she was a member of the European Analytical College of Local Authorities on Urban Safety and a visiting tutor on the violence against women course at the Police Staff College in Bramshill. She enjoys the challenge of working across sectors but is challenged more in raising her young son.

Coral McDonnell is one of the founders of the Duluth Domestic Abuse Intervention Project (DAIP). Prior to her work with the DAIP, she was active in developing Duluth's shelter for battered women. During her 18 years at the DAIP, she has been involved with every aspect of program development discussed in this book. She has worked on many of the materials published by the DAIP, particularly a manual on developing a coordinated community response to domestic violence. She also has worked with battered women and facilitated groups for women who have been charged with domestic assault.

Martha McMahon is Associate Professor in the Department of Sociology at the University of Victoria, British Columbia, Canada. She teaches in the areas of qualitative methods, feminist theory, and ecological feminism. She worked for many years in community-based programs for immigrant women, women on social assistance, and women entering nontraditional occupations in trades and technology in Toronto, Canada. She is the author of *Engending Motherhood: Identity and Self-transformation in Women's Lives,* which won the 1996 American Sociological Association Sex and Gender Section Book Award.

Fernando Mederos, Ed.D., has been counseling physically abusive men since 1980. He was at Emerge from 1980 until 1989, when he left to cofound and become director of Common Purpose, a batterer intervention program in Boston that now provides services to 350 to 400 court-mandated clients per week. Presently, he is an independent consultant, trainer, and supervisor for batterer intervention programs. He coordinates part of a project funded by the Center for Disease Control to create a coordinated community response system in Dorchester, Massachusetts; he consults with the Massachusetts Department of Social Services, the state child protection agency; and he is the clinical supervisor for three batterer intervention programs in the Boston area. He also has conducted many trainings nationally and abroad, and he is particularly interested in developing culturally competent intervention models for physically abusive men and in deepening the connections between batterer intervention programs and the communities they serve.

Kersti Yllö is Professor of Sociology at Wheaton College in Norton, Massachusetts. She received her Ph.D. in sociology in 1980 from the University of New Hampshire, where she was associated with the Family Violence Research Program. She has published numerous research articles and several books, including *Feminist Perspectives on Wife Abuse* (with M. Bograd) and *License to Rape* (with D. Finkelhor). She is very interested in researcher-activist collaboration and has done evaluation research with AWAKE, a battered women's advocacy program at the Boston Children's Hospital, and with the U.S. Marine Corps' coordinated community response to spouse abuse. She also serves on the board of Common Purpose, a batterer intervention program based in Boston.

Printed in the United States
98554LV00003B/114/A

10160317R00178

Printed in Great Britain
by Amazon.co.uk, Ltd.,
Marston Gate.